❋ ❋ ❋ ❋

# THE GREAT PLANTATION

❋ ❋ ❋ ❋

*By Clifford Dowdey*

❋ ❋ ❋ ❋

# THE GREAT PLANTATION

## A PROFILE OF
## BERKELEY HUNDRED
## AND
## PLANTATION VIRGINIA
## FROM
## JAMESTOWN TO APPOMATTOX

❋ ❋ ❋ ❋

*by Clifford Dowdey*

RINEHART & COMPANY, INC.
NEW YORK          TORONTO

PUBLISHED SIMULTANEOUSLY IN CANADA BY

CLARKE, IRWIN & COMPANY, LTD., TORONTO

To the memory of the grandmother,
and all the Virginia grandmothers before,
of my daughters—
Frances Blount Dowdey and Sarah Bowis Dowdey

# CONTENTS

✿ ✿ ✿ ✿

# THE AGE OF
# THE FRONTIER

## CHAPTER I

# THE DESPERATE MEN

**1**

*Berkeley Hundred,* a working plantation still in operation after three and one-half centuries, is older than any English-speaking settlement in America outside Virginia. In fact, a Thanksgiving was celebrated on its river front and an experiment made there with corn whiskey before the Puritans, setting sail in one of the boats bound for Virginia, were blown off their course and landed in New England.

One of the very first plantations settled in the New World, Berkeley evolved out of the wilderness to become the demesne of the Harrisons—presidents of the United States, governors of Virginia, a Signer of the Declaration of Independence and an ancestor of Robert E. Lee. The Harrisons helped shape their immediate region into one of the most powerful and fabled sections of Virginia. Their home place sat between the Westover of William Byrd and the Shirley of the Hills and Carters; President John Tyler lived nearby, and his brief term as William Henry Harrison's vice-president was probably the only time in the country's history when a president and his vice-president had grown up in the same neighborhood. The wife of George Washington and of Thomas Jefferson came from that section, and Lee's mother was born there.

The aristocratic pattern which was to characterize the Old South was created in that region, and the first democratic form of government on the continent was introduced there. The men were America's first Indian-fighters, first patrician grandees and first rebels, resisting the power of England one hundred years before the successful revolution. Underlying all things, they were the country's first planters.

The plantation seems remote today, almost legendary, intertwined with the half-romantic and half-barbarous myths of the antebellum South. In these myths of the slaveholding South, the plantation seems always to have existed in some perpetual and semitropical feudalism, where time ceased in the slumbrous heat, the seasons never changed, and the cast of characters in the white-columned mansions, identical on each plantation, were as impervious to the mutations of life as the characters in a familiar play.

*The* protagonist was always Old Massa. Ridden with debts and vice, but jealous of personal honor, always booted and spurred, with a whip in one hand and julep in the other, this high-born and arrogant wastrel kept a harem of mulattoes, a stable of blooded horses (on which he repeatedly ruined himself by betting), and, when he wasn't out dueling under the live oaks, he was entertaining friends with prodigal lavishness. Actually, to this composite image, many gentlemen in the South would contribute aspects of the whole.

Some were debt-ridden (as was William Byrd, III), some were always booted and spurred (as was John Randolph even in the halls of Congress), some were addicted to drink and some to horse racing (as was President Andrew Jackson), some were impoverished by hospitality (as was Thomas Jefferson) and some had Negro mistresses (or there would be no mulattoes). Certainly all held a high sense of personal honor, and dueling in protection of personal honor was an established custom, though the actual number of duels was small. But plantations were neither developed nor maintained by men who embodied *all* these traits.

These personal domains were built by men who, whatever their weaknesses of the flesh, contained the same ingredients that have built large successes throughout the ages—ambition and energy, self-discipline and resourcefulness, and the power to conceive boldly. For the plantation was, above all things, a most bold concept: it was a private principality, a self-contained world that required a unique amalgam of talents of the very first order.

2

Stripped of romantic connotations, the plantation was both a large-scale agricultural operation and a commercial center. In Virginia, where plantations were first established, the money crop was tobacco. For this operation, the virgin forests were cleared, the seeds planted, the plants tended, the leaves cut, stripped and hung, then packed into hogsheads made on the place and shipped to England from the private wharf.

The plantation was also a commercial center. The large ones bought tobacco from small planters, the plantation masters acting as exporters; they also shipped in from England goods beyond their own needs which they handled as importers. In addition to tobacco, the planter raised food for his own people (sometimes as many as one thousand), milling the extra and selling the meal or wheat. Some river plantations baked hard biscuits which they sold to ships' crews as at the plantation of the Berkeley Harrisons' kinsmen. Artisans made the clothes from cotton, wool and tanned hides, built the outbuildings and sometimes boats (as at Berkeley Hundred). From their sawmills, the planters sold planks and clapboards to England.

With a village of artisans, with buying and selling, importing and exporting, banking and storing, the plantation center conducted a vast and complex co-ordinated operation, which in towns would be separate enterprises of many individuals, each taking his cut from the farmer. On the plantation, master got it all.

The plantation master was also responsible for every detail and the total group life of his microcosmic world: he represented law and order, the Church and the courts. The mayor, judge, sheriff and preacher combined would not be so powerful as he. All such offices are dependent upon the economic life of the community; the planter was all of these offices and the economic life, too.

The outright master of all he surveyed, with no other will to question his own, he co-operated with other masters to form the ruling bodies of his immediate country, his state, and from their ruling class they sent their own chosen representatives to act for them in London or, later, Washington. If you accused the planter of not being democratic, he would look at you in surprise and say, "Of course not. I am an aristocrat."

Manifestly the successful planter had little time for all the wanton and imperious sins attributed to him. Where a planter ran into debt, as did William Byrd III, he lost in a single generation all that his ancestors had built. When hospitality became too continuously lavish, as with Thomas Jefferson, the planter became impoverished and his plantation lost. Within reasonable limits, the plantation merely supplanted the town as a center of hospitality. Towns were bitterly opposed by planters and, except for their capital, where the ladies and gentlemen gathered on court days, the plantation was the center of social life as of everything else. It was a parish, a political entity, and to sustain this vast power all pleasures had to be enjoyed in moderation. When excesses of any kind occurred, or weaknesses were revealed, the plantation was soon lost to the family.

Because excesses did occur, and various heirs of great establishments simulated the mythical Old Massa, there was a steady turnover in the ownership of the plantations. Families rose to prominence and fell into obscurity in a dramatic fluctuation of fortune.

In time, the society based on the plantation and the planter class became relatively static in comparison with the dynamism of the industrial North, and a slave-labor economy began to appear feudalistic in comparison with Northern industry's use of cheap labor-pools of foreign immigrants. But these were nineteenth-century developments. Plantation culture lagged in this period of crucial change because the planters were satisfied. There is no dynamism in paradise. They had what they wanted, and their only concern was to keep it—and keep others out.

That, however, was a late development in the South, and it is a mistake to associate the plantation essentially with the antebellum era. It was only then that the whole South, the thirteen states which were to comprise the Confederacy, had built the plantation system, dominated by the planter-class and identified with a common culture. That had been over two centuries in evolving. By then new-sprung Bourbons wore the purple and the families of the generic masters lived largely in the afterglow of the power and the glory. The continuity was the plantation, not the individuals.

In a way that no other section was ever one thing, the South was plantations, and the destruction of the plantation system during and immediately following the Civil War caused the dislocation that affected three generations and leaves its effect today. For the plantation was always (and is now in retrospect) more than an economic system and pattern of life: it was a perfected ideal, designed and executed and hard won by hard men who came to a naked wilderness with a dream of a new life.

## 3

Virginia was the first "land of opportunity" in the New World; but only briefly—no longer than the span of a single lifetime—did opportunity beckon the small man. Though the illimitable land of the continent was there for everybody, and the access to wealth through the golden leaf of tobacco, the quickly evolving plantation system early gave the rewards to those who conceived largely and executed masterfully. In less than a century the planter *class* had emerged, forming a new and tight aristocracy which, in turn, formed the character of Virginia as an insulated, aristocratic republic. By 1701 a governor of wide experience in the Colonies observed the self-sufficient clannishness of Virginians, and said, "they begin to form a sort of aversion to others, *calling them strangers.*"

Within four and, at the most five, generations from the arrival of the first obscure settlers in Indian country, families such as the Lees, the Washingtons and Jeffersons, the Harrisons of Berkeley Hundred, had grown sufficiently imperious to challenge the might of Great Britain and lead an armed rebellion that a new nation might be created on earth—for themselves.

They not only had imperiousness, they possessed the true leadership, and this, too, developed from the plantation culture. These men had the habit of authority, they were familiar with the assumption of responsibility, and making decisions was second nature. In the period of the Revolutionary and post-Revolutionary leaders (the Virginia Dynasty), covering roughly the half century from 1770 to 1820, when Virginia produced more giants in a single era than any other region in America before or since, the plantation culture reached its fullest flowering and the aristocratic republic attained its "golden age."

Obviously the Old Massas of the legend do not create such a great epoch, nor was the society which produced the leaders built by a tropical and neo-Romanesque decadence. This society, with its splendor and

[7]

its arrogance, its graciousness and its cruelties, its greatness and its inequalities, was built by men who came to America's first frontier seeking to improve their lots in the new land of opportunity. They did not come as grandees; they came to become grandees. Their difference from all other frontiersmen lay in the nature of the dream which evolved during their conquest of the wilderness.

Totally at variance with the impression of static feudalism, plantation society resulted from an evolutionary process in which the masters and the system were born of the union of the dreams of men and the hot, rich land, and conditioned by a single curious circumstance—the British Civil War which sent the royalists (so-called cavaliers) to Virginia. The plantation master and the plantation came so close together that, in perspective, they seemed to have sprung up simultaneously. They did not; not quite. The plantation came first, and before the plantation came the dream.

The aristocratic republic which the early Virginians created was far from the consciousness of the first settlers, and certainly very far from the plans of England, to whom the experiment in colonizing came under the grandiose purposes of "for Crown, for Church, for Empire"—though this soon became translated into riches for the mother country at the expense of the colonists. For the first settlers the dream was simple and crude—gold. They came seeking a new Eldorado.

Tobacco early changed the goal of the search, refined the dream and created the plantation as the means to fulfillment. In turn, the plantation beckoned a more substantial class of settler, who conceived the magnificent dream of the private baronies. From these New World principalities—bound by common interests and sharing common concepts—came the final perfected dream of an aristocratic republic with its ruling class dedicated to responsibility for the whole.

The rapid changes from the first crude dream of quick riches into the concept of the plantation republic fell into three clearly defined, though overlapping, phases in Virginia's Frontier period.

The first waves of adventurers who came to Jamestown Island, and mostly died there, represented England's earliest fumbling attempts at colonization. In this venture, British financiers risked capital and men of desperate fortune risked their lives. Fittingly enough, "adventurer" was the technical term both for the men who invested money and for those who personally adventured. Of the original band of 105 who landed in Jamestown, not one left a descendant in Virginia; and of the less than 200 survivors of the nearly 800 who came in the first and most perilous period (1607-1610), not five by record left descendants in Virginia. These descendants, however well-connected and personally elegant, are not listed in that roll of the ruling planter families (Carters, Randolphs, Harrisons, Lees, etc.) who loosely comprise the royalty known as the F.F.V.s. For F.F.V. does not mean the first families who came to Virginia. It means the first families who achieved power *after* the settlement had been won.

The initial phase of privately backed enterprises lasted no more than a quarter of a century. During this phase, beginning with the discovery of Virginia tobacco (1614), individuals began adventuring on their own in small planting operations, and by the 1630s the small hard-working planter had superseded the financiers and the misfits seeking an easy fortune. The emergence of this yeoman class marked the second phase, which lasted nearly half a century. The existence of a stout yeomanry continued indefinitely and individuals arose from that class to become plantation masters, but as the dominant economic-social element—as the class giving the colony its character—the yeomanry began to decline with the coming of the cavaliers.

It was these royalists, with their background of English country life and ideals of gracious living, who (from the middle 1640s to the 1660s) brought the influences that were to give the permanent formation to the character and structure of Virginia society.

Virginians today live under some awesome misconceptions about the cavaliers, which contribute to the legend of the perpetual enchantment of the plantation world—what someone called "a time in thrall." In the legend, all cavaliers were noblemen and Virginia was settled entirely by cavaliers. This is similar to the countless living people who claim descent from Pocahontas, with never a mention of the six hundred contemporaries of the Indian princess who would also be ancestors. There was a Pocahontas who had a son, and there were loyalists of the Stuart kings who settled in Virginia during Cromwell's reign. But Virginia was settled before the cavaliers came, and the Lees, the forerunners of the Byrds, and the Harrisons of both Berkeley Hundred and Brandon were all in the colony before the cavalier influx.

"Cavalier" was a political and not social term (actually one of derision), and, while some cavaliers bore noble blood and many were well born, as a group they brought essentially an attitude and a style rather than pages from Burke's *Peerage*. As royalists they opposed the republicanism of the Cromwellians, as Anglican churchmen they opposed the dissidence of the Puritans, and they brought to the receptive land of Virginia a passionate conservatism and a distrust of republican dissidents in all forms, especially Puritans. They also brought that ideal of the life of the British country gentry, which served as a model for the energetic men of ambition who worked as planters. The cavaliers articulated the dream into its final form of a new-world society of land-baronies which grew out of the wilderness into a self-made and untitled aristocracy.

The cavaliers, then, were the dominant influence in the third phase of Virginia's frontier period, the phase that completed the transformation of colonists into Virginians. However, they never regarded themselves as colonials, and were extremely self-aware before the cavaliers came. In fine, the cavaliers gave the ultimate definition to the dream that began, crudely, on Jamestown island in 1607.

4

To begin at the beginning, England, in 1607, consisted only of the British Isles. Spain, the great rival, was the nation settling the New World. In addition to their conquests in South America and Mexico, the Spaniards had secured settlements in Florida, Georgia and South Carolina, and briefly—before the Indians wiped them out—had established a mission in Tidewater Virginia. The British needed to supplant Spain in the colonization of North America for the most practical of reasons to a most practical people—natural resources.

The island kingdom had won its mercantile position through its ships, and the limited area was running short of timber, of pitch and tar, and other essentials of shipbuilding. More acutely, in the lag between the passing of feudalism and before the age of industry, dispossessed country people crowded the cities and starved. We read of Shakespeare's London. True, the theater was a spot of glamour (though the immortality of the playwrights could have held little meaning to the audiences); wits found pleasure in the taverns and men of great learning, like Bacon, also in perspective cast a luster on the period. But to the hungry, diseased hordes, hoping for no more than the anesthesia of gin, the times were anything but romantic. Artisans were poorly paid, men of small businesses and modest gifts could find little in the future, and "the restless, pushing material" could find no place to push for opportunity.

The resources of this unexplored territory called Virginia (after the Virgin Queen, Elizabeth) could provide the essentials for ships, could open new pathways to wealth, and could offer opportunity to that restless, pushing human material. These were the practical considerations. Religion was another consideration not without its practical aspects.

The Anglican Church's renunciation of the authority of Rome was then so recent that England was filled with Catholic families from the days of the Pope's episcopacy. From the Calvinist movement, the Anglican Church was afflicted with dissenters (of whom the Puritans were a sect) in the rising tide of the Protestant faiths. Caught between "schismatics and papists" in their own country, the Anglicans added a realistic zeal to a colonization which would contain the spread of Roman Catholicism through the Spaniards.

With state and Church working hand in glove, men of substance contributed money, time and thought to the establishment of a permanent settlement on the unexplored continent. All previous attempts had failed. The most recent, at Roanoke Island in North Carolina, had been mysteriously abandoned, giving rise to strange and sinister rumors. To support the new attempt at empire, in 1606, under James the first, financiers chartered the Virginia Company of London with rights to settle the new continent, and 105 men volunteered for the ocean journey to the unknown, primeval land.

This first band, which included that literate and belligerent swaggerer, Captain John Smith, were not the founders of the colony in the form which Virginia was to assume. The forty survivors of this first wave established the barest foothold on a river island, and the following waves in the next three years did no more than cling to this precarious three miles on the edge of a three-thousand-mile-wide continent.

As the Crown and the London Company expected to find in Virginia the mineral riches that the Spaniards had found in Mexico and South America, so those first deluded individuals came for a quick fortune. They were illy selected by fate for the "adventure."

The majority were privileged to write "Gent" after their names, and it is difficult in our time to approximate the precise status of these gallants. Products of a fluidly stratified post-feudal society, they might be younger sons of the lesser nobility or pleasure-minded sons of some successful character who had been knighted; they could be dandified offshoots of the untitled country gentry or urban lads of decent connections and a flair for fashion. It is commonly presumed that most of them had squandered their modest estates in the London fleshpots and were seeking to repair their fortunes. It seems likelier that most possessed no estates to begin with, that they were picaresque characters who lived by their wits and their credit, and were taking the big gamble to get out of hock. In all there must have been a certain reckless courage and for a certainty all seemed to exercise that perquisite of "Gent" which rendered them superior to gainful employment and manual labor.

Since some brought starch for the ruffs that set off their doublets, pointed garters for their knee breeches and silver buckles for their shoes, it is obvious that the gilded bucks lacked the faintest conception of the demands of settling an Indian-infested wilderness. Few survived, and those who succumbed to malaria or Indian arrows or starvation doubtless died in the lonely land without the meager solace that their lives were sacrificed so a colony might be established.

The less numerous and more useful members of the band, those of "the common sort," were listed as artisans and as laborers, but in them, too, must have run a strain of reckless courage to make that desperate gamble. They lost, along with their social superiors, and the precise nature of their ends went unrecorded, as names simply vanished from the records.

For this doomed group, Captain Newport, an experienced mariner, and a council of six were appointed as leaders. They were feuding among themselves before they even reached Virginia. The president, Edward-Maria Wingfield, came of a family of professional soldiers and was himself, at forty-seven, a graduate of "that university of war, the Low Countries." Evidently capable in his previous career and certainly brave, Wingfield found nothing in his experiences to equip him for the uncharted frontier assignment, and he had no luck. Factions in the council turned against him and within a year he was back home, writing that "there were never Englishmen left in a foreign country in such misery as were we in the new-discovered Virginia."

The historically best known of the leaders was Captain John Smith, and at least part of his fame rests on the fact that he was by all odds the best writer. According to his accounts, he was the only capable man of the lot, and his adherents claim that the only reasonably good times in the first three years came in the period of his presidency. Son of a farmer, Smith was a soldier of fortune, very powerful physically and very ambitious, but boastful and contumacious and usually at odds with his fellow councilmen.

He was always taking small parties off in boats on exploring trips up the various rivers, mostly seeking a passage to the South Seas and the great glory. On one trip he was captured by Powhatan's Indians. After being given up for dead by his fellows, Smith unaccountably reappeared at Jamestown and years later, back in England, wrote a very moving story of having been saved from death by the chief's little daughter, Pocahontas. In essence, the story is probably true. He, too, returned home before the first three-year period ended.

Of the original six councilmen (excluding Captain Newport who was not a permanent resident), one died, one was killed by Indians, one was executed by his fellows, and Smith and Wingfield were both imprisoned before they returned to England. Only one, John Martin, remained in Virginia to found a plantation.

The one bona fide nobleman among the group was twenty-seven-year-old George Percy, who, not of the original council, was to outlast most of the others and have his turn at the presidency. He was the brother of the Earl of Northumberland, at the time imprisoned in the Tower for political misadventures, and young Percy unmistakably made his adventure to recoup his family's fortunes. He failed with the rest and returned to England, leaving no descendants in Virginia.

One other who came with unmistakable purpose was the Reverend Mr. Hunt—"Maister Hunt," as they called him. This devout Anglican dedicated himself to the religious life of the new colony. Though he prayed too much for the taste of some of the gallants, the clergyman always found willing helpers to provide the first makeshift places of worship. Maister Hunt was an early casualty; but, whatever its other failings, the Virginia Company always supplied the colonists with clergymen.

What no one supplied for the first period was a single, common practical purpose for those bands who came seeking an Eldorado and found instead a remorseless struggle for survival to which most were unequal.

5

Despite the long voyage, the 105 men and forty sailors reached the new continent in good spirits, the three small ships (*Susan Constant, Godspeed* and *Discovery*) sailing between the capes into the broad bay which the Indians called Chesapeake. It was a Sunday morning in late April when they first beheld the flowering wilderness, and the vine-entangled foliage was in its full semitropical bloom. The land was flat, contoured with gently rolling hills and sliced with shadowed ravines of clear-running streams and swampy creeks. The men observed with pleasure "the fair meadows and tall trees," and the dense fragrant vines of honeysuckle, wild grape and creeper. Wildflowers and bright berries grew among the creepers that draped the trees. The heat had not settled down then, breezes blew off the water, and the warm air was indolent and fragrant.

The men used the anchored ships as quarters, from which they made tentative land explorations, discovering Lynnhaven oysters, "very large and delicate in taste." They built a shallop, and in this light boat explored the broad tidal river (which they named the James, for their king) in search of a place to settle. Before the three ships sailed for the permanent settlement, the party experienced their first attack from the Indians, and two men fell wounded by arrows.

These Virginia Indians belonged to the confederacy of the great Powhatan and consisted of forty tribes whose demesne extended from the Potomac down into North Carolina, and from the ocean about one hundred miles westward to the head of tidewater in the large rivers. This mighty Powhatan is something of a figure of mystery. It has long been assumed that Powhatan, not a proper name, meant ruler, as Caesar. Now there is a belief that Powhatan did not mean ruler but, applying only to this one Powhatan, was a soubriquet meaning "falls in the current," after his stronghold on a hill in the present city of Richmond, where the falls mark the head of tidewater in the James River.

His brother or half brother, Opechancanough (Opie-can-canoe), who succeeded him, was not called Powhatan. He was involved in rumors regarding a sojourn in Mexico, but the rumors have shifted to Powhatan, placing his origin in Spanish-dominated Mexico. All that seems known for a certainty is that Powhatan was a most powerful and sagacious chieftain, under whose rule the widespread confederation enjoyed victory over their enemies and prosperity among themselves.

Powhatan's people were very superior savages. Though the "bowmen" (warriors) ranged far for fighting and hunting, the Indian society lived in villages of small huts and also tilled the soil. They enjoyed a finely balanced diet of fish, fowl and game meat, corn and peas, which were easy to grow, and fruit which they picked from the trees. They had their own religion and rigid tribal laws. Though polygamous marriages and divorces were a custom, unmarried sexual relations were not acceptable and infidelity was regarded as "the most unpardonable of crimes." Women were neither traded nor given against their will but, as the Virginia historian Beverley put it, "may manage their persons as they see fit."

They were a fine-looking people, and all stood so straight, with such uniformly well-formed limbs, that the Englishmen marveled at their physical formation. They were of a tawny color in youth, turning darker, more coppery, as they grew older, and extremely vain of their personal appearance. The women were small and well made, very pretty, with round, firm breasts that seldom hung even in old age. Quite the opposite of the stoic Indian, they were "full of spirit . . . Mirth and good Humor . . . extremely given to laugh, which they do with a Grace not to be resisted." They were also volatile and of violent emotions.

The men stood at about the middle height of the Englishmen, though some were relatively tall. As "bowmen," the men shaved one side of their heads to keep their long, coarse, black hair out of their bowstrings, and on the other side a scalp lock fell to their shoulders. They bedecked their hair with small feathers and were much given to ornaments, beads and bracelets and the like. Upper arms were tattooed with the tribal insignia and for war they painted their faces most hideously. They had light beards, which they pulled out by the roots with shells, and all Indians vastly admired the heavy-bearded Englishmen. Apparently one of Captain John Smith's appeals to Powhatan's daughter was his impressive beard.

The men's faces, like those of the women, were well featured with rounded foreheads, and the skins of both sexes shone with oil. In the summer, men and women went naked to the waist and wore about the middle something like a double apron. In the winter they wore over this middle-cloth a "matchcoat," a long, loose-fitting, sleeveless garment made of furs.

When the British came to their Eden, the Powhatan was of vast years and a great dignity, a man of treachery and loyalties and, in his way, of humor. Apparently white men had been seen by him before. There were strange tales of survivors of the Roanoke Island colony and of a blue-eyed Indian among Powhatan's people.

From the beginning his policy toward the new settlers was ambiguous, though he certainly did not welcome them as co-inhabitants. Sometimes the Indians fought and sometimes they professed friendship, trading corn for trinkets and guns. Mainly they observed from the shadows of the tangled vines, picking off strays. Occasionally they made full-scale attacks. Individual Indians became friends and individual whites who deserted the colonists were well received by Powhatan and lived in his town. Apparently he could form personal attachments but understandably resisted this strange, undeclared invasion.

The strangers were divided between a need to make friends (along with a vague purpose of Christianizing the savages) and the necessity of self-defense. The whites always fought hard against the Indians—though not always well—but it would seem that, for a variety of understandable reasons, they preferred to be friends of the natives. In any event, after their rude introduction to the Indians, the first band proceeded in wary alertness rather than in hostility up the broad James, on whose shores the dense, heavily vined forests rose like soft, green palisades.

On the fourteenth of May (old calendar) the ships came in on the evening tide to the river island selected by the council and, "in six fathoms of water," they were moored to the trees along the shore.

The boats were unloaded quickly. The gentlemen along with the vulgar sort lugged ashore their personal belongings and all gave a hand to the equipment supplied for their settlement.

Heeding earlier warnings and their own brief encounter with the Indians, the men made their first chore the erection of a log palisade, "pallizado," they called it. The gallants bent their backs with the rest behind the axes, because they were then only performing a necessary chore in order to get at the riches of the unexplored continent. Since they had landed on a projecting point of the island, the "pallizado" was built in a triangular shape—420 feet across the base on the shore, and each side some 300 feet, the length of a football field. Rude forts were erected at the corners, guns from the ships placed there, and, though such accomplishment was remote from the thoughts of the weary little company on the lonely land, America's first permanent English colony had been established.

6

For three years, with successive waves of immigrants, the settlement did not progress appreciably beyond this beginning. As it turned out, despite its convenience for mooring ships, the island of James Fort or James Town was an unfortunate selection as a site. Actually connected at that time with the mainland by a narrow isthmus, the low-lying land was swampy and damp. When the smothering, enervating heat of the Virginia Peninsula closed in on the men, who called the summer "the sickly season," the torment of mosquitoes added malaria to the general illnesses that afflicted them.

They managed to construct crude cottages in two rows, called streets, a storehouse facing a market place, a blockhouse for the guard, and did themselves proud on a chapel. This wooden building was sixty by twenty-four feet, with cedar pews and pulpit, "fair broad windows," and the air was kept fragrant by "divers flowers."

Interspersed with the wooden structures were rotting tents, the ground was muddy, and on the whole the town probably presented a depressing spectacle. A few men tried gardens outside the walls, and some corn was raised, but mostly the band depended on relief ships and the uncertain trade with the Indians. During friendly periods, the half-naked dusky children played freely on the streets and even the great chief's daughter, Pocahontas, turned cart wheels with the rest. ("Pocahontas" was the affectionate diminutive given by her doting father, and the Englishmen's translation into "Little Wanton," carrying none of the later-day connotations, meant gay and impulsive—or, as we would say, "full of life.")

In 1609, to begin the third year of the colonizing effort, the Virginia Company tried to vitalize the experiment by sending out nine well-supplied ships loaded with five hundred men, women and children. (Women had come to the colony before. In 1608, a man's wife came with her maid, Anne Burras, who married John Laydon, no "Gent." They produced Virginia Laydon, the first child of America's first permanent colony. No F.F.V.s have claimed descent from this humbly born girl and, as far as is known, there is no record of her fate.)

Two of the relief ships were lost on the way, and many passengers on the other seven died during the voyage. To join the 100 survivors of the first two years there were only 250 unacclimated newcomers, and among them were carriers of the London plague. Instead of revitalizing the colony, the added numbers made the following winter, 1609-10, the worst period that the settlers were to experience. Called "the starving time," the dreadful winter could as well have been called "the time of the plague" or "the time of the Indians." As a result of the three menaces, more than one half of the 350 alive in October were gone by the following June, and the survivors were in hard case.

Their shoddily built dwellings were decaying and part of the palisade had been torn down for firewood by men too weak to go wood-chopping. A push would have demolished the rest. George Percy, the nobleman, had his turn at the presidency during this period, and, under his mild leadership—if such it could be called—men chased despair by bowling in the weed-grown streets.

Though skilled artisans had continued to come in small numbers after the 1607 band, and there were fewer of the feckless "Gents," there were too many city casuals—the rogues, the shiftless and the drifters—who had come to the wrong place for an easy thing. Those who did not succumb to the rigors of the frontier succumbed to the apathetic aimlessness of life on the hot, malarial island. Indeed, the dispirited band, with dreams of gold forgotten, were in the act of abandoning Jamestown island when, in the summer of 1610, a new batch of leaders arrived with a new and—at last—effective chain of command. This was the turning point for the Virginia colony.

7

An advisory council had been appointed in London, and a permanent governor was selected to serve for life. To assist him or to serve in his absence were a deputy governor and something like an assistant deputy governor who, for want of a better term, was called "high marshall."

The first to arrive, preceding the governor, was Deputy Governor Sir Thomas Gates. Knighted in 1596, Gates was an old campaigner who had been to America before, as lieutenant in the Raleigh-Sidney expedition of 1585. Because his interests in England kept him going back and forth, his contributions to the colony's growth were not to bulk large, but at least he brought authority.

The high marshall came last, stayed the longest and accomplished the most. This relatively unsung character was the recently knighted Sir Thomas Dale, another graduate of the war in the Low Countries, where he had fought with Essex. A shrewd man-of-results, Dale was not the stuff of which legends are spun and a pompous hardheadedness won him few friends. He possessed, however, a practical grasp of the colony's needs and an unvainglorious competence in meeting them. As an incidental of which he was probably unaware, the old soldier had the distinction of introducing into Virginia the first strain of horses, having brought with him "seventeen horses and mares." The earlier half-dozen animals had been eaten in "the starving time."

Before Dale arrived, and after Gates had prepared the way, the pomp and ceremony of empire came to Virginia for the first time with Lord de la Warre, "Lord Governor and Captain-general, during his life, of the Colony and Plantation in Virginia."

Thirty-three years old at the time of his appointment, the third Lord Delaware (as commonly spelled), was an Oxford graduate, who, in addition to rendering distinguished military service, had also been a privy councilor to Queen Elizabeth and currently to James the first. A strong supporter of the Virginia colony since its founding, the first permanent governor was among those who for a certainty was motivated by a zeal for empire and for Church. Though the stout Anglican churchman lacked the physical constitution to adapt to the climate, his interest was deep and sustaining, and while he tarried, Delaware saw a solid impetus given to Britain's experiment in empire.

When Lord Delaware arrived on a Sunday in early June, 1610, his ship was met by the uniformed company which Sir Thomas Gates had brought over with him, and they presented arms smartly enough while the colors hung limply in the hazy heat. The magnificently caparisoned governor stepped ashore, followed by his own guard of fifty halberdiers in His Lordship's livery of "fair red cloaks." On the marshy shore, Delaware knelt and prayed silently. Then, followed by his personal guard in their resplendent red, the councilors and "other gentlemen," he marched to the little chapel in the center of the "pallizado."

After His Lordship's ceremonial arrival among the half-dead remnants of the colony, he immediately sought to project a working policy. Abandoning the duality toward the Indians (hoping for help, but fighting when necessary), he pronounced them enemies and, except for those who were proven friends, made war on the savages wherever he found them. At the same time, Delaware tried to make the colonists self-sustaining.

For growing Indian corn and garden crops, for hunting, fishing and general adaptiveness to the frontier, he had the help of those survivors called "the ancient planters," who "by use were grown practique in a hard way of living." And he had 'in the hierarchy of his command able and tough-bitten men who, some out of greed and some out of duty, were to strengthen the settlement.

Captain Samuel Argall was a greedy, ruthless young man, barely thirty, of real ability. As a mariner, he founded the new direct sea voyage to Virginia, and in the colony he was to get his chance at riches while acting as deputy governor. George Yeardley, who came over first with Gates, had started life as a tailor's son, risen as a professional soldier, and was later to be knighted and serve as one of the colony's best governors. He was a man of duty.

Then there was well-connected, tobacco-smoking John Rolfe, a sad and mannerly man of close to fifty when he came. No soldier, he held the lucrative post of secretary to the new Council and, an experimenter in planting, the black-coated middle-aged gentleman was to become associated in history (all unbeknownst to himself) with the romance of the first recorded marriage of an American white man with an Indian maid, the Princess Pocahontas.

The former "Little Wanton" had become a young woman of about sixteen, married to an Indian, when in 1612 she was captured by tough Captain Argall to be held as a hostage in bargaining with the Powhatan. The colonists found that they needed peace in order that planters might work in safety beyond Jamestown's "pallizado," and they needed Indian corn for their chronically borderline subsistence. As Pocahontas was the apple of the old chief's eye, the truce was made, and on the whole kept for some years.

While the princess was in captivity at Jamestown, she became a companion of Rolfe. Recently arrived in Virginia, he had lost a baby daughter on the voyage over and buried his wife soon after his arrival, and he was understandably lonely. A devout Anglican, Rolfe was disturbed at his deepening affection for a "heathen" and, probably disturbed about the whole affair, wrote to practical-minded High Marshall Dale an emotional letter of sentiment and justification about "these passions of my troubled soul."

Under Dale's own guidance, Pocahontas was converted to the Anglican Communion and, with Indians and whites amiably gathered in the little chapel, was joined to Rolfe in wedlock by the Reverend Mr. Richard Buck. John Rolfe was to enjoy only three years of married life with his tempestuous princess (1614-1617), before she died in England, leaving one son. This Thomas Rolfe, judging by the Virginians who claim descent from Pocahontas, was truly the Adam of the continent. The facts are that John Rolfe married again and died in Virginia in 1622, at the age of sixty, having made an incomparably greater contribution to the colony than tinting its early struggles with the color of romance. Through experiments with Indian tobacco, he discovered a sweet-leafed variety that revolutionized the use of the plant and provided the base upon which the Virginia colony was to grow.

8

Even measured by today's accelerated rate of changes, seven years was a brief span for the conversion of unknowing British settlers in a raw land from the chimera of gold to the reality of tobacco-making as a way to fortune. Planting, tending, curing and packing tobacco is hard physical work, requiring skill and patience, and this was no easy way to Eldorado. Indeed, for most of the settlers, making tobacco was a means of subsistence and—if they were resourceful and lucky—of improving the lot they had endured at home. However, when the adventurers turned from seeking easy fortunes to long-range work for their own betterment, Virginia began to change from a discouraged foothold of empire into a solidly based colony.

By the time of Rolfe's discovery (roughly 1614), the use of tobacco had become a fashion in England and in other parts of Europe. A world market was waiting for the hitherto neglected riches beneath Virginia's soil. Though the Virginia Company, as the sole proprietor of the colony, continued to try to control all operations, individuals began to plant tobacco in a small way on their own.

With a temporary truce existing with the Indians, men and families braved the unprotected stretches beyond Jamestown's overcrowded and unhealthful "pallizado." The original James Fort fell into decay and was gradually abandoned as settlers erected new houses paralleling the river. Some built near the grassy walk along the riverbank, called "the highway," and some on the "back street." Others developed small holdings farther away from what was becoming the "New Town," in isolated little clearings along the three-mile shore front. A few went to the inland side of the island, separated from their fellows by the great "pitch and tar" swamp.

More and more left Jamestown Island altogether. By 1618 the separate little tobacco-growing colonies had spread along both banks of the James River, to a depth of roughly five miles, seventy miles west from the mouth of the river to The Falls, at the present site of Richmond. South of the river, mining operations were begun for iron; a city——variously called Henrico, Henricus, Henricopolis——was planned near there; and a university was founded with a lower school for Indians.

During these years of expansion, adventurers still came and still failed to survive their first year. By 1618 the survivors numbered 600 out of the 1,800 who had put out from England. Since mortality rates in the early days ran as high as 80 per cent, this over-all 66⅔ per cent mortality rate for an eleven-year span indicated that the later arrivals were taking advantage of the mistakes of the "ancient planters" and that a strain of sturdiness ran through a cross section which still contained the useless "qualitye" and the shiftless among the "vulgar sort." Of fundamental importance to the initiative of the adventurers, and to the character of the newer arrivals, was a change for the better in the conditions offered the adventurers by the Virginia Company. Those men of business and large affairs had also to learn as they went.

One of their basic lessons was that English-speaking people do not thrive well under "communism," as *they* called it. In the beginning, colonists came to Virginia in two ways: they bought a share in the company for twelve pounds and ten shillings and came as freedmen, or they came as indentured servants. The word "servant" has a connotation to us which does not rightly place the indenturers. The individual indentured his services for a period of time, usually five years, during which he worked for free in exchange for his passage and his upkeep. Then he was on his own.

In the earliest days, the Company made it harsh for these settlers who did not pay their own passage. It offered the poor devils future "profits" in exchange for working on a communal basis for the Company. Since there never were any profits, and since the gentlemen of quality and the urban casuals more or less gave the character to the early days, there was no inducement for any man to work at a common harvest. One stout soul, who did cultivate a few acres of his own and built a house on it, gave to his holdings the only name of a plantation in early Jamestown. It was "Labour in Vaine."

As the Company caught on to the scant appeal this communistic enterprise held for the adventurers, more liberal terms were offered through reforms initiated by hardheaded High Marshall Dale. Ancient planters (who were held in high esteem by later arrivals) were

used as an indication of the early stirrings of democracy in Virginia. It really wasn't that way.

This assembly, the House of Burgesses, was granted the colonists through the liberalism of factions in the Virginia Company, and was supposedly to act something as a counterbalance to the more lordly Council. It was much later, after people became accustomed to exercising a voice in their government, that this *habit* of self-government influenced Virginians in their assertions and demands for personal liberty. (Even then, it would be a distortion to represent the House of Burgesses as representatives of the people as "the people" is meant today. Members had to be landowners to begin with, and actually the Burgesses was used as a proving ground and training course for promising young politicians in the ruling class, like Jefferson and Washington, the Lees and the Harrisons, who were being groomed for leadership.)

It can reasonably be assumed that during brutally hot July in 1619 when America's first electors met in assembly on Jamestown island, these sixteen men were more aware of their discomfort than of the historic fact that they were serving as precursors of democratic forms of government. Dressed in their Sunday best and stiffly on their dignity, the new "representatives" gathered in the chapel, still the only public building on the island, and suffered so acutely from the heat that they were happy to adjourn after five days and get back to their small holdings and tobacco planting.

Most prophetically in that same year came the first black slaves from Africa, twenty of them on a boat carrying the Dutch flag. They were introduced as a substitute for indenturers; unlike them, slaves could be bought outright and would not be free after five years. As a commentary on Western civilization as of that time, it is significant that chattel slavery was introduced into Virginia by Britishers. The colonists did not invent the system, and the small planters did not take readily to the idea. For the next fifty years the slave influx was small and slave labor exerted no influence on the colony until the large landowners designed their tobacco baronies.

In the year 1619, of far greater consequence to the lonely settlers was the first boatload of females, to be sold (for the price of their passage money, like indenturers) as wives. The sales were restricted to freedmen and supervised very carefully. Apparently the historically anonymous ladies made as good wives as the next and helped found frontier families—though, if genealogical-minded Virginians are to be believed, they were all barren. In any event, no claimant of descent from them has yet been found.

10

Even with wives and a "popular" form of government, with the Indians quiet for the moment and riches coming from the earth, seven hundred or more souls scattered along a seventy-mile strip on the edge of an unexplored continent still formed only a wild frontier that seemed remote from fulfilling the grand dreams of empire, of Church and of fortune.

Certainly fortune had come to none of the backers of the Virginia Company, men who subscribed for hundreds of pounds, and tales of distress trickling back from the New World discouraged new subscribers. Jealous bickering among the colonial leaders led to one faction vilifying another by painting horrendous pictures of life in Virginia, and naturally people were found to give credence to the worst.

The unscrupulous Captain Samuel Argall abandoned the colony with his plunders, and the last years of John Rolfe were saddened by Argall's enemies turning on him for the apologias which, as secretary, he had written for the acting governor.

Lord Delaware, the governor in absentia, had been prevailed upon, in 1618, to expose his health once more to Jamestown's debilitating climate, but he died on the way. Though Sir George Yeardley, appointed governor to succeed him, was a sound and dedicated colonist, in applying himself to Virginia (and accustoming himself to the style of the Governor's House, with thirty-five hundred acres attached), he could do little to calm the unsettled atmosphere around the Company.

In England, the King was growing impatient for the large profits. Except in tobacco, the colonists were not yielding to any extent products off which the home merchants could prosper, and the importation of raw materials was negligible. Then too, with less than one thousand survivors scattered along one river in the wilderness, there were not enough people going to Virginia. Actually, the time was running out for private enterprise as a system of colonization; the yeomanry was unobtrusively establishing the system of small individual operations.

Yet, considering the existing ignorance about the raw continent, the confused motives for and the fumbling methods in colonizing, the Virginia Company had accomplished incomparably more than it was given credit for. Their center originally made the yeomanry possible. Some of the Company's supporters maintained a high and intelligent idealism in the adventure, while others still wanted to see profits on their investments. Fighting to hold its charter as the proprietor, the Company adopted a plan which was something like a sublet of portions of the limitless land, by which smaller companies could take some of the load.

In these sublets, called "priorities," the Virginia Company granted tracts of land to groups of substantial citizens who would undertake to plant small colonies within the whole. The Company made no profit off these priorities. It was simply a method of getting more settlers in Virginia without paying out more cash themselves.

The Britishers who formed these priorities came for the usual motives of profit, of fascination with the project, or because they had been talked into it. Despite the discouraging stories of life in the New World, Virginia was still a magic name to the English mind and still evoked the image of opportunity.

The priorities still attempted the colonizing experiment by which absentee investors sought to gain from the personal adventure of individuals dependent upon the corporation. It was the last attempt.

The Hundreds, which the plantations of the priorities were called (either because one hundred settlers was the ideal figure for a plantation or because of the hundred-acre basic grant for a share of stock), served as a transition between the first phase of the private enterprise and the second phase of the yeomanry's rise. The Hundreds were a most costly transition to all involved.

❋ ❋

## CHAPTER II

# THE PLANTATION IS BORN

1

"The town and hundred of Berkeley in Virginia," the most thoroughly recorded of all plantations, was patented in 1618 by four British gentlemen who were all related by blood or marriage. The leader of the partners was John Smythe, Esq., of Nibley, not to be confused (as he was) with Captain John Smith. An Oxford graduate and lawyer, both learned and practical, Mr. Smythe had married a very well-endowed lady, and this fortunate circumstance permitted him to pursue his abiding fascination with Virginia. He had earlier subscribed seventy-five pounds to the Virginia Company, once risked fifty shillings in the Virginia lottery and donated sixpence to the college at Henricus. When he decided to form a private company for the founding of a plantation (originally the name of a private colony), Smythe turned to his substantial kinsmen.

Sir William Throckmorton, who had been created a baronet in 1611, had earlier shown interest by subscribing in the Virginia Company, and it is probable that he and Smythe secured the priority from the hard-pressed colonial financiers. Richard Berkeley, who bore the proud name which was given to their Hundred, appears to have become interested in Virginia only after Smythe and Throckmorton started forming the company. The fourth, George Thorpe, Esq., was a most dedicated Virginia colonist.

Less affluent than his cousins, Thorpe was extremely well connected. A "gentleman pensioner" and "captain," he was a member of the King's privy chambers and of the Council of the Virginia Company, though he had been able to subscribe only twenty-five pounds. Thorpe's particular interest was the conversion of Indians, and he had already experimented successfully with one. Soon he was to make the personal adventure to Virginia, where he could work with Indians in the lower school of the college.

Under the guidance of John Smythe, the lawyer, the partners went about the founding of their Hundred in businesslike fashion considering the gamble inherent in the venture. In wordy and repetitive charters, they covered every legal aspect in protection of their investment and redundantly clarified the means by which all profits would revert to them. Though from perspective the risks seem fantastic, even then the partners must have been to some extent motivated by the romance of a distant plantation. They appear to be similar to investors today who support some long chance out of interest in an enterprise.

According to the terms of their charter with the Virginia Company, the partners allotted to themselves as individuals one hundred acres for each share subscribed, another hundred acres for each passage of a person paid by them individually, and granted the Company fifteen hundred acres as communal property, reaching a total of something over eight thousand acres. Because the early expenses were heavy, they tried to bring in Governor Yeardley for a fifth share. Sir George, the tailor's son who had risen to eminence by ability and integrity, declined on the grounds that further private enterprise in the colony was inconsistent with his official position, though he offered to give them his support.

Then they tried to interest Captain John Woodlief, early adventurer to Virginia and their selected governor, in a fifth share. Woodlief might be willing to gamble his life, but not his money. On this point a misunderstanding developed between the home partners and the plantation manager which was basic in the relations between all British financiers and working planters, and eventually extended as a basic misunderstanding between the British government and all colonials. The Berkeley partners, then, as the British mercantile class later, failed to perceive that men would not expose their families to the risks and hardships of a frontier only for the profit of distant investors.

Woodlief himself was a man of some substance. (The name was spelled variously Woodliffe, Woodleaf, Woodleefe: Woodlief is the spelling of his Virginia descendants today.) Privileged to write "Gent." after his name and a subscriber to the London Company, he had adventured to Jamestown in 1608, survived the "starving time," and prospered as a planter sufficiently to import four indenturers to join his wife and children. The "captain" seems to have been an honorary title, doubtless to dignify his responsibility as plantation governor.

For serving as captain of the colony—supervising planting and directing the commercial center—Woodlief was specifically enjoined against taking any personal profits. Aside from subsistence for himself and family, his monetary gains were to come from sharing the partners' future profits. This was the genesis of the trouble. Soon John Smythe was complaining that Woodlief was evading the letter of the contract by such measures as using company servants to work his own tobacco acreage, and Smythe lamented to Throckmorton that "he hath deeply sophisticated with us."

Because communications were restricted to letters that were months in going back and forth, and self-interested parties in England and Virginia were forever spreading partisan rumors, it was easier for any misunderstanding over a conflict in details to grow out of hand than to be intelligently resolved. Woodlief's "sophisticating" would seem to consist of a realistic attention to his own affairs while serving to the fullest of his considerable capacities as plantation manager. His conduct would be similar to that of a company worker who, after full time on his job, followed personal interests on his own time by making some use of company property. The relationship between financial planters and working planters was tenuous at best, and these areas of obligation had not been clearly defined: the partners assumed one condition, the manager another, in a foreshadowing of the schismatic relationship between England and the Colonies.

None of these misunderstandings were even hinted at while the colonists were being gathered for Berkeley Hundred, and Captain John Woodlief supervised the chartering of the ship and collection of supplies. As that then rare man, an experienced planter, he knew the ways of the wilderness, the needs of the settlers, and he worked with hard practicality in fitting out the cargo and the colonists for the adventure.

The thirty-eight men who signed for the voyage were selected with care. Nobody can ever know the exact status of each. The charters refer repeatedly to "tenants and servants" and to "wages." Presumably the tenants were those who paid their own passage and, after three years of planting, came into fifty acres for which they paid the Company only twelve pence a year. During the three years of establishing residence, they were required to allot some of their time to community enterprises in exchange for the protection and advantages of the Hundred.

Some of the servants were obviously hired employees. William Clement was given an advance on his "wages" to get his tools out of the pawnshop, and a carpenter was paid three years' wages in advance in order to settle his debts. The wife of Richard Godfrey, a joyner, was loaned money against his wages, and the wife of John Cole was advanced money against his wages. Godfrey was drowned and Cole later died of causes unknown, but in his first year he earned forty shillings plus found. The surgeon (a graduate barber and not an M.D.) even then was highly paid, thirty shillings a month.

Which were straight indenturers is not known. These, for their period of years, worked entirely for the Company, without wages, against a thirty-acre stake on becoming free.

Among these tenants and servants (employees) and indenturers, there were oddly enough no farmers. There were carpenters, a sawyer, cooper, shoemaker and shingler, gunmaker and smith, cook and gardener, one "for hops and oade" and one "for pitch and tarre." The presence of city artisans and lack of farmers was typical of the whole colony. The unemployed urban workers would "set their life upon a cast," but landholders, however small the property or poor the yield, were reluctant to abandon their piece of earth. On the other hand, the dispossessed artisans sought their own pieces of earth. Thus, the generic colony of the agricultural South was built by urban fugitives, with their own dreams, subject to the transmutation of an unexplored continent.

To Berkeley Hundred came only three "Gents," at least so

listed, and these were not the foppish wastrels of the type whose corpses rotted in unmarked graves in Jamestown. One at least was a respected friend of the substantial partners and he with another, "ancient" Ferdinando Yates, served on the staff of five assistants (an informal council) to Captain Woodlief. As an indication of the partners' businesslike methods, the other three assistants were Godfrey, the valued joyner; a handyman artisan listed as "carpenter, smythe, fowler and turner"; and another friend of the partners, probably a clerk, Rowland Paynter. At least, John Smythe and his kinsmen selected workers.

With their band of adventurers formed, the partners demonstrated their mastery of the details of the settlers' needs in establishing a private colony. Including the charter of the ship, the forty-seven-ton *Margaret* of Bristol, and the passage of thirty six men, the cost of sending the first batch of adventurers came to 733 pounds— and that thirty-six hundred dollars in round figures represented considerable in those days. Though every pence was meticulously figured, the Berkeley Hundred company did not stint anywhere.

Heading the list of supplies were twenty-four muskets, powder and powder casks, matches and match casks, swords and bandoleers. Following the items for physical defense came the spiritual supports—Bibles and the Anglican Book of Common Prayer, with two of the popular religious sellers of that day, "The Practice of Piety" and "The Plain Man's Pathway to Heaven," *Wherein every man may clearly see whether he shall be saved or damned.*

Every manner of tool was supplied, every article for equipping buildings; cooking utensils, wooden dishes and spoons, sheets and blankets, pillows and bolsters, and a drum. For food there was fish, bacon, meal and wheat, peas, cheese and butter, bread and water (probably for the voyage), and "a ton and a half of beer." The men were supplied with two suits of clothes, shirts, shoes, stockings and caps. There were even six rugs, doubtless for the officers' quarters. Small sums were loaned or advanced to various of the wives who were left behind.

Without women, the small band left England at eight o'clock of a Thursday morning (September 16, 1619) for the long voyage from home.

2

The *Margaret* was at sea two and one-half months and anchored near shore in the Chesapeake Bay on the last day of November. The weather was mild and, though the flowers and most of the leaves were gone, the men found the country surpassingly fair, even exceeding the happy descriptions. They came on up the broad tidal river, where on both banks the wilderness at wide intervals was indented with small clearings. What lay beyond did not intrigue their imaginations, as dreams of gold and South Sea passages had beguiled the first group who came twelve years before. These people had come for a chance to earn their livelihood, much as the unemployed in our time moved to new places during the Depression.

Nobody can ever hazard their thoughts as, on reaching Jamestown, they beheld the small, crude houses, frontier versions of the feudal houses of England. At the governor's new house, outside the "old town," the officers received from Sir George Yeardley their patent to a very choice site. The governor had kept his word of supporting the partners and overrode a claim of Francis West, Lord Delaware's brother, to place Berkeley Hundred in the section destined to become (as Charles City County) one of the richest areas in Virginia.

The eight thousand acres of meadowland and virgin forests, with three miles of river front, was about thirty miles west of Jamestown by land (if there had been a road then) and much farther by water because of the huge loops (called "curls") in the James River above Jamestown. On the third of December the small ship anchored off an open stretch of shore line and the thirty-eight men were rowed ashore. When they placed their personal luggage on the hard ground, they gazed at the woods enclosing them and listened to the complete silence. Then, at a command from Captain Woodlief, with which they were profoundly stirred to comply, the homesick men knelt on the dried grass to pray.

Explicit orders in their charter commanded that the day of arrival be celebrated as Thanksgiving, and the date, as ordained, "shall be yearly and perpetually kept holy as a day of thanksgiving to Almighty God."

Some version of a thanksgiving celebration was as old as recorded history, going back to the Hebrews and the Greeks, and the Romans who copied it from them. In England, a thanksgiving was celebrated as a Harvest Home Day, and it was this custom that the Berkeley Hundred settlers followed on their safe arrival. Because New England had the better propagandists, Thanksgiving has passed into legend as an invention of the Pilgrims. Actually, before the religious dissenters called Pilgrims ever set out from England, the ancient custom of a thanksgiving celebration was introduced in the New World by that cross section of Britishers who founded a plantation in Tidewater Virginia.

After their religious ceremony had been celebrated, the little band set earnestly to work with a clarity of purpose that had never come to the first settlers at Jamestown. Before the ship was unloaded, the men built two public buildings—a stout storehouse for their food, implements, powder and shot, and an assembly hall, where the group gathered for meals and worship. Most such buildings, erected quickly before the ship unloaded, were crude affairs of logs peeled and split ("clove"), stacked vertically with the removed bark then applied as a coating. The average ran to twenty-five feet by eighteen, and were twelve feet high, though the assembly hall might have been larger. Probably individuals began building their own small dwellings on home models before the *Margaret* sailed.

When the ship left them in late January, the Berkeley family, though lonely enough, did not suffer the complete isolation of their predecessors. There *were* fellow Britishers, even if seldom seen, in the same naked wilderness. Gradually they grew accustomed to the howling of wolves, to the sudden sight of bears and wildcats, and to the rustling of unseen animals in the brush. The tenuous truce with the Indians continued and as a result, men could work without the nagging fear of unseen menaces lurking outside their range of vision.

Instead of building a fortresslike "pallizado," the colonists built a light palisade to contain their cattle and hogs, and to keep wild animals from their plantings and gardens. The London partners, trying to profit by the mistakes of the earlier colonists, made gardens and general planting the basis of the new Hundred. Tobacco of course was to be the big money crop, but the little private colony was not to subsist on the golden dream, even of the sweet-leaf beneath the foot.

First, the settlers must establish a self-sufficiency and not depend for sustenance upon relief ships and the uncertain Indian bounties (which, in trade, built up the savages' supply of firearms). Then, beyond both self-sufficiency and the money crop, the businesslike backers conceived a totality of agricultural operation which was to characterize the later great plantations, especially Berkeley. Through the then highly esteemed Captain Woodlief, the Hundred was to operate a commercial center in which subsidiary profitable products would tend to equalize the extremely unequal exchange between planters and British merchants.

After the first high tobacco prices passed, planters were always forced to sell cheap and buy dear (first with the British and then with the Yankees), and the design of the proprietors of Berkeley Hundred was to establish a broad spread of selling through which the plantation would not be dependent upon the fluctuations of a single crop. Human cupidity was to create a shortsightedness which caused many Virginia planters to defy this system, and later in the lower South the cotton barons were to ignore it almost completely; but the adventurers at Berkeley conceived soundly within the limitations of their knowledge of what the country would yield.

In the spring planting of Berkeley's first settlers, time was to be lost in experimenting with mulberry trees for the nurture of silk worms, with grapevines for the making of wine, and with the search for iron deposits—which, though worked south of the river, were never to be found in their part of Virginia. Nor did the men do too well with pitch, tar and hemp, to fulfill the British need for its ships. However, they at least made a start with their Indian corn, English wheat and garden crops, tended cattle and hogs and sold some fish, clapboards and timber for shipbuilding, along with a little tobacco.

Yet, the very diversity of the activities of inexperienced urbanites, with high rates of illness and death in the first year's pitiless test of adaptability, caused them to fall short of the primary goal of self-subsistence. The partners in London blamed this failure on Captain Woodlief, who seemed to them to be doing very well by himself. Actually no one could have done better than this frontier-wise plantation manager, but in the following year (1620) the British financiers, knowing little of local conditions, made some fundamental changes.

Bitterly complaining of the need to send a relief ship (whose cost of more than seven hundred pounds was called "insupportable") and insisting that the settlers *must* become self-sufficient, the Company made a change in personnel. "One Woodleefe," as they then called their energetic governor, was fired. In his place went George Thorpe, the Indian converter, and a new partner, William Tracy, a sad and mysterious mortal in Virginia's early settling.

### 3

Willi Tracy, as he signed himself, was obviously a gentleman of fine connections. He was the kinsman of Sir William Throckmorton and of Richard Berkeley, and other kinsmen were well placed and extremely loyal to him. His own brother had been knighted. Also, he must have maintained a certain position. His residence adjoined the estate of the recently widowed Lady Delaware, with whom Tracy was on friendly terms, and for his family of wife, son and daughter he had four maidservants whom he undertook to transport to Virginia. But at the time of his adventure, Tracy was in acute financial distress.

By some family arrangement, he was assigned his kinsman Throckmorton's share for 75 pounds with the understanding that he would pay in 300 pounds to the partners. The bulk of this, 175 pounds, was his fourth share for outfitting the second ship, the *Supply*. During the late winter, spring and early summer of 1620 Tracy raised something over 200 pounds on his share, though evidently it was hard for him to come by the cash. In the same period he moved his family to Bristol, in preparation for the voyage to Virginia on the *Supply*, and it was at the port city that his troubles began.

From his piteous letters of appeal to John Smythe, of Nibley, it would seem that Willi Tracy had impoverished himself in order to raise the stake in the Company and to settle his family temporarily in Bristol, where they were to subsist on credit until the *Supply* sailed for Virginia. It can only be assumed that his fortunes were already low and his adventure represented a desperate gamble, for the delay in outfitting the *Supply* drove him frantic as his debts mounted. In his one bitter outburst, inspired by fear, he wrote Smythe, "You have Nibley and he (Berkeley) has Stoke, but I have nothing but Virginia, and that I am held from, to live in shame and disgrace in England."

No appeal could move the partners to hurry. By the summer of 1620, the dedicated George Thorpe had left for Virginia to investigate the situation, Throckmorton had sold out, and Richard Berkeley showed himself to be unresponsive to the plight of Cousin Willi. Though John Smythe must have professed some sympathy to Tracy, the master of Nibley was a practical-minded man who paid meticulous attention to details, and his practicalities did not include assuming personal responsibilities for a rush job on outfitting the *Supply*, even to help the stranded family of the new partner. The result of the delay was that William Tracy, Esq., was jailed for debts —providing a handy fact for those who wished to prove that Virginia's earliest settlers contained "jail-birds."

Then the family was aroused to action. Through the importunities of various cousins (not including Richard Berkeley), Sir William Throckmorton and Smythe got the wretched man released. Within a matter of days, the *Supply* was made ready to sail with fifty people. Smythe had reached an agreement with Tracy over the rest of his share and had also paid out of pocket the 175-pound share of George Thorpe, already in the colony. The venture had been rushed at the end and Smythe's detailed reports reveal that many items had arisen in the one year of colonization to plague the reduced partnership, in which he was in effect the only actively responsible person operating in England.

Some five of the workers had, for instance, petitioned to have two servants each sent to them. They had to be put off tactfully, as servants for a few would create discontent in the majority. Besides, with the limited space on the *Supply*, it was important to ship as many artisans as possible. Even Willi Tracy, with his brood, wrote that "men being the more usefull and excellent creatures, it would be ill to go Chasing for women." (Mr. Tracy's spellings are all recast, as he was the poorest speller of all who formed the Berkeley Hundred Company, including that "ancient" Ferdinando Yates.)

Settlers already in Virginia were petitioning for their wives, and John Smythe decided it the point of wisdom to send over the wife, son and daughter of their fine carpenter, Coopy. Also, a number of the new settlers would go only with their wives. Monies were also involved with personnel, and in fine, Smythe the effectual partner had to contend with a number of troublesome problems to which Willi Tracy was not privy. As it turned out, the new settlers were selected with less careful screening than the first.

One died before the ship left Bristol, a maid of the Tracys decided at the last minute not to go, several others jumped ship on the stop in Ireland (as they had it, "went not but stayed in Ireland"), and two came back after one sight of the wilderness. There were more gentlemen, too, more women and children, and the whole supporting shipment was more haphazard than the first— even with the replacement of George Thorpe and Willi Tracy for realistic Woodlief, who went south of the James River to found a private plantation that lasted until the Civil War.

Finding that a number of the original Berkeley colonists had already died could not have put heart in the new arrivals. George Thorpe had a most significant comment on the high mortality of the first-year arrivals. He wrote to Smythe that he was "persuaded that more do die here of the disease of their mind than of their body."

The Indian converter believed that the newcomers were disappointed at the victuals in contrast to what they had been led to expect and "not knowing they shall drink *water*." This drinking of water and not spirits was a matter that the good Captain Thorpe set himself to rectify.

The miserable quality of Virginians as propagandists is attested to by the fact that not one bourbon whiskey is called "Old George Thorpe" after America's first distiller of corn. In his own words, Captain Thorpe wrote, "We have found a way to make so good a drink of Indian corn as I protest I have divers times refused to drink good strong English beer and chosen to drink that (of his own brew)." The drink was probably like an ale, and for generations to come this corn-distilled drink provided comfort to the early Virginians.

Without knowing that he was to exert as profound an effect

upon the South with his precursor of bourbon as did John Rolfe with tobacco, Captain Thorpe turned the plantation over to his co-manager, Willi Tracy, and moved on to the college across the river at Henrico—pronounced Hen-rike-o.

This college, the first in America, was located on the south side of the river on one of its great loops, about ten miles southeast of the present site of Richmond. The settlers conceived of the river as a central avenue in the colony (a watery Main Street) and at that time the south side of the James was more populated than the north side, which later came to dominate. The City of Henrico was designed on the river site of the college, but only the college was well advanced in its physical buildings. It had been surprisingly well endowed by Britishers interested in educating their less fortunate cousins across the sea, and George Thorpe's mission of educating Indians to Christianity through the lower school was in no sense chimerical. He had a soundly based and working proposition, to which he brought a selfless zeal rarely equalled in those early days.

Thorpe also co-operated with Willi Tracy at the Hundred during the winter of 1620-21, and in the spring Captain Thorpe had to become sole manager. Poor Willi's desperate gamble had not paid out. After all his troubles and humiliations and hopes in the adventure, he became one of the first-year casualties. Tracy had written Smythe, on his belief in the colony's welfare, "God grant that we labor to gain it more for the soul than the body." Dramatically it was unsound for him to die in April. Yet, perhaps, the long silence in a faraway place came as a mercy.

His son returned to England and Tracy's wife died after him at Berkeley Hundred. His daughter married powerfully connected Captain Nathaniel Powell, a councilor with a plantation outside Jamestown, and one of the maidservants—who had romantically married on the boat coming over—went with Mrs. Powell. They were all soon to die horribly and, as the little-recorded Tracy family, their family unit illustrates the true desperateness of the long gamble on Virginia.

4

It is not possible to establish the exact population of the private colony at the time of the second spring planting at Berkeley Hundred, 1621. Eighty-odd men, women and children had come in the two shiploads, and four more men had come with Captain Thorpe. Of these approximately ninety settlers, several, including the original first assistant, "ancient" Ferdinando Yates, had returned to England. Among the others, the death rate ran very high during the first year; however, the dates of the individual fatalities were not given.

Though brick-work for houses was beginning by 1621, the large majority of homes were still constructed—in various makeshifts—primarily of wood; and, from the rapid decay of the early Jamestown houses, it can reasonably be assumed that only those men who were both hardy and skilled built tight houses. Log houses of the sort that came to be called log cabins were not used, though the settlers are now known to have developed before mid-century an understanding of construction with logs. When Berkeley Hundred was being settled, most settlers still tried to copy the feudal English houses they had known at home. Since carpenters were few at the beginning and all at Berkeley Hundred were early casualties, most of their do-it-yourself efforts on dwellings (of which not a trace has survived) achieved inadequate shelters for the damp, bitter winters.

Judging from medical studies in later periods in the same climate, many of the settlers fell victim to respiratory infection and, lacking both medical attention and home nursing care, died in effect of neglect. Then, the sticky enervating summers brought malaria and "the sickliness" which, compounded by the disease of the mind as mentioned by Captain Thorpe, carried off the despairing who lacked the will to fight for life.

The uncertainty over the survivors at this time was the same in all the plantations strung out east and west from Jamestown on both sides of the river. Approximated figures for the total population of the Colony in 1621 run something over eight hundred survivors and newcomers of the two thousand adventurers who had put out from England. Outside of the small planters who worked in the environs of Jamestown, these settlers were scattered in about fifty plantations generally along the James River. Some of these plantations were private colonies, such as Berkeley, and others were individual operations on various scales. Most of these were relatively modest affairs, listed as "Mr-So-and-So, His House." A few, like Martin's Brandon and the grandly y-clept Flowerdieu Hundred, were sizable plants for their day. Probably none was larger than Berkeley Hundred.

The practice for these isolated plantations was to form loosely in groups near some center. For instance, on the south side of the James River (south of the present Richmond), where a company worked the iron mines at Falling Creek, Sheffield's Plantation was listed as "some three miles from Falling Creek," and the next in turn was "about two miles from Sheffield's Plantation." In other sections, locations were given as "about the precincts of" and "as the plantation next adjoining." However, outside of Jamestown and the embryonic city of Henricus, there was nothing remotely resembling a town or a road (travel was by boat or on foot), and fifty-odd, unconnected little clearings comprised the merest fringe of civilization on the edge of a savage wilderness. At the same time, the colonists did represent a firmly planted foothold of empire; no matter how small and lonely, it was there to stay.

A grim realization of this came to the Indian population.

In the early days, the Indian leaders had waited patiently—with little prods of their own—for the band of white invaders to perish as had their predecessors. Instead, from the spring of 1621 to the spring of 1622, Virginia made its strongest spurt in growth of that time. With new arrivals, the colony rose to something like twelve hundred settlers. Though a proportion of these represented the unacclimated, at least two thirds of the whites had passed the test of the frontier and could be definitely regarded as permanent residents of the country the Indians had regarded as their own. The Indians decided on punitive measures for clearing their land of the unwelcome co-inhabitants, and their decision became the best-kept secret in the history of Virginia.

Who conceived the Indian plot was never discovered. Its design and execution were so masterful that some observers believed the Spaniards had a hand in it. Outsiders would not have been necessary. A strain of great power ran through that generation of chiefs, and the current chief, Opechancanough, the younger brother of Pocahontas's father, had always been more forthrightly hostile to the whites than the Powhatan who became Captain John Smith's friend. While the truce continued in the four years following the death of the old leader, who had made the peace as ransom for his daughter, Opechancanough obviously had been brooding over the expanding white colony. It is obvious because his plot could only have been the result of long maturation.

During the winter of 1621-22, the Indians made themselves particularly friendly. New settlers, such as those in the small colony at Berkeley Hundred, had never experienced any Indian hostility, and the gestures of friendship convinced them that racial enmities were a thing of the past. The Berkeley family were easily persuaded to trust the Indians because Captain George Thorpe, their surviving leader, had not only made strides with his conversion of the savages but established an intimacy with Opechancanough.

Captain Thorpe had especially pleased the Indian King by building him a new house "according to the English fashion." Previously the chief had abided in a cottage made with sticks and poles and covered with mats "after their wild manner." But Captain Thorpe's feudal replica included a door, and the Indian thought "no device in all the world was comparable" to the lock and key. He locked and unlocked his door one hundred times a day and, in his admiration of Captain Thorpe's civilization, confessed that the English God was a good God, better than theirs.

Captain Thorpe then told Opechancanough that if he would worship the English God, he would partake of the good things the whites had, and things "far greater than sense or reason ever could imagine." The Indian chief appeared to ponder favorably about these promises, and the whole Virginia Colony was pleased at the devout Captain Thorpe's success with the savages.

On other isolated plantations the settlers traded freely with the Indians—beads and trinkets for corn—and received them in their own homes at meals. In Jamestown, with the "pallizado" all gone, and three trading vessels standing off the shore, the new secretary did not even mention Indians in his letters. This former gentleman of fashion was more fascinated by the doings of the common sort, who strutted about in gaudy clothes and gave themselves unseemly airs. He also pined for clever conversation about the arts and gossip of the great world, though he consoled himself that his soul was ennobled by hours of contemplation in the vast silences. It removed vanity from his mind.

In such freedom from anxiety, the settlers entered the Lenten season in 1622.

### 5

Early in the morning on Good Friday (March twenty-second that year) friendly groups of Indians drifted into the settlement at Berkeley Hundred. The survivors among the colonists had reason to feel full of the Christian impulse in that religious season and they were happy to include the peaceful savages in their good fellowship.

The winter was behind them and, during the bleak season, the people had worked at building up their settlement. Men inured to hardship had cut wood, and the sawyer had helpers on his make-shift mill, and the houses and the two public buildings had been made more snug. Other men had experimented with brick-making and more fields had been cleared for the spring planting. Already the former city dwellers, grown wise in the way of the land, had planted their tobacco seeds and covered them with the rich earth. Most of their cattle had weathered the winter and their hogs, which ran as wild as boars in the woods and ate acorns, had yielded a curiously dark and flavorsome ham (the precursor of the Virginia Smithfield ham).

As the Indians approached, on good Friday morning, the colonists' fierce mastiffs set up a roar, but masters quickly quieted them. Captain Thorpe was indignantly opposed to loosing mastiffs on Indians and, over the angry protests of some planters, had killed dogs who attacked Indians. In fact, he would have "gelded" all the mastiffs in the colony if he'd had his way. The manager was absent on Good Friday, across the river at the college, but he would have been pleased at the reception his people gave the Indians. Some were invited by the bachelors into the assembly hall where the trenchers were being loaded with gruel, and a few went into private dwellings.

No white man or woman saw a signal given, but as if by some

group impulse, the unarmed Indians suddenly snatched up the muskets which the unsuspecting settlers had propped in corners. Some grabbed up carving knives and the staves that were used to drive animals, others reached for hatchets and all the implements of peace which could be turned in a moment to deadly weapons.

Despite the surprise, few whites were killed at the first onslaught. In John Rowles's little house, he went down with his wife and child. But where only men shared a house and in the assembly hall, the toughened settlers fought hard for their lives. While they fought, dwellers in other private houses had the chance to escape behind the smoke screen of the burning buildings.

Elizabeth Finch, who had survived her husband, and remarried, escaped with her daughter Frances. Elizabeth Webb, one of the maids who had come with the Tracy family and married in the colony, also got away, as did Elizabeth Coopy, who had been sent on the second ship with her mother and brother at the importunities of Thomas Coopy, one of the five original assistants of Woodlief. Coopy and his wife had previously died and what became of their son is not known.

The records are not complete on the fate of the individuals who came to Berkeley Hundred. In the massacre on Good Friday morning, eleven are listed as being "slayne," at the plantation. As forty-eight are listed as "dead" by 1622, it is probable some of these had died of wounds. Seven others besides Coopy's son are unaccounted for, and five of the Berkeley Hundred emigrants were killed at other places. For, unknown to the Berkeley colonists, similar friendly groups of Indians had drifted peaceably into almost all the plantations in Virginia at the same breakfast hour on Good Friday, and followed precisely the same pattern.

At the college, where twelve workers were killed and all the buildings burned, one man ran to warn Captain Thorpe. The devout converter and friend of Opechancanough would not believe ill of the Indians. He stood quietly, unbelieving, as four of them clubbed and stabbed him to death. His body, like those of the other corpses, was horribly mutilated.

The last of the Tracys in Virginia, Mrs. Joyce Powell, "great with child," was slain along with the maid who had come over with her (and romantically married at sea). Her husband, councilor and captain, Nathaniel Powell, who had obtained four hundred acres through the offices of his father-in-law, went down with all his people.

John Howlet and his son, working by some wage arrangement away from the Hundred at the ironworks on Falling Creek, were killed along with most of the company of ironworkers.

In addition to the ironworks and the college, some twenty-five plantations were attacked, and many were completely wiped out, women and children falling along with the men. At that stage of the colony's development, there were relatively few women compared to the male population, and the status of all is not clear. Those listed as "maid" were maidservants, working for one family. Those listed as "female" could either have come as indenturers or in later shiploads of women sent to be wives; perhaps they had failed to find husbands or were widows and not so listed. A breakdown of those slain at the separate plantations reveals the structure of the frontier society as of 1622, the fifteenth year of the colony.

On one plantation where twenty-seven were killed, there were living two wives, each with a child; on another where the Indians claimed nineteen victims, were one wife, one "female," a father and son; where eight were slain, the total group included two brothers, a man with his wife, child and sister, a boy, and a female provocatively listed as "Goodwife Redhead," evidently a widow. Ten were killed on a plantation where a wife, child, and two maids were living; six at another which listed "one old maid called Blind Margaret" among the inhabitants. Captain Powell's plantation sheltered his wife and her maid, two females and seven other men; a "Polander" lived on another, along with three other men, a wife, and two boys; and at still another was a "French boy," three men, a wife and child. One little family unit consisted of a man, his wife and child, maidservant and boy-indenturer.

There were also strictly male settlements, as revealed by the death lists: three out of five men were killed at one plantation; at another, two out of three men and a boy fell victim. Captain West's plantation, adjoining Berkeley Hundred (and later to become the Byrds' Westover) held three separate units of two men each.

The most wholesale murders occurred on two new plantations, private colonies like Berkeley. At Martin's Hundred (not to be confused with the earlier Martin's Brandon) seventy-four were killed, including ten wives, one with a suckling child and four other children, and five either maids or females. At the very new Bennett's plantation, where fifty-three were killed, the only women were the manager's wife and her child, two maids and five females.

The total death rate in the colony came to 349, close to one third of the total population. The casualties struck most deeply at the foundations of the foothold of empire because the majority of the victims were seasoned adventurers, with at least the first fatal year behind them.

Yet, the timing of the Indians was off. Four years before, when the great Powhatan died, the mass slaying and incalculable destruction of properties might well have been the blow (so experienced observers believed) that would have set up the struggling colony to be finished by continued Indian aggressions. But the blow came too late and the colony had enjoyed one stroke of luck, one happy result of the effort to convert Indians.

A man named Perry had converted a single Indian, and the two of them had moved in with a planter on the mainland near Jamestown. This planter, Richard Pace—who called his holding "Pace's Paines"—had treated the Indian convert like a son, and this one Indian responded to the affection. On the night before the massacre, the Indian's brother came for a visit, and divulged to him the grand plot, in which his part was to kill Pace. The Indian struggled with his new-found Christian conscience until near morning and then broke down and told the whole thing to the white man who had befriended him.

At first light, Richard Pace rowed across the backwater to Jamestown Island and gave his historically neglected warning to the officers. The result was that when the groups of Indians drifted idly toward the island on Good Friday morning, they found the whole population waiting for them with loaded muskets. No attack was made on Jamestown island, and the center of the colony remained intact as a haven and a core for the recovery of the Virginia colony.

6

As no poet made a "Paul Revere" out of yeoman Pace, so Virginians made no to-do about what they simply referred to as "the massacre." The survivors of the largest Indian massacre ever on the continent were more outraged at the treachery of good Captain Thorpe's converts than aware that America's first college, along with the city and the ironworks, had been wiped out of existence.

When they began to rebuild, the colonists had no heart then for another college (certainly not for converting savages) and the city to replace Henricus waited a century to be reborn as Richmond. The day of dreamers and idealists such as Captain Thorpe was over, and soon the Virginia Company would pass, too. Gone forever were the vague abstractions of "for crown, for Church, for empire." Virginia had established Britain's first base of empire and this colony of plantations could yield riches from tobacco. Let the survivors pick up the pieces and go on realistically from there, killing Indians where they found them. There was no more talk of conversion; the order went "to make war, to kill, to spoil. . . ."

There is no record, such as that meticulously kept by John Smythe, Gent., of Nibley, of the heartache and the travail of picking up the pieces. Immediately following the massacre, the survivors on the outlying plantations were ordered to come under guard into James City, like people evacuated today from disaster areas. This move was not only for their protection but because hundreds were without food. The Indians had killed the cattle and, in setting fire to the buildings, burned the stores of corn.

As time passed without further depredations, various individuals (such as Richard Pace) petitioned the Council for permission to return to their holdings. The yeomanry wanted to get at their tobacco, and they had no fears of being surprised by Indians again. On other plantations, there was no one to return. Some of the abandoned holdings reverted to the colony and were repatented, others went to heirs in England who sold the land. The land remained to be worked again, but the buildings vanished and the wilderness reclaimed the sites where private towns had been bravely planned.

Though some privately financed Hundreds (like Martin's Hundred) poured more money into the wreckage in efforts to revive their plantations, most were slowly abandoned and eventually sold. While it was not recognized at the time, the massacre marked the beginning of the end for absentee proprietors, both the Virginia Company and the priorities. As personal survivors patented their own holdings and swelled the yeomanry, the British financiers lost heart in risking more capital on settling the colony. The settling of Virginia began to shift to those who made the personal adventure.

Of the ninety who had adventured to Berkeley Hundred, fourteen returned to the charred ruins: four women and ten men, including the drummer and two cooks who had managed to survive all hazards of famine, illness and Indians. All of their leaders were gone.

Woodlief, the first, was then working his own plantation; Willi Tracy had died and Captain Thorpe had been killed; three of the original five assistants had died, old Yates early returned home, and John Blanchard, Gent, was unaccounted for. One of the two surviving gentlemen, Thomas Kemis, was appointed governor by John Smythe.

By then, with two of his partners dead and Richard Berkeley taking little active part, the whole burden had fallen on Smythe. At first the master of Nibley seems not to have realized the extent of the disaster, for he still expected a good tobacco crop the following year. But by the summer of 1623, Smythe knew the worst. He joined other Britishers in pledging relief to the colonists, Smythe specifically for his own Hundred, and from then on his venture went steadily downhill.

Kemis, the last appointed governor, died, and the managership devolved by default on a Richard Milton, neither "Gent" nor "Mister." It is not known whether Milton had come as tenant, servant, or indenturer, but he was to stay longest. In the ten years following the massacre, all the survivors except Milton and one other disappeared from the records. Some doubtless died and others, having worked out their tenancy or indenture, moved on to patent their own fifty acres and join the growing class of the yeomanry. The other survivor, John Gibbs, an able and ambitious man, evidently unable to get along with Milton, had hired out for wages with the plan of buying the plantation for himself.

When Gibbs made an offer in 1632, no remnants of the buildings remained and the site of "the town and hundred of Berkeley" was almost obliterated. However, the rich land on the river was there, some of it cleared, the company still owned hogs and cattle, and Richard Milton was still around, trying to care for the animals and breed the cattle. As the sole accredited resident of the eight thousand acres, Milton wished to revive the plantation with himself as "Captain," and asked the Company to send over three servants for him and three for the Company, to rebuild the center unit and plant tobacco again.

A Mr. Thomas Combe, representing John Smythe, investigated the situation and wrote the last active partner a very clear letter on the conditions. Though Mr. Combe believed Gibbs to be the better man and preferred the two survivors to work together, since Gibbs was set on becoming a planter himself, he thought the plantation should be revived under Milton even though, as he wrote Smythe, "we adventure but a small matter."

He pointed out that settlers at that period would be better able to sustain themselves, and the company need invest only in the clothing, weapons and corn for half a year, for three men—ignoring Milton's request for three servants for himself. In urging on Smythe the revival of the plantation, Mr. Combe pointed out that many other commodities besides tobacco were then coming from Virginia. Pot ashes made soap "the rarest in the world"; there were cedar and black walnut, beaver and deer skins, and for colonists there was a plenty of bread and butter and cheese. Though Mr. Combe was restrained in his optimism and tried no persuasion, clearly he longed to see the plantation recapture its lost glory. He was more correct than he realized in believing that the times were riper for adventure in 1632 than they had been in 1622, for the early history of Virginia came to be divided—actually and in the peoples' minds—into before and after the massacre.

John Smythe, deep and constant though his interest ran, had had enough of financial participation. He was then sixty-five years old, with nine children, and, as he said, he had "spent upon

Virginia a very great matter." Though the time might be riper for colonists, the time had passed for the British-backed plantation. The end had come with the passing of the Virginia Company in 1624. Though the old adventurer was not aware of the historical second phase which the colony had entered, he recognized that the day of the yeomanry had come.

When the Crown took over Britain's colonizing, the Virginia governor became responsible to the King—then Charles the First —and at Jamestown the governor fell under the influence of the growingly powerful Council of landowners. In England Mr. Smythe's friends in the Virginia Company (to which he had subscribed and through which he had received his patent) ceased to be useful; he needed friends at Court and on the scene in the colony. Gentlemen of the standing of poor Willi Tracy and the devout George Thorpe could probably have protected his interests in Virginia, but the governor and the Council brushed aside the likes of Richard Milton. He could not even hold on to the cattle against the claims of the Council's friends.

It would have been difficult to find a new manager of the caliber of the old; such gentlemen were beginning to make their personal adventure to build private domains, not for absentee landlords but for themselves and their heirs. It was too late, in all ways, to revive a Company colony. With whatever repinings, the master of Nibley resigned himself to writing about Virginia and no longer participating in its events.

Yet the learned and practical-minded colonial adventurer had participated in a symbolic phase of Virginia history—the transition from the raw frontier, in which financiers speculated with their money and the desperate with their lives, into an established settlement of permanent colonists with new dreams in the world. Historically unheralded, his Hundred, and others like Berkeley, had done their part in the conquest of the wilderness, opening the way for *residents* to form a society of independent, self-reliant, small planters.

So rapid were the changes in The Frontier Age, phase following phase like waves, that, even as the era of the yeomanry supplanted the era of the privately financed expeditions, there were already in Virginia men of ambition and substance who were

to design, execute and dominate a culture that doomed the hard-working planters who desired modestly.

South of the James River lived the first of the line which was to become identified with the Hundred founded by the aging Mr. Smythe, and by an odd coincidence this first Benjamin Harrison (whose grandson was to establish the family at Berkeley) had occasion, as clerk of the Council, to write John Smythe in 1634. Thus the founder of Berkeley Hundred not only reached back to the past and symbolized the transitory phase from it, but touched the hand of the future.

Before Smythe's death in 1641, Richard Lee—whose blood-lines were to cross with the Harrisons and who was to sire the greatest of all Virginia families, one of the greatest in the country—had already planted in Virginia; and John Stegge, whose descendants, the Byrds, were to intermarry with the Harrisons of Brandon and become the neighbors of the Harrisons of Berkeley, was already trading in the Colony.

These men represented the new wave, already forming to wash over all that had gone before. Men destined to become plantation masters were buying up the Hundreds, where not even graves marked the bitter and violent ends of men and women, who, seeking to better their lots, had won the great tracts on which a more fortunate generation were to build personal empires.

Those first of America's pioneers were the most unlucky and the least remembered. They had no flair for success, and the chroniclers (then as now) liked to record the doings of the celebrated. Even John Smythe, of Nibley, is known only because, in his meticulous attention to detail, he kept records and letters. History's final slight was to confuse him with that boastful swaggerer, Captain John Smith, and his revenge for that indignity was most modest: in his own writings on Virginia, Smythe did not mention Smith. But history treated him shabbily to the end. Few read his writings, possibly because there was no Pocahontas at Berkeley Hundred.

His Hundred is known because of those successful men who prospered after he was dead, and used his link in the chain with grand indifference to those who had gone before.

❀ ❀

## CHAPTER III

# THE FLIGHT OF
# THE CAVALIERS

1

*The* first Benjamin Harrison might be called, for purposes of definition, one of the larger yeomanry. Of somewhat more substance and with more advantages than the average member of that class, he did not adventure to the colony with the means of, say, Richard Lee and some of the later large landowners. He did, however, possess at least sufficient education to become clerk of the Council, he enjoyed sufficient standing in his locale to be elected to the House of Burgesses, and he laid the foundation on which his family was to rise into the ruling class. Of the conditions under which he made his adventure, nothing is known. In fact, nothing is known at all concerning the origins of the founder of the Berkeley Harrison dynasty; and, considering the Virginian's passion for genealogy, it is clear that the emigrant came and settled as an obscure person.

It is probable that Benjamin Harrison (the spelling was changed from Harryson) arrived some while after the massacre (1622) when, as John Smythe's representative wrote, circumstances were more favorable for colonists. By March of 1633 he was established as clerk of the Council, so Harrison had obviously been in the colony long enough to make the proper connections, though it is probable that friends from England were well placed when he arrived. The clerkship was not a position of power, but it carried a certain prestige and was certainly a plum for anyone in modest circumstances.

The year following his known occupancy of the clerk's job, Harrison bought two hundred acres outright—a good average holding in that day of the yeomanry's small agricultural operations—and at an unrecorded date he married a woman whom history can only know as Mary. She was illiterate, signing an X for her name, though this was typical for the times. This paucity of information about the Harrisons' progenitor is also typical of a time when few records were kept on a frontier in flux, when even the few records were often destroyed by fire, and it proves nothing about the Council's clerk except that he did not spring from some heraldic line. Those who did usually were known.

Perhaps through his salary, more than through his small holding, the dimly perceived figure in the settlement on the narrow frontier prospered sufficiently to buy in 1643 a five-hundred-acre grant on the south side of the river, across from Jamestown Island. The year before that he was elected to the House of Burgesses, and that is all that is known for certain of the emigrant's brief career—except that, in September, 1645, his wife bore a son.

Within a short period after his son's birth, this sire of presidents died at an unknown date and at an unknown age. As his wife lived on for some forty years, this would indicate that the first Harrison was a comparatively young man at his death. Besides the acreage he had acquired, apparently he left no wordly goods (his will, if it ever existed, has not been found).

It was unlikely that any house built in Virginia before 1650, and few before 1725, would represent anything of great value as an inheritance. The quality of dwellings passed through the quick transitions which reflected the early phases of the colony, and the first Benjamin Harrison died before the more solid and relatively imposing brick houses began to appear. Within his own time in the colony, there was a distinct improvement over the crude cottages that marked the early days of Jamestown, and the settled part of the island began to assume the aspects of a real town. A brick chapel was built, a brick statehouse, some "stores" (more like warehouses) and on the highway a half mile of timber-framed and brick houses faced the broad James.

If Harrison followed the standard building during this period, he probably had a dirt-floored brick-walled basement with a fireplace, and two rooms above, more likely of timber than of brick. The windows would be lattice casement, the doors would have decorative iron hinges, and probably a mantel would have some decorative design in primary colors. There are excavated examples of polychrome decorations for interiors, indicating that the settlers even then liked a splash of color and nonutilitarian touches.

Since his family was small, with only the one known child when he died, the house probably did not have the dormered half-story above the main floor. At that time the colonists lacked the present-day passion for privacy, and the uses of rooms were not so clearly defined as they were by more affluent successive generations. A family room, with the large fireplace, served for all the activities of the waking hours, and in the bedroom small children would sleep in trundles and cribs. To a family without servants, more rooms meant more fires to build and more lamps to clean, and there is no record that the first Harrison had servants. It does seem likely, since he was much across the river in Jamestown, that he might have paid the passage of an indenturer or so to help with his planting.

In any event, the house was essentially utilitarian and, however snug, a plain affair that characterized the yeomanry's era. The yeoman planters were simply too hard-pressed in maintaining their families to have time or thought for style.

In following generations, during the rule of the plantation masters, those families who continued in the yeoman class came to be called plain people, or just "plain." In the contemporary South the word plain connotes commonness (as "plain common," it is a term of social derogation) but historically, "plain" merely applied to a humbler class as distinguished from the privileged. In this historic sense, the distinction could not have applied during Harrison's lifetime. Before the rise of the planter class, no caste structures had developed and there were few families in Virginia, however successful, who would not by definition belong to the yeomanry. One of these was the family of Richard Lee, who obviously was well-to-do and well connected when he came to Virginia; he sat on the Council and was a personal friend of the royal governor. However, it was more usual in that period for the members of Council to be colonists who had risen by their successful ambitions *within* the yeoman class.

It was this intangible of ambition, a future-acting element, which was later to differentiate the members of the mid-century yeoman society into the planters and the plain. Above all, the son of the first Benjamin Harrison was a man of ambition.

While we know that ambition is not an inherited characteristic, certainly there must be some genetic content which causes individuals of succeeding generations to respond to an environment of opportunity with a self-disciplined determination to succeed in it—to master conditions for a known goal. Benjamin Harrison II could have received no direct influence from his father, who died before the child remembered him; his mother remarried a yeoman named Sidway whose life apparently was uncomplicated by the goads of worldly success. What young Harrison did receive from his father was a good name, then as always in Virginia at least as valuable as gold for those on their way up. The value of this good name was extremely practical.

When the second Benjamin Harrison was born, the county system of government, which was to form Virginia's permanent political structure, was already in operation. After establishment of this system, there were no more representatives from Hundreds or locales dominated by a Hundred; the state was divided into eight great shires, or counties, each semi-autonomous. In time, as the population grew, the counties would be divided into smaller areas, and new ones came in when the colony spread westward. But the unit never changed.

The unit was always controlled by a very few men, usually the twelve vestrymen of the church. These included the substantial planters recognized for their sagacity and discretion, the justices and members of the court, the important and honored sheriff (really the tax collector and invariably a planter), the "colonel" of the county militia (usually the biggest planter) and, of course, the members of the House of Burgesses. Since the senior Harrison had served in that Assembly, his son began life within the protective interest of the controlling group of the then powerful Surry County, and he grew up as one of them. This would seem to have been his only tangible advantage, beyond the five hundred acres repatented in his name when he was four years old, but he knew how to use it.

When second husband Sidway died before Harrison's mother, her estate had not been increased. In her will, besides two small bequests, she simply divided the estate between her son, Benjamin Harrison, and his half brother, Thomas Sidway. What Sidway did with his share is not known, and his line followed the more typical yeomanry history of drifting off into obscurity. When Benjamin received his share at the age of forty-two, he was far beyond the need of any help from his mother. He was on his way to riches which would have seemed fantastic to the good woman who willed her granddaughter only "the horse colt that sucks on the black mare."

For the second Benjamin Harrison came into the world with the coming of the cavaliers to Virginia and, from the first, they served as models and symbols of power, the like of which had scarcely existed during his father's time. Though his home surroundings were those of the moderately well-to-do yeomanry, and his immediate family belonged contentedly in that then dominant class, young Harrison belonged in the future. His lifetime was to span and embody the evolutionary period from the day of the yeomanry to the big planters with their private ruling class, of which he became a member.

2

The cavaliers had a forerunner to Virginia in the elegant person of the royal governor, Sir William Berkeley (no connection with the Berkeleys of the Hundred). The brother of a lord, a young nobleman of fashion and wit (as a dilettante, he had written a successful play in London), Berkeley reflected the difference in the colony from the days when professional soldiers like Dale and Yeardley were fighting to maintain a foothold.

When Sir William came (1642), Jamestown, with its immediate environs, was an established settlement. Compared to an English town, the little river-island capital would be a raw affair, with tobacco fields and slumbrous swamps interspersed with houses. Scenically its situation was charming, with the broad tidal river in front, the forests of cypress and oak and chestnut, pine and black walnut and poplar as a background, and flowers and flowering vines everywhere. The thirty-four-year-old governor found it delightful.

True, there were no theaters or taverns, and no grand houses for social life, but the transplanted courtier found his own way of remedying those deficiencies. Two miles from Jamestown, on the mainland, he built the first great house in Virginia, called Green Spring. Measured in the scale of the British Jacobean mansions, Green Spring would have been a modest country house. Set down on the frontier, on the fringe of an unexplored continent, it was most inposing and—to those planters of soaring ambitions—inspiring.

Berkeley found a piece of rising ground and along the crest built an L-shaped block, with three large front rooms facing down to Jamestown island and the river. The house was unique at the time, for England as well as Virginia, because of the wide central entrance hall, with flanking rooms, which was to become the characteristic not only of the early Virginia mansions but of houses all over the South.

It is presumed that the rooms were paneled in oak, and the furnishings along with books and wines were shipped from England. Great orchards were planted around the house and a road built down to the capital.

Amid this colonial splendor, the erstwhile gallant of the court of Charles the First entertained his new friends and tried to elevate the conversation above the mundane subjects of planting and shipping— with which, as he said, the planters were understandably preoccupied. The governor discovered that emergencies would divert their minds from crops, and he was quick to unite them in action against the Indians who made forays on the outlying plantations.

When Berkeley came, the relatively settled area of Jamestown was the only section free of hostile Indians. Though their numbers had dwindled considerably since the massacre, any collected band was physically too much for a family on an isolated plantation, and planters would go anywhere to get tobacco land on or near a river. Berkeley's actions against the Indians, his intelligent interest in the problems of the colony, and his gracious manners made him immensely popular. He soon developed a coterie of planters who shared with him a common interest beyond both crops and emergencies. This was the plight of Charles the First.

This stupid tyrant had alienated all factions in England and brought to a climax the bitterness between the religious factions. It is difficult for us today to conceive of English-speaking people taking their religion seriously enough to go to war over it; though even in England's Civil War, the religious differences were involved in a complex of many causes, including class struggle.

Basically, since the Church of England had renounced the authority of the Bishop of Rome, the Church had been divided within itself between Anglicans and Puritans. The Anglicans (as they do today in the whole Anglican communion, which includes the Episcopal Church in America) wished to retain the apostolic succession of the clergy, the episcopacy as a system of bishops, and many rituals of their traditional church. This was the orthodox church, the church of the state.

The Puritans, under the influence of Calvinism, denounced everything that smacked of "popery" (as they called it), including specifically the episcopacy and the ritual. The Puritans in turn were divided between the Presbyterians, more or less the conservative dissenters, and the Independents, who were the extremists or radicals.

The nobility naturally favored the orthodox church of the state, of the King, while the Puritans attracted the commercial class of shopkeepers, merchants, their employees and the like. There was nothing hard and fast about this: some noble families were Puritans and many Anglicans were humble people. Where the religious factions formed the bases of political parties, doubtless many political adherents of the Puritans were something less than messianic about religion, and undoubtedly many royalists were Anglicans in name only, if that.

The personal exacerbations arose from the Puritans' intolerance in imposing their anti-pleasure codes on everybody and the indignation of the Anglicans, with a blander attitude about sin, over having their pleasures interfered with. As in all times, these personal differences could be accentuated into symbols of hatred: all Anglican loyalists became Nero-esque sinners, and all Puritans became religious fanatics out to make a gray world. Yet, all these divisions were not sufficient to cause a civil war; they were the explosive elements in need of a fuse. By a series of blunders, Charles provided the fuse and the people took to arms.

The loyalist followers of the King got the worst of the fighting, largely because of the military aptitude of Oliver Cromwell and the disciplined ferocity of his Independent troops. After the King's forces were defeated, Cromwell turned the power of his Independents against the conservative Presbyterians, threw them out along with the loyalists and established a military dictatorship of the radical Puritans. Religious intolerance such as never before known was inflicted upon Britain and, to demonstrate at the beginning the finality of the end of royalty, Charles the First was beheaded in 1649.

Virginians, in a loyal crown colony and predominantly Church of

England, were shocked at the news of the monarch's execution, and none was more outraged than Sir William Berkeley. The former courtier became a passionate leader of Virginia loyalists and turned the colony of yeoman planters into a sanctuary for the King's followers. In achieving this Berkeley showed great strength. Not all the settlers by any means felt any loyalty to a distant king, and some very definitely held grievances against the Crown. But, in less than half a century the colonists *had* developed a self-awareness as Virginians and, prophetically, revealed that they could be aroused to a unity of action by a threat from the outside.

Actually, Cromwell's only definite threat was to their Prayer Book, which he demanded be abolished. However, under Berkeley's leadership, the Assembly passed an ordinance prohibiting the abolition of the Prayer Book in Virginia and went on to proclaim Charles's son, Charles the Second, the rightful King of England, Scotland and Virginia.

During the civil war the small band of Puritans in Virginia invited three ministers from New England to come in as missionaries. The Puritan ministers had been forbidden to enter the colony and the governor gradually rescinded the earlier tolerance which Virginians had shown nonconformists. By the time of the King's execution the three hundred Puritans were so uncomfortable that they accepted an invitation to migrate to Maryland. This episode has been used as an example of a strain of religious intolerance in early Virginia. The opposition to the Puritans during the tensions of the civil war was really political. After all, Puritans as viewed by loyalists were enemies of the established government, hence, enemies within their midst; and one of the leading Puritan preachers, on leaving Virginia, did rise to prominence with Cromwell's government. Yet, even this minor action tended to solidify the power of the Church of England loyalists and to discourage, at least, outspoken dissent in any form.

Then in 1651, for the first time in their history, Virginians were called "Rebels and Traitors." When this name-calling letter, published in London, was read to the Assembly, the Burgesses and Council joined to draft an angry vindication of their allegiance to the King and openly defied any authority of the dictatorship over them. Charles the Second had already been sent a personal letter offering him a haven in Virginia, and his adherents were coming over by boatloads.

With all his troubles at home, Cromwell was forced to act against a colony which stood, in effect, in a state of war. He sent over a commission armed with authority to call out the British Navy and to raise recruits in Virginia. The commission was met by a colony under arms. The counties' militia was called out, batteries were ranged along the riverbanks, and Dutch vessels were impressed into service.

Berkeley did not want war, any more than did Cromwell. He wanted a favorable truce—until, as he confidently expected, the monarchy was restored. The terms were more liberal than he could have hoped for; they read almost like terms dictated by a victorious Virginia. Everyone was forgiven any acts or words against the Cromwellian government; no taxes were to be imposed without the consent of the Assembly; except for omitting the prayer for the King, the use of the Prayer Book was extended for one year (it continued indefinitely); and Virginians were free to elect their own governor, naturally excluding Sir William as a candidate.

Virtually as a victor, Berkeley retired to the magnificence of Green Spring, surrounded by a growing "court" of loyalists, to await the passing of the ugly interlude.

### 3

As it turned out, the eight following years of Cromwell's Protectorate became the most prosperous period in the colony's early history. This period represented the pinnacle of the yeomanry's power; it was the full flowering of the era of the small planters, who exercised their power through the House of Burgesses.

Under the Crown's rule, the royal governor appointed the members to the Council, the secretary of state (Berkeley appointed his friend, Richard Lee), and the county commissioners—very lucrative posts. Under Cromwell, the House of Burgesses, whose members largely represented the yeomanry, elected the secretary of state, members of the Council and the county commissioners, as well as the governor. As governor, they elected the most successful member of their own class, Captain Samuel Matthews.

This "Captain" Matthews revealed just how far an early adventurer could come by shrewdness and industry, and the type of industry needed to succeed. Coming to the colony before the massacre, he had acquired large tracts of land on the tip of the Peninsula, where the James, three miles wide, flows into the Chesapeake Bay near the present city of Newport News. Some forty miles from Jamestown, he had established on his domain something of a private city—the dream of the old Hundreds and a precursor of the big plantations.

One of the first large investors in slaves (he had forty), Matthews trained them as artisans. He had spinners and weavers for his hemp and flax, tanners for his hides and eight shoemakers; his beeves were dressed and sold to ships, and he sold wheat at four shillings a bushel. In addition, he raised hogs and poultry and kept a "brave dairy." His large earnings *in cash* (not merely the credit and barter value of tobacco), enabled him to build a fine, well-equipped house and win the daughter of a British knight. Yet, in this thirty-year career of acquisitive industry, Matthews remained hospitable, mannerly and devoted to the interests of his locale and the colony. The people evidenced their liking and respect by sending him to the House of Burgesses, and when fellow yeomen elected him governor, he was paid the highest compliment of his time and place: "(he) keeps a good house, lives bravely, and is a true lover of Virginia; he is worthy of much honor."

Except for a couple of mistaken gestures of authoritarianism (on which the rampant Burgesses quickly set him straight), Matthews served ably, without airs, and he is forgotten because his class, and their hour in the sun, were historically cast into obscurity by the myth which identified Virginia's beginnings with noble cavaliers—*i.e.*, F.F.V.s. Yet the brief hour of the yeomanry's full ascendancy coincided with Virginia's first experience as an independent republic, which is what its status under Cromwell amounted to. Virginians were never to forget this taste of independence until it was won permanently in the Revolution. They were to forget that the yeomanry had any part in it (and this, much later, was to prove costly to the state).

While the yeomanry governed in the era of prosperity during the 1650s, the cavaliers kept coming, into the thousands it was estimated. They were highly personable, with a graciousness of manner that the colonists had lacked the circumstances to cultivate (though native courtesy had always been esteemed). They had a flair for fashion, which some of the natives admiringly noted, and a taste for good living that was welcomed by those long exposed to the harshness of a dangerous frontier. Most of all, underlying everything, was the attitude that revered the life of the country gentry with its gallant code of honor. This exerted a strong appeal on a few who were reaching a stage of success where they wished to look beyond making another crop of tobacco, paying the passage of another batch of indenturers and clearing more acres of virgin timber.

In our American West, the frontier people renounced everything Eastern as effete and sissy, and culture was made suspect into our own times. The switch on America's first frontier, in Virginia, was that they looked at what the British had and determined to do it better. They determined to do it on their own terms. Of course, this was not articulated. It happened, and very quickly, though not all at once.

The cavaliers came during the Protectorate, and though many yeoman families regarded them with indifference or even hostility, the attractive fugitives from a reign of Puritans found many doors open to them, and, more practically, many hearts. The charming gentlemen were very successful at marrying widows whose husbands had worked themselves to death acquiring land and clearing acres for tobacco, or, as bold traders, had fallen afoul of Indian raiding parties. Then, as now, fathers who had known a hard, rough life were pleased to place their daughters in the hands of a young gallant who could advance her socially. Loyalty to the Stuart kings paid off well in a raw country where the successful were just beginning to glimpse a kind of New World aristocracy for their own. It was something of a preview, in more practical terms, of the daughters of American millionaires who marry foreign princes—and the terms were very practical. The land still had to be worked; the husbands had to become planters.

Others of the émigrés went straight to planting. Virginia loyalists offered those with cash choice tracts of land in fee simple, gave them advice and lent them servants, and some of the cavaliers did very well on their own. The important point is that they were assimilated while they influenced, and many soon became devout Virginians. George Washington's family came over then, and the Carters and the Randolphs.

Some of them, of course, traded their charm for hospitality. Like Governor Berkeley, they were merely waiting for the fantastic interlude to end. Among these transients were the boon companions of Sir William, who gathered at Green Spring to drink toasts to Charles the Second. "Come the monarchy . . ."

All in all, allowing for all the legendary aspects of the cavalier influx, their impact was tremendous and decisive. Virginia was never the same again. For better or worse, their influence made it as it is today.

4

It was during the influx of the cavaliers that Benjamin Harrison II grew up, and under the influence of their impact that he matured. Among his first conscious memories, beginning around the age of five, he must have seen fashionably turned out and courtly gentlemen in his neighborhood, and about the same time he saw neighbors build houses of a grace, size and solidarity not seen before in Virginia, except in the case of the Governor's Green Spring. Though the new houses would appear relatively modest beside the mansions that were to come later, still they were beautifully done—as can be seen today from the surviving examples in Surry County.

In young Harrison's country, across the river from Jamestown, the south shore rises sharply to a plateau that stretches for miles in all directions in a flatness remarkable for no undulations at all. What was then Surry County spreads like an endless billiard table. To the west from the Jamestown crossing, John Martin, the only member of the original 1607 Council to survive in Virginia, had operated one of the first plantations in the New World, Martin's Brandon (in what is today Prince George County).

Directly across from Jamestown, on what is said to have been property of John Rolfe, a charming red-brick house was built, in Harrison's boyhood, on the Green Spring model of a central hall with flanking rooms on either side. The brick-walled basement was nearly fifty feet long on the inside and more than twenty feet deep; the high-ceilinged rooms above were spacious, bright and handsome, and the dormer-windowed bedrooms on the second floor had a good height. Now called Smith's Fort House, a replica of this pleasant dwelling is a fine example of native Virginia architecture, in which the colonists, breaking away from the English houses they remembered, were building more indigenously. Of course, by the 1650s, there were hundreds of adults in Virginia who had never seen England.

At the opposite extreme from the Smith's Fort House, and several miles to the southeast, was built the largest and most elaborate house in Virginia in the high Jacobean style, with features going back to Tudor England. The Harrison boy must have watched in awe as two high stories rose above a full basement and were topped by a steep-roofed attic story. The outside chimneys had the Jacobean characteristic of three grouped stacks, and projecting from the front and rear were towers of porch and stairs. Inside he could glimpse the great timbered ceilings, with double-crossed girders that formed a series of six panels. Called Bacon's Castle and enclosed by holly and magnolia, it stands out today as it did then like some ancient castle on the flatland.

These new homes must have made their impression on the ambitious boy, as did the furnishings that were being brought into his neighborhood from England as he grew into his teens. With the coming of the cavaliers, the successful planters—both those who had come well endowed and those rising out of the yeomanry—began to become aware of their position and to seek the tangible symbols of rank.

Silver plate became the thing. Silver came in dram cups and caudle cups, sillabub dishes and wine bowls, even gallon basins for punch, and drinking vessels of all kinds. Silver dishes and silver plates were used to decorate the dining room, and the silver began to be engraved with coats of arms. Younger sons of thrice younger sons harked back to distant origins for coats of arms, and members of modest collateral lines investigated the armorial bearings of some long-dead first cousin four generations removed.

Tapestry hangings were imported and Oriental rugs, and chairs and tables of the latest styles were shipped from England. Pictures began to arrive for the high walls, and crates of books. With all these touches of high fashion installed in houses in their clearings in the brushy forests, hospitality began to become more formalized.

From the beginning, as on most frontiers, the people had been friendly with visitors and generous in sharing. In the early days their lives were spent largely in isolation and hard work with the tension of danger a constant, and a visitor offered a welcome change. Even with the affluent in the mid-century, plantations were isolated and, with Jamestown the only city of any kind, the home continued to be the center as social life became a recognized and fashionable custom with styles and standards of entertaining. The cavaliers and their forerunner, Sir William Berkeley, most definitely exerted an influence in changing primary human exchanges, which served to break the lonely monotony, into a formalized social custom which came to characterize Virginia.

One of the reasons for the lavishness of their hospitality was the bountifulness of food. Not only did they raise their own cattle, hogs and poultry with comparative ease, but the woods were full of deer and rabbits, the tidal rivers of oysters and fish, and the smallest streams offered good fishing. Where in England the "deer park" made hunting the privilege (indeed, a symbol) of the landed gentry, in the boundless wilderness the poorest one-room planter followed the sport of the nobility for pleasure (and perhaps a sense of privilege) while loading his table with food.

Corn grew in great abundance, with little tending, and it formed the basic diet of Virginians as of the Indians. The easily ground meal was fried on top the stove in bacon fat—either flat as corncakes, or hand-shaped and hand-sized with thick crusts and called corn pones. Formed into a batter with water or milk, corn was baked into a large rectangular shape, two inches deep, served hot with butter melted on it and called batter bread—a heavier, less soupy version of spoon bread. All these varieties of cooked cornmeal have remained a staple of the Virginia diet into the present.

In the woods surrounding the holdings, fruit grew in profusion— grapes, peaches and pears, plums, persimmons and cherries, all kinds of berries and especially a most tasty strawberry. For "fruit and nuts," a favorite dessert after the heavy meals, families need only send the children to gather walnuts, hickory nuts, chestnuts and the small flavorsome chinquapin.

The planters, living outdoors in nonintrospective action, "ate hearty." By piling victuals on their guests' plates they were only offering friends what they themselves enjoyed. There has been no satisfactory explanation for their concentration on alcoholic beverages. Perhaps they needed a stimulant to achieve the desired conviviality after periods of aloneness with thoughts only on things of the land. Nothing in their religious faith forbade the use of alcohol; in fact, orders were sent to restrain some of their ministers from overindulgence and "public riot."

Again to the cavaliers, perhaps their escape from the blight of a

Puritan England had sharpened their appetites, and here, too, they exerted an influence. In any event, the openhanded and gregarious planters developed a certain stylized hedonism which centered around hospitality in the home. They felt no need of cities, since they shopped in London, and their pleasures, as well as their pride, were focalized in the country estate.

Finally, in their burgeoning world of country fashion, the planter families also imitated the cavalier models in dress. Great bolts of silk were imported, along with laces and perfumes, powder for the hair and other items of elegance. It was after the fiftieth anniversary of the founding of Jamestown (which went unobserved) that the newly privileged planter-families began to bedeck themselves in the finery which, in the mists of legend, supposedly comprised the attire of all Virginians from their first arrival on the continent.

All these grand doings developed as the world of Benjamin Harrison II unfolded before him. These formative stages in the evolution of the planter class coincided with his own formative years. What education he had is not known. That he received an adequate education for his day is evidenced by the offices he held—sheriff, speaker of the House of Burgesses, and finally member of the Council. Mere wealth (or, as they said in those rougher days, "land and niggers") would never have been enough to win him those places of honor and power. Essentially he was acquisitive, broadly ambitious and early developed that sense of community responsibility without which none of them achieved a position of real power.

Irresponsible meteoric success was unknown: control was too tightly held by a few. Part of the individual's conformity to the group was a sharing of group responsibilities before one could share in group rewards.

It was natural for an ambitious boy on a plantation to develop a sense of responsibility early. Young Harrison, with only his contented and younger half brother to share the operations of a five-hundred-acre plantation, obviously had to learn the management of his land at an early age. And when very young he must have identified his course with the embryonic planter class, developing as he developed. He was only fifteen years old when the rule of the yeomanry received its death blow, and the division between classes began to sharpen and harden into the caste system which was to mold the Virginia character. The division began in 1660 with the return of a Stuart king, Charles the Second, to the British throne.

5

In England, the Restoration became a glamorous period. Theaters were reopened with a flowering of talent in mannered comedy, public places brought cheer to a thirsty generation (as did saloons in America after Prohibition); following the repressive Puritans, life in general assumed a certain gaiety and all the frantic recapture of fleshy pleasures was symbolized by that most fleshy and charming monarch, Charles the Second.

For Virginia, however, the persuasive charm of the restored King had no meaning. Virginians experienced only the effects of his deceitful, selfish irresponsibility. If Charles II did not persuade England to be done with kings, nobody will; but this divine-right playboy started Jamestown on the course that ended a century later at Yorktown, on the other side of the Virginia Peninsula.

From the beginning, this Stuart King conceived of England's first foothold of empire as his own property from which he milked personal riches and with which he could reward his friends. Totally indifferent to the colonists' loyalty to him, he gave away small countries of their land to his favorites. He gave away whole counties where pioneers had fought Indians to secure their holdings and had cleared the primeval timber to build their plantations, some great but mostly small. Of course, the people fought to hold the land they had won, but their struggles made ugly complications that endured for years and promoted in Virginians a litigiousness about land that never died.

Then, affecting everyone, was his revival of the Navigation Acts. Cromwell had introduced a Navigation Act which restricted planters to selling their tobacco only to England and to shipping only in English boats. His reason, to hurt the Dutch trade, had led to a war with Holland, and during the Protectorate the planters had managed to some extent to evade the restriction by selling tobacco directly to Dutch merchantmen. Charles II's restrictive policy was more personal and rigidly enforced. The natural result of reducing a world trade to a single market was to glut the British warehouses, and the price of tobacco completed its decline from a high of four shillings (about one dollar) a pound, to one pence, about two cents.

Out of that one pence, the planter must also pay British taxes, the cost of shipping and a commission to a British factor (who also charged a commission on imports he bought for planters), and it is evident that the profit would be negligible at best. On the one thousand pounds that a single man might hope to plant, cut, cure and pack, the net had fallen from a high of better than fifty dollars to something under fifteen dollars. At best, with the cost of manufactured articles from England rising, small planters could scarcely replace their farming equipment. At worst, as it gradually became, the small men could not squeeze out enough profit to make ends meet.

The immediate result was to place them in debt to mortgage holders—*i.e.*, big planters, Indian traders, and speculators in land and indentures. Beyond the immediate was the inability to save cash to replace their indentures. To the small operator, the indenturer was as important for the fifty acres he brought as a headright as for his labor. Tobacco wore out land in about four years, and the need of new acreage was the basis of the planters' constant grasping for land. Running in debt, acquiring no new land, with planting reduced to what his own family could do, the small operator was getting smaller.

Obviously unless some relief came, or changes were made in methods of production, the yeomanry faced ruin. But not even loyal Sir William Berkeley could move Charles when, as royal governor, he made a personal trip to see the son of the King whose court he had graced. There was nothing the small planter *could* do; the economic division between the yeoman and the big planter became a clearly defined and ever-widening chasm.

The big planter could by volume operate on a smaller margin of profit. Because of the size of his operation, which included trained artisans, he could also turn to other products in addition to tobacco. Also, as the big planters formed into a closed corporation for the rule of the colony, they developed a caste loyalty and, through the influential offices they held, could always obtain land for one of their own. Since these expedients placed them beyond the need of getting fifty acres by headright on indentures, the big planter abandoned the system in which he was forced to pay twelve pounds every five years for an indenture. He turned to buying chattel slaves for only twice the cost of an indenture. He could own their labor for their lifetime, and their children would become his property.

This cold solution to the effects of Charles the Second's irresponsible selfishness did not consider any of the effects inherent in the solution itself. At that period in the Western world, no moral judgments were involved; indeed, the Puritans were quick to seize the opportunity to trade in human flesh and supply the planters with their needs. Whether or not the big planters were aware of the immediate effect, they would have been indifferent in any case. The immediate effect was to drive the small planter slowly out of business and to undermine the yeoman class as a factor in Virginia's political and economic life.

The rise of a class of plantation masters was inevitable as a result of the drift of ambitious planters before the Restoration, with or without chattel slavery. But it was the introduction of the Negro slave as the labor system of the big plantation that began the elimination of the sturdy yeomanry which had built the colony, from the days of the privately financed adventures, into a prosperous settlement.

Because new blood was constantly coming into the colony and a yeasty movement still sent the ambitious to the top, the loss of the backlog of the yeomanry power was not felt for more than a century. Then, as the ruling class grew apathetic in contentment and the blood thinned out, the yeomanry as a class had been too long separated from power to rise as replacements. Countless thousands of the more aggressive—that "restless, pushing material"—had migrated to the Lower South or the Middle West. Without replacements among the powers, Virginia's sun was quickly to set.

An immediate tangential effect of Negro slavery was to stigmatize manual work, even of skilled artisans. As early as 1662, when an irate citizen wanted to denounce the justices of peace as unfit for office, he called them, "coopers, hog-trough makers, peddlers, cobblers, tailors, weavers." This was considered a deadly insult to gentlemen of pretensions, who might be seeking dubious connections with some armor-bearing family that they might frame and hang a coat of arms to proclaim to all their *inherited* superiority to manual work.

The establishment of the slave-labor system, coming on the heels of the cavaliers, changed the colony rapidly along the line of "the rich get richer and the poor get poorer."

To Benjamin Harrison II, growing into young manhood during these dynamic changes, the pattern of the big planters determined the course of his own ambitions. In his late teens, when Charles's Navigation Act began to crush the small planter, Harrison was, in practical terms, among the relatively small himself—except that he did not think as they thought. Seeing the fate of those trying to hold on to what they had, Harrison followed the example of those who tried to get more.

In any emergency for the many, there is opportunity for the few. Harrison was among those men, of all ages, who can turn a time of crisis into personal advantage. Since profit depended on volume and volume depended on workers, he must get more workers; further, since profits from small acreage were insufficient for the purchase of new indentures or slaves, he must find another way to cash profit. He found it in trading and began to operate a river-front store.

A planter's "store" bore slight resemblance to stores as we know them. It was something of a combination wharf, tobacco warehouse and importing storage house. Harrison had small boats built and he plied up the back creeks to take on the tobacco hogsheads of small planters. Shipping the odd lots with his own from his wharf, the quantity lowered his freight charges. In London, the tobacco would be credited against goods which he imported, and from his store some of the goods would be taken by the small planters in exchange for their tobacco. Some he sold for cash. He profited both from a charge on handling their tobacco and a mark-up on the goods. By these manipulations he established favorable credit balances with his British factor and could sell his own tobacco for cash—to buy more people and get more land. There is no record that he traded with Indians, as did William Byrd's uncle, though he was sharp enough to barter with traders.

These economies enabled Harrison to acquire five tithables by the time he was twenty-three years old in 1688—and this right when hard times were at their worst. Some were Negro slaves for the tobacco fields, one or two were white artisans to make subsidiary products and to build boats. The cycle was completed. He was not then a big planter, but he was in their system. Each year he would extend his trading, get more people and more land. His operation would grow bigger, and he would be recognized as a planter of substance—"discreet," as the coldly sagacious were called—worthy to share the honors and the burdens of the ruling group.

Except for the few who came well endowed to the colony, this is the way they all got to be Old Massa, and those who arrived with substantial property had to show the traits to hold it and increase it. These were not soft men. Such shrewdness as Harrison's—demanding constant calculation and the most disciplined industry—was not characteristic of the average yeoman planter, any more than it is of the average citizen today.

After a day's toil over tobacco plants, the typical yeoman wanted to relax with his family and enjoy his children. On rainy days, he worked around his house and barn at odd jobs that pleased him. On Sundays, he went to church and visited his neighbors. After he packed his tobacco in hogsheads and a British merchantman or some planter like Benjamin Harrison took it off his hands, the yeoman did not want to go in the house and figure over minute calculations for the future. He went hunting. Maybe he could get a bearskin for the bedroom floor. When times grew hard under Charles II, he did not envision changing his scheme of life and going in for the bold gambles of the big planters. He tended more to his vegetable garden and went fishing more to assure his family of sustenance, and complained with his friends over the terrible conditions. It did not occur to him that he could change them.

He would listen in bewilderment if you told him that his class was vanishing. He did not know he belonged in a historically defined segment. He could not have conceived that his way of life was jeopardized by the arrogant planters, with their "niggers" and fine airs and fancy clothes from London. After all, the members of the House of Burgesses were their neighbors and friends, and they had shown that they could run Virginia to suit everybody.

However, the House of Burgesses after the Restoration was not acting with the assertive independence that the people's representatives had showed during Cromwell's Protectorate. Sir William Berkeley was back as royal governor, with his friends on the Council, and the aging royalist had the Assembly under his thumb. Maybe some of them were afraid of the King's representative and maybe some intended to align themselves with the real powers. In any event, the House of Burgesses was not looking after the yeomanry's interests.

The more enlightened and more aggressive yeomen grew aware of the neglect they received, and rumblings of discontent became loud in the colony. These people had known their hour of power, had experienced a people's government, and they were not going to give up without a fight.

Benjamin Harrison was on the outside in the struggle brewing between the embittered yeomanry and the power represented by Sir William Berkeley. He had married a lady named Hannah, whose last name, as with his mother, has remained undiscovered by the most diligent genealogists. From the imposing record of her children, Hannah was a good breeder, with stalwart qualities of her own. That her last name is unknown indicates that Benjamin II had married within what was then his own class and not into the well-recorded ruling class to which he was striving.

In 1673 Hannah Harrison was delivered of a son and he, like all the first born, was named Benjamin. (The numerals affixed to all the Benjamin Harrisons are purely an historical means of identification; the Harrisons never used any dynastic numerals after their name.) This newborn Benjamin Harrison, the third of the same name, was the one who would acquire Berkeley Hundred. While he was still in his crib, the Hundred which Mr. John Smythe had patented in 1618— and which had been revived as the plantation of a London merchant-family named Bland—was to figure once more in a transitional period.

This transition was to be violent and dramatic, marking the final, definite cleavage between the yeomanry and the plantation masters. It was the yeomanry's last stand, and the beginning of the unques-tioned rule of the big planters.

❀  ❀

## CHAPTER IV

# THE FORTUNE BUILDER

**1**

*The* violence in Virginia, which erupted into America's first Revolution, was fifteen years in building to a trial by arms. As in all armed clashes, and especially civil wars, the opposing factions were represented and led by individuals who became symbols of the cause.

Until the fifteenth year of the struggle, the yeomanry, in effect betrayed by the House of Burgesses, lacked a leader. Even the basic elements of their cause—poverty and a sense of injustice—were negative and vague.

The glut of the British tobacco market had reached the point where the small planters had trouble selling their tobacco at all. The big planters, selling larger lots (and, in turn, buying more goods from England), consumed the shipping space on the reduced number of British merchantmen, and the warships of the greedy King kept the Dutch merchantman out of the rivers.

The small planters could still pay their quitrents (in effect, property tax to the King) in tobacco, as well as poll taxes, parish taxes and various requisitions, but for necessities they sold off land, cattle, anything, or went hopelessly into debt. The inequities caused by the British King, which the big planters used to their benefit, were accompanied by nature's gratuitous misfortunes, where hurricanes unprecedented in violence laid waste the tobacco fields and garden crops, and a stock disease took off half the cattle in the colony. Bedevilled by the slow accumulation of disasters and faced with the spectre of ruin, the yeomanry began to center their resentments on the groups forming into a ruling class.

Charles II was too far away. At home they saw that the church vestries, instead of being representatives elected by all the parishioners who paid parish taxes, had become self-perpetuating bodies of gentlemen with a common group interest. They saw further that their vestries were composed of the same men who held the profitable and important posts in the counties, and sat down as friends of the Governor's Council. They saw that even the House of Burgesses, supposedly their own representatives, had not had a new election since the restoration of Charles II returned Sir William Berkeley to Jamestown. When, through a death or a resignation, a new Burgess was elected, he was a man concerned with making his own way and not with making enemies in important places. Slowly the yeomen perceived the extent to which a planter oligarchy had arisen in their midst and was running the colony—in indifference to the majority—for its own aggrandizement.

(The *noblesse oblige* of the planter class was developed after their rule was established and the political system of the aristocratic republic perfected. In the formative stages, when the class grouping was loose and flexible, the big planters were acquisitive individuals with the ruthlessness of men embroiled in a dog-eat-dog struggle for control. Their responsibility then was only to their own kind: it was their descendants who, secure, spread their sense of responsibility in benevolent paternalism to the whole.)

The growingly bitter resentment of the yeomanry, accompanied by minor and futile outbreaks of violence, could not be directed against all the individuals of power in the colony. Because of great distances in a land without real roads or any public communication, the yeomanry lived in a narrow parochialism in which they did not even know the names of the big planters outside their immediate region. Nor, in the widening cleavage of classes, did the yeomanry know any details of the life of the big planters on the river.

Actually, the big planters were having a hard time of it themselves. The low tobacco prices and high costs required of them tremendous resourcefulness, constant application and bold speculation to maintain their big operations. Some of the planters were heavily indebted to British factors, and nobody was making any cash in that period. The yeomanry saw none of the planters' struggles. They only saw that from the outside the big planters were doing all right, and lived with a lavishness that mocked their own poverty and despair.

The one gentleman in all the colony who lived with the most ostentatious splendor was their governor, Sir William Berkeley. This royalist became the symbol of the yeomen's grievances, and certainly the former courtier acted the role of villain with magnificent gusto.

2

It is true that, as a nobleman, Berkeley had always despised the common people, and had always liked to do well by himself. However, when he returned to the governorship, he acted as if Cromwell's interregnum had transformed him into a harsh and ruthless tyrant, who ruled Virginia like some divine-right monarch of the olden times. Countless explanations have been offered for the change that made Berkeley appear like two different men—before and after. Yet, his change was not that of a man who ceases to be one person and becomes another. It was more as if his experiences with the Protectorate had debased his more genial qualities and accentuated all that was arrogant and despotic, selfish and cruel.

It should be recalled that he had come to the colony at the age of thirty-four from a favored position in the Court of Charles I, and he might well have nurtured ambitions which envisioned the colony governorship as a steppingstone to greater place. He offered a hint of this late in his second term as governor when he said, "Though ambition commonly leaves sober old age, covetousness does not."

His avarice, then, which he had always revealed, only increased. It happened that his flagrant greed stood out in sharp contrast to the welfare of most of the colonists. While carrying on his profitable private trade with Indians, he accepted the twelve hundred pounds along with cash gifts which the Assembly was pleased to give him each year, over and above the upkeep of the spacious Green Spring mansion. The upkeep included seventy horses and a coach, probably the first one in Virginia, in which he rode the two miles to the capitol. All that money came from the taxes paid by starving people.

The grandeur of his scale of living grew even more sumptuous after he married a young widow, the beautiful and high-spirited Lady Frances Berkeley, who was quite as greedy and as aristocratic-minded as her husband. She would have fitted well into a contemporary French court. The comparative youth of the fascinating Lady Frances has been offered as one of the reasons for Berkeley's change of character. While attentions to her and the lady's own support of his arrogance might well have been factors, it seems likely that he had become soured by the republican uprising which reduced him for years to useless exile and then fixed his career permanently, at the age of fifty-two, in a starving colony that had become the plaything of his light-hearted king.

Since there is no doubt that his change came after Cromwell's interregnum, obviously the assertion of *people* against the fixed order profoundly affected the aristocrat. Passionately subscribing to the divine right of (Stuart) kings and the perquisites of the Crown's noble satellites, as he was to be committed for life to the colony, he began to rule it as a satellite of the King—in effect, a colonial monarch.

Always despising the people at a distance, he came to hate them, because people had killed his King, caused a rupture in his own career, and showed themselves to be untrustworthy and dangerous. Hatred of the people became a canker in him, and this canker—with his sourness about his own life and his newly dedicated despotism—promoted the personality change which observers noticed most. In brief, he had lost the desire to make himself attractive.

As age came, with all of its disagreeable changes and intimations of mortality, Berkeley simply gave vent to irascibility. He could afford to do what others would like to do, and he played his role of tyrant like an actor. His young dilettantism had been expressed in the theater, and there was doubtless something of the ham in the ex-courtier.

When young and in one circumstance, it had pleased him to be the charming and benevolent representative of the King; in age and under different circumstances, it pleased him to play the highhanded tyrant. He delighted in calling people "rogues" and "dogs," in refining insults, and, when we regard some of our own contemporaries who have achieved success by epithet, it is simple to comprehend Sir William making of himself something of a character. There was nothing else for him, as he grew into his sixties, when personality problems were intensified by arteriosclerosis and approaching senility.

None of this is to imply that he was not a cruel man by nature, or that he was merely acting when he arrogantly humiliated people and callously tended his own orchards while his subjects were starving. Berkeley was a man of his own times. Inequalities were accepted along with the divine right of kings (they would have to be). In accepting them, with himself on top, the British nobleman simply used the existing conditions and his own convictions to express those native drives (which psychiatrists today assure us are quite healthful) through a flair for the dramatic. When he had wanted to be popular, he had been charming; when he wanted to be a tyrant, he was hateful. Circumstances, in the form of Cromwell, had changed his role, but nothing changed his character.

From the beginning, he made friends with the local powers. In the fifteen years of the growing despair of the yeomanry, he continued to make friends with the powers. If the times had been good, he might have continued to be an able administrator, with all his despotism. He did try to persuade Charles II to introduce a "stinting" of the growth of tobacco—probably the world's first experiment in "ploughing under." He tried various long-range methods for control of the tobacco crop. His stupid King would have nothing to do with the experiments. Being a devout monarchist, his own failures in the colony's interests hardened his indifference and intensified his selfishness.

He was a complex figure in the fluctuating of large forces, this villain of the people. Totally brave, learned and able, he was shrewd and strong and became mean on an heroic scale. In 1676, when the yeomanry finally got a leader of their own, the once-popular governor was by his own choice symbol of all that was greedy, tyrannical, callous and regally self-indulgent.

He was a horrible old man of sixty-eight by then, using all his brains for the advancement of favorites who would support his reign and using all his powers to suppress any threat, however just, to his despotism. He did have powerful supporters, entirely among those either solidly entrenched or those allying themselves to the entrenched in hope of future advancement. The nature of his adherents, all big planters, fixed this Virginia monarchist in the yeomanry's mind as the author of all their evils. He gorgeously personified the Enemy.

After their villain had gradually assumed his role, the yeomanry suddenly found their Hero overnight. Ironically he belonged to the villain's class.

### 3

It is probable that the yeomanry would never have found a hero in their own class. Members of that class with education, some privilege and connections, had striven beyond it, like Benjamin Harrison II—though neither he nor the other aspirers were in any sense renegades. The yeomanry were not class-conscious when Harrison was young, and he and the others on their way up began their strivings before disaster developed in the yeomanry an awareness of their common plight. Those individuals with the capacity for leadership had gone on by 1676 (Harrison was then thirty-one) when the yeomanry found a leader among the enemy.

Twenty-eight-year-old Nathaniel Bacon was perfectly cast by nature and circumstance to become history's foil for the avaricious old tyrant. A young and slender aristocrat, dark and intense, of dash and courage, Bacon spoke with a fiery eloquence that moved men's hearts, and when the men were ready for action, he led them. That rare combination of natural leader and spellbinder, Bacon added the fillip of social philosophy: he was the first leader on the continent to speak of "the people," as we mean it today, and his burning lines on the rights of man could have been paraphrased by both Patrick Henry and Thomas Jefferson.

Seen dramatically from the outside, this privileged champion of the people and precursor of the American Revolutionaries appears as a backwoods beau ideal, a bright meteor flashing across the grayness of poverty, despair and the evils of man's inhumanity to man. Yet there was more, or less, in America's first rebel than would appear in the gallant role in which he was cast by his duel with Sir William Berkeley.

Motives are obscure. Bacon's change into a champion of the people—
or of anything—was more sudden and more of a switch than
Berkeley's change.

Nathaniel Bacon was born into an aristocratic family of solidly
entrenched country gentry, of which the shining light was his kinsman,
Lord Francis Bacon. He was sent young to Cambridge and, after
some youthful extravagance, was withdrawn for a spell. He returned
to get his degree, took the Grand Tour, and was the forty-ninth
member of his family to enter Gray's Inn for the traditional study of
law. At the age of twenty-two or twenty-three, having established the
customary background of his class, Bacon took up residence on his
father's estate to enjoy the nonutilitarian life of the young gentry.

Probably he would have lived out his years in innocuous and
unheralded leisure except for the bumpy course that true love took.
He fell in love with a girl of his own class and county, Elizabeth
Duke, and no one knows why her father, Sir Edward Duke, so bitterly
opposed his daughter's choice. However, when young Bacon came to
the colony, men spoke of his "pestilent" talk and accused him of
tending "to atheism." In his time this would mean that he was what
we would call a nonconformist, and one might hazard that Sir Edward,
finding him "irregular," suspected that the young gallant was not a
sound man. Whatever the reason for the father's disapproval, it went
so deep that he threatened to disinherit Elizabeth if she married
Bacon; and when she did, he did.

Bacon's father-in-law died soon after their defiant marriage, and
Bacon's father and his bride's brother got together to arrange a settlement on the young couple. John Duke gave them eight hundred
pounds in cash (for which Elizabeth Bacon relinquished all future
claims on the estate) and an annuity of sixty pounds; the elder
Bacon settled five hundred pounds on them and added a forty-
pound annuity. Though no fortune, the settlement—considering the
properties they had access to—should have supported Nathaniel and
Elizabeth Bacon in a style commensurate with their position. But
the young husband again displayed the tendencies toward extravagance revealed at Cambridge. Like many another trying to make a
quick killing, he got involved with the professionals and wound up in
such financial difficulties that his father decided, for his own good, to
send him "to the colonies."

Thus, the young aristocrat who was to be the people's champion arrived in Virginia as something of a high-grade remittance man. He was high-grade because his father did not put him on remittances. Thomas Bacon settled a sizable sum on his son, eighteen hundred pounds (nearly three times as much as used for thirty-five people to settle Berkeley Hundred), in order for Nathaniel to establish himself in the New World.

Bacon and his wife were not coming over cold. His father's first cousin, Nathaniel Bacon the Elder (fifty-four and twenty-four years in Virginia when Bacon the Younger came), had already established a successful plantation and joined the ruling class, as member of Council and friend of Governor Berkeley. Through the good offices of his older cousin, young Nathaniel was able to purchase a working plantation on the James River for five hundred pounds. This low price for land (some of it cleared) with river footage, with house and outbuildings and servants, was made possible by the low price of tobacco and because the owner was a friend of Nathaniel Bacon the Elder.

Thomas Ballard, who sold the property, was the elder Nathaniel's fellow member of the Council and a Berkeley supporter. Doubtless he assumed that the young Bacon was a conforming member of his own class. At that time, there was nothing to indicate that young Bacon was not. He and his wife settled in 1674 into their frontier barony at Curles Neck (so-called for the loop of the river at that point), and the transplanted young squire began to study the growing of tobacco and the operation of a plantation. In addition to the tract of land at Curles Neck, Ballard had thrown in a more distant and smaller plantation which was being worked by an overseer. This was called Bacon's Quarter, within the present city of Richmond, and into our day a stream running across the land was called Bacon's Quarter Branch.

This Bacon's Quarter was located at The Falls in the James River—the last outpost of the relatively settled area and the beginning of the rude frontier. The old references to The Falls make it sound like some minor Niagara. Actually The Falls was a series of rock formations in the river, over which the water tumbled and roared, and marked the head of tidewater and navigation in the James. Since all commerce was handled by boat, all the choice land lay by rivers, and only the small planters then went to the wilds beyond tidewater.

[ 81 ]

At The Falls on the south side of the river was the stone house and the trading establishment of young William Byrd. He had inherited both the land and the trade from his hugely successful uncle, Thomas Stegge, and was himself an extremely enterprising young man of ambition. No substantial planter along the James River was as isolated as Byrd, some ten miles above the ruins of the town and college of Henricus. Given the wilderness spaces of that day, Byrd's nearest neighbors were Nathaniel Bacon and the other planters near The Falls on the north side of the river.

By 1674, when Bacon came, plantations had been settled along all the other rivers which, loosely paralleling the James, empty into the Chesapeake Bay. North of the York was the rich Gloucester area and north of the Rappahannock was the Northern Neck, where the Lees and Carters operated fat estates. These regions too were more settled in the tidewater and their own "frontiers" to the west were composed of the small, isolated holdings. Naturally, the yeoman families on the frontier got the burden of the new Indian uprisings, and this opened the way for the strange career of Nathaniel Bacon as the people's champion.

4

In all civil wars, after the causes are defined and leaders provide a galvanizing symbol, there must be incidents. In Virginia, in 1676, before the Indians provided the incidents, there were the involvements of personalities which led to Nathaniel Bacon's leadership.

Bacon, apparently still alert for a quick fortune, had applied in Virginia for a license to trade with the Indians. Even with his inexperience, it had taken him only a short while to discover that Charles II's policies made it difficult to grow rich as a tobacco planter. Bacon was refused the license by Berkeley who, heavily committed himself to Indian trading, did not wish more competitors. As a sop to Bacon, and indirectly to his powerful cousin, Councilman Elder Nathaniel, Berkeley appointed the younger Nathaniel to the select Council. Though his way to the big money had been blocked, the newcomer in the colony was placed among the powers, as his older cousin assumed he wanted to be.

But Bacon had made friends, along with the conservatives of

Berkeley's group, among highly articulate men bitterly opposed to the governor. He seemed to have a natural affinity for other irregulars. Among his friends were two gentlemen who kept the finest houses in Jamestown. William Drummond was a Scotsman with a fearless anti-Berkeley wife, and himself had been a former colonial governor (of the Albemarle colony in North Carolina). Richard Lawrence, a scholarly Oxford graduate, had long resented Berkeley for a decision that went against him "in estate" in favor of one of Sir William's pets. "The thoughtful Mr. Lawrence," as they called him, was a most curious inhabitant of early Virginia.

Apparently endowed with a private income, he appeared in Jamestown for no particular reason and became one of the first white men in the South to be condemned for amorous doings with a Negress while also among the first white men to be publicly concerned with "the people." No Old Massa (he didn't plant tobacco), the prurient Mr. Lawrence turned his reflective mind to the philosophical aspects of the injustices wrought by those becoming Old Massas, as exemplified by Berkeley's friends in power. This curious character out of America's first colony was very adept at making a cause of the injustice suffered by the yeomanry, and some believe he played Svengali to Bacon's Trilby. Undoubtedly the analytical mind of the Berkeley-hating miscegenist attracted young Bacon and they became fast friends.

There was still a third student of affairs in Giles Bland, the most neglected of all early American romantics. He was the son of John Bland, a highly successful and esteemed London merchant, who, with his brothers, bought Berkeley Hundred and the Westover plantation. The brothers, Theodoric and Edward, had come to settle the great tracts, which had struggled along since the massacre. Edward soon died and Theodoric and his wife settled at Westover. Evidently the merchant brothers were connected with Berkeley's clique, for Theodoric was appointed to the Council and established himself as a friend of those powers hated by the yeomanry. In 1671, Theodoric died at Westover, leaving a widow and two sons, age six and eight, and at this point the complications involving Giles Bland begin.

It is without profit to puzzle over the details of one of those litigations which run like a leitmotif through so many Virginia-British families. Just in time for the climaxing struggle between yeoman and

Berkeleyites, Giles Bland was sent from London by his father to settle the estate left in the hands of Theodoric Bland's widow. The young man was well received by the powers, given the lucrative post of Collector of Customs, and settled at Berkeley Hundred—in a house built there in 1652—leaving his aunt-in-law and young cousins at adjoining Westover. Giles Bland, trained as an international merchant, was in Virginia specifically to settle his father's interests in the joint estate and evidently had no intention of staying permanently. He certainly showed no respect for the colonial governor's clique of powers.

It happened that, while trying to arrange for his father's share of the three brothers' investment, young Bland spent an evening in the home of the colony's secretary of state, Thomas Ludwell, Gent. Thomas Ludwell and his brother Philip had come to Virginia during the cavalier influx from the same town as Sir William Berkeley, and it is possible they were distantly related to him. For a certainty, the crotchety old despot welcomed them in his circle, gave them every privilege and received in turn a feudalistic allegiance from the quickly entrenched Ludwell brothers.

Because of the caste loyalty among the new powers, Secretary Ludwell would support the widow of his former fellow Councilman, Theodoric Bland, over the claims of a young interloper. On the night of Bland's visit, under the influence of a few too many brandies, Ludwell spoke disparagingly of Giles Bland's father. Young Bland was no eager toady of Berkeley's favorites. Having had a few brandies himself, he answered the powerful secretary in hot anger in defense of his father. When the insults began to fly, Ludwell was shocked to hear himself called "pitiful fellow" and "puppy" and, finally, "son of a whore."

According to Bland's story, gloves were exchanged, and he went the next morning to Jamestown to meet on the field of honor. When Ludwell failed to show, the still raging young Bland nailed the secretary's glove to the Assembly door and scrawled under it some unrecorded but apparently fighting words.

The big powers were, as the saying went, "discreet," and Thomas Ludwell did not chose to fight with weapons nor, any more, with words. Instead, as colony secretary, friend of the other Council members and the governor, he fought in the traditionally discreet way of a suit. He claimed that his hospitality had been abused by an unwarranted verbal attack, that his glove had been stolen, and such irresponsible behavior as nailing the secretary's glove to the Assembly's door should be punished by a five-hundred-pound fine. When the Council found for him, Bland, by then outraged beyond the thought of consequence, denounced the Council. For this, Berkeley forced an apology, removed Bland from his collector's post, and left him to seethe at Berkeley Hundred.

While seething, Bland also studied the colony with an anti-Berkeley viewpoint and wrote to London a letter recommending remedies for the ills of the Colony. It was an extremely clearheaded exposition of the impossible conditions. He pointed out, as an example of the causes of the yeomanry's discontent, the allowance of one hundred and fifty pounds of tobacco a day for a Burgess's expenses and another hundred pounds for his man and horse, causing a county to contribute five hundred pounds of tobacco a day to its two burgesses. Two days would mean a year's toil of one single planter. Whether or not Giles Bland came to see the colony from the yeomanry's viewpoint because of his feud with the Berkeley clique is of no consequence. An impulsive and strong-minded young man, he, Drummond, and "the thoughtful Mr. Lawrence" became forces for the oppressed people against the ruling powers.

Though there is no record of these three men talking conspiratorially over their mugs with Nathaniel Bacon, obviously they influenced him in his course when, as the people's champion, he switched the object of the fight from the Indians to Berkeley. It is possible that the "people" provided Bacon with a cause to suit his unstable ambitions.

While the fighting was limited to the Indians, Bacon had many supporters among his solidly placed friends who, more than Lawrence or Drummond, helped him to the original position of leadership. Among the most influential in preparing the way for his leadership against the Indians was his neighbor, William Byrd I, whose family and Bacon's were natural friends.

Byrd was only twenty-four at the time and had come to Virginia only six years before, on the death of his rich and powerfully connected uncle. Though himself the son of a London goldsmith, his inherited position in the colony gave him the opportunity to win the daughter of one of the cavalier officer-emigrants of good family, and Mary

Byrd and Elizabeth Bacon were of the same English background. Young Byrd, with a two-year-old son at the lonely plantation on the outpost of tidewater, grew disturbed over his family's safety when the Indian uprisings began, and he was among the first to promote his friend as the leader to go against the Indians.

Byrd, and others like him who originally supported Bacon, never contemplated carrying the fight beyond the Indians. Bacon never mentioned that he did either. It is possible that he had no intention beyond the immediate course against the Indians; but clearly he had become receptive to the larger course when the Indians provided the incidents that began the action.

### 5

For many years the remnants of the tidewater Indians had lived, almost necessarily, in peace. The various tribes were reduced to 725 hunters, or warriors, and under Virginians' protection lived on something like large reservations. Because of the riches to be made from Indian trade, with Sir William himself one of the biggest traders, the Indians were treated very tenderly by the government, and occasional small forays against a lone family were overlooked.

But in 1675 some Northern Indians, the Susquehannocks, were driven southward by the Senecas. They forced themselves into the territory of the Doeg Indians in Maryland, and from that base swarmed across the Potomac, killing surprised settlers and burning property across Northern Virginia. Virginia militia, with George Washington's grandfather as a leader, went after them, and one of the officers let his spirit of vengeance get out of hand. He killed five Indians who came into his lines under a flag of truce. Then the fat was in the fire.

The Susquehannocks started out again, very guilefully this time, skirting always to the westward along the fringes of the frontier, where they could pick off the isolated families one by one. They were aided in these deadly tactics by the formerly peaceful Pamunkey Indians in tidewater. Like old war horses sniffing the battle again, the warriors came slithering out of their villages and joined their racial brothers in a war against the whites.

The widespread murder and pillage provided the incidents that unified the still leaderless yeomanry, and under their protests even their timid representatives petitioned Berkeley to call out the counties' militia for protection of the citizens. Incomprehensibly, Sir William refused to do it. His refusal was certainly not, as was long suspected, because of his own trading with the Indians. It seems to derive more from the same source that changed his personality—a fear of "the people." After all, *people* formed those militia units. Once they united with arms in their hands, there was no telling where they would stop. They had killed Charles the First, a divine-right king. Along with this apprehension, there was the stiff-necked attitude of the despot which would harden under pressure.

When Berkeley refused, for whatever reasons, to provide defense, the small planting families began to abandon their holdings, formed together in armed bands and drifted eastward. They were already an undisciplined fighting force when the final incident occurred. Bacon's Quarter, barely fifteen miles from his home plantation, was ravaged— the overseer killed, buildings burned, tobacco destroyed and cattle run off. That was too close to home.

Totally apart from the factional fight between his friends and the Berkeley cabal, Nathaniel Bacon felt a natural horror at savage atrocities coming to his own people, and it was as a leader of the armed mob against the Indians that the young dandy first defied Berkeley.

For some time before his overseer was killed, Bacon had been asking Berkeley for a commission to go against the Indians, and he had said, "If the redskins meddle with me, damn my blood but I'll harry them, commission or no commission." His words had gotten around and it was known that he wanted to be a leader—though it was assumed that he wanted to lead only against the Indians.

When the armed mob of frontier planters reached Tidewater on the south side of the James, Nathaniel Bacon and William Byrd, with several of their friends, after a few afternoon drinks, crossed the river to talk to them. Immediately some of the men recognized the young planter and a shout went up: "A Bacon! A Bacon!"

In a matter of minutes, he was made leader by acclamation. His beginning as a people's leader was that simple, and there is nothing documentary to indicate that at this time his purpose went beyond the suppression of Indian outrages.

His men were hardly on the march southward, where the Pamunkeys and their Northern allies were retreating, when an order from Berkeley reached him. It demanded that the extemporized militia disperse at once and Bacon return to Curles Neck. His blood was up then and he ignored the order, as did most of his followers.

While his band marched on through the hot spring woods toward the North Carolina border, Berkeley set out to raise a force to go after him. The Governor's own divine right had been challenged, and from that stage onward the fight became a duel to the death between Berkeley and his fellow aristocrat.

Bacon's men, some three hundred, defeated the Indians in a bloody fight and turned back northward. As the news of their victory ran ahead of the tattered mob, Bacon became a popular hero. Families all through the colony armed themselves and declared for Bacon. The old governor, facing the dreaded assertion of people, beat a strategic retreat to Jamestown.

By then, group electricity was crackling. Excited by action and unified by a personal symbol of leadership, the people began to give voice to their long resentments. They demanded a new election for the House of Burgesses, to throw out Berkeley's puppets, and they got it. This people's victory, the first election in sixteen years, was attributed to Bacon's actions, and somewhere along the way Bacon was transformed from a leader against the Indians into a popular leader against the established government.

6

It is impossible even to guess at his total purpose in the beginning or at what stage he made the shift. He could have been changed at successive stages by the changing events. Everything went very fast in the summer of 1676, after he returned from his first Indian campaign.

In the new election, though still a councilor, he was elected to the Burgesses from Henrico County. When with his personal guard he sailed for Jamestown for the session of the Assembly, his sloop was run down on the James River by a man-of-war and Bacon's party was arrested.

By this time, the politic elder Bacon was shocked at all the goings-on, and hurried to advise his impulsive nephew on the ways of restoring himself to the governor's favor. The fifty-six-year-old substantial planter could not conceive of any other course for a sane person. He explained to the younger man that the domineering old governor only wanted a public confession in which Bacon would admit that he had been wrong to go chasing Indians without a commission and, indirectly, acknowledge Berkeley's supreme authority. Thus placated, Berkeley would show magnanimity. Bacon's followers would be freed, he would return to his rightful seat in the Council (forgetting all that Burgesses foolishness) and, in all likelihood, he would be granted a commission.

Whether or not Bacon sincerely agreed that this offered the course of wisdom, or went along with it simply as a matter of expediency, he allowed his disturbed uncle to write out his admission of guilt and lent himself gracefully to the little drama that Sir William staged the next day in the new statehouse.

The statehouse, built ten years before, was a wide and shallow redbrick building, seventy-seven feet by twenty feet, of two stories. The Council chamber was on the first floor. In there, the regal governor, with his double chins firm, sat with the Council on a raised platform with a railing in front of it, and Nathaniel Bacon was called to the railing. There he knelt on one knee and read aloud the prepared confession.

It was a great hour for the old tyrant and he made the most of it.

"God forgive you, I forgive you," he intoned, and then repeated twice more, "God forgive you, I forgive you. God forgive you, I forgive you." Then the act was over and Bacon, following his uncle's advice, resumed his seat in the Council.

Nothing really had been resolved. Berkeley delayed granting the commission, if he ever intended giving it; Bacon grew restless in Jamestown, where he was staying with his bachelor friend, Richard Lawrence; and friends warned him that the governor planned some treachery against him. Most likely Berkeley merely wanted to immobilize Bacon indefinitely in the capital, but by then action had become essential for the young leader. At night he stole out of the dark capital and put his horse at a gallop along the dirt road to Curles Neck. Berkeley was infuriated at losing Bacon and vented his spite by having Lawrence's home ransacked.

Within a few days, Nathaniel Bacon returned to Jamestown with his armed force and, in effect, took possession of the town. Six hundred men swarmed over the public green and Bacon, with a picked group of musketmen (probably the most presentable), marched to the statehouse where he formed his men in two lines. The governor, as if on cue in this act of the drama, stormed out on the porch. Striking a dramatic pose, he tore open the lace on his chest and shouted, "Here I am. Shoot me! 'Fore God, a fair mark, a fair mark. Shoot!"

Bacon, not intending to have the play taken away from him, answered with the courtesy due Berkeley's age and rank, and without theatrics stated simply that all he wanted was the promised commission. Frustrated and determined to give no commission, Berkeley, followed by his loyal Council, strode on to his nearby townhouse. Bacon appeared stalemated.

At that point, the members of the House of Burgesses began poking their heads out of the upper windows to see what was going on. In angry impulse, the musketmen aimed their weapons at the startled Burgesses and Bacon himself did a little strutting and saber-rattling, threatening to kill the whole government unless he got the commission. The Burgesses promised to get it for him, and the next day they prevailed upon the smoldering governor to grant the commission which made Bacon general of an army to fight Indians.

The struggle between Bacon and Berkeley was still ostensibly over the Indians, and, as far as Bacon revealed to his conservative followers then, getting at the savages was his sole concern. As soon as his forces had withdrawn from the southern border, the Indians had reformed to begin a second war on the settlers on the outskirts, and Bacon the Younger clearly purposed their extermination—or, at least, defeat so destructive that fighting bands could never form again.

While Bacon started his second and larger expedition, the popular uprising that had begun with the election of new representatives, continued in Jamestown. All manner of laws were rammed through to break the control of the ruling power.

These changes showed that the yeomanry clearly understood the details of the structure built by the oligarchy. Suffrage was restored to all freedmen and not merely land-owners; the self-perpetuating vestries were ended by returning the elections to the whole parish and limiting the terms to three years; sheriffs' terms were limited to one year; no man could hold more than one office; the clergy and the council must pay taxes; and the excited Burgesses went after officials who had taken excessive fees and those whose actions had been outright fraudulent.

It was a great day for the people while it lasted. Probably none of them suspected they were enjoying the final flare-up before extinction. The headiness of success and the climate of change kept the whole colony in a state of excitement and unrest.

Nathaniel Bacon, with more than a thousand armed men, mounted and on foot, was affected by the emotional swell. Remorselessly running down the marauding Indian bands with his large, hardened, frontier-wise force, Bacon became carried away and grew highhanded in making impressments of food, arms and animals of private citizens. Some of these happened to be Berkeley supporters and their protests gave the badgered governor an excuse to go whole hog against the young hothead who was casting such a blight on his declining years.

He issued a proclamation, naming Bacon and all his followers as rebels. Declaring that Bacon's commission was void because it was issued under duress, the enraged royalist issued a call to arms to suppress the threat against the established government. The strange contest of wills had reached a showdown.


7


Bacon's army had just completed a tough four weeks of marching and fighting in the July heat, finishing off for all time the Indians in eastern Virginia as a menace to planters, when ally Richard Lawrence reached him with the chilling news that he was proclaimed a rebel. Ordering a forced march, Bacon hurried his men along the narrow dirt road to Middle Plantation, a village (which became Williamsburg) midway between Jamestown on the James River and Yorktown on the York River, midway up the Virginia Peninsula. There with his friends—Giles Bland and Colonel Hansford, Drummond and Lawrence—he held a council.

Apparently many others talked and everybody held a different opinion of what to do. Some, clearly cooled off by the rebel status, wanted to make terms. Others, like Drummond the Scot, advocated working through the Burgesses and deposing Berkeley, as Harvey an earlier governor had been deposed. This would have seemed to be the sanest course. Berkeley was getting nowhere in trying to rally people to the royal banner. When it came to numbers, his few supporters were a handful compared to the people.

But Bacon cried, "I'm in over shoes; I might as well be in over boots."

This sounds like an impetuous man grown reckless, and maybe it was no more. On the other hand, Berkeley and his cronies were to Bacon at best equals; he regarded them with no more awe than did Giles Bland, and he profoundly hated them. He was intoxicated by his leadership and—who can know?—ambition might have suggested that he could supplant Berkeley and himself become governor. On the surface this meant defying the King, though Bacon had earlier written an apologia to Charles II. According to one witness, Bacon believed that even if a few redcoats were sent over, these would be finished off. Then he might become ruler of an independent Virginia.

Possibly no one, including Bacon himself, knew clearly his ultimate purpose. A leader of an armed force he was, like Cromwell on a smaller scale, suddenly the most powerful man in his country. As is the case with many military heroes who become dictators, twenty-eight-year-old Bacon was by then a creation of the forces in which he participated. He knew only to keep going, to meet Berkeley's new attack with new defiance. Proclaimed a rebel, he made a counter-proclamation defying Berkeley's authority, and supported his position with his army.

When he reached the decision that, whatever its motivation, inaugurated civil war, Bacon made the most famous of his speeches. "If virtue be a sin, if piety be guilt, all the principles of morality, goodness and justice be perverted, we must confess that those who are now called Rebels may be in danger of those high imputations. . . . But . . . if to stand in the gap after so much blood of our dear brethren bought and sold; if, after the loss of a great part of his Majesty's colony deserted and dispeopled, freely with our lives and estates to endeavour to save the remainders; [if this] be treason— God Almighty judge and let guilty die."

(Patrick Henry must have read that.)

To most of his simple followers, the words probably meant only that they were going to carry their fight to the top, and with Bacon they were ready for that. The more thoughtful recognized Bacon's counterproclamation for what it was—civil war—and a number of these resigned from his army. His friend, William Byrd I, and other early backers, began to remove their support when Bacon left off attacking Indians and began to attack the royal governor. Byrd, in fact, sent his young son, who was to become the great dandy, to safety in England, when he realized that Bacon's course would open the colony to the horrors of a civil war.

Bacon himself brought the first horrors. These acts alienated many substantial planters who hitherto had merely observed or, like Byrd, had simply withdrawn active support. Harried Berkeley had caused a breastwork to be built across the narrow isthmus which connected Jamestown to the mainland, with several hundred musketmen planted in houses to pick off any invaders. The means by which Bacon placed guns on the breastwork revealed how far the young aristocrat had gone on the road to conquest. He had his men capture the wives and daughters of the councilors, including Bacon's own aunt-by-marriage, and placing clearly visible white aprons on the ladies, forced them to parade up and down the parapet. Under their shield, the men occupied the works and made ready to charge.

"My hearts of gold," Bacon called them, in urging his irregular soldiers forward. "He that dies in the field lies in the bed of honor."

Berkeley's halfhearted defenders made no contest of it against these ruthless people. Nathaniel Bacon's forces moved in and the capital of Virginia was burned—for the first time. Governor Berkeley fled in a boat across the wide Chesapeake Bay to the Eastern Shore, that stretch of two counties between the bay and the ocean, and Bacon sent Giles Bland after him.

Then, seeming not to know what to do with his armed success, Bacon turned to a campaign of ravaging the estates of the Berkeley supporters. None of his actions in August and September seemed to proceed from any logical purpose toward any clear goal. It was as if he had a wildcat by the tail. Among the Berkeleyites whose estates he plundered were the ancestors of George Washington and Robert E. Lee; Richard Lee II was imprisoned for seven weeks. Bacon's own bewildered and outraged uncle was sacked for a loss estimated at one thousand pounds. Of course, the Ludwell brothers, Thomas and Philip, the enemies of lieutenant Giles Bland, came in for their share of damage.

But Philip Ludwell, who was to be the father-in-law of Benjamin Harrison's daughter, showed that he was made of tough and tricky stuff. By a treacherous and bold stratagem, he got men aboard the boat commanded by Giles Bland, and had the satisfaction of capturing his brother's enemy. Young Giles Bland never got to settle for his father the estates at Berkeley Hundred and Westover. He was among those to be hanged.

Then in October, the whole brief rebellion collapsed when Nathaniel Bacon, very mysteriously, died in camp. It is said that Richard Lawrence caused the body to be weighted with rocks and sunk in the York River. Nobody knows. The inarticulated dreams of the irregular young aristocrat died there in the marshes of tidewater Virginia, and his body disappeared. So did Richard Lawrence. The "thoughtful" young bachelor of Jamestown was not around when Colonel Hansford and twenty others of Bacon's more literate followers were hanged by the senile, vindictive Governor Berkeley.

8

The whole episode, from beginning to end, was over in seven months, yet those months encompassed a period that profoundly affected America's history. Nothing much has been made of Bacon's Rebellion, since for generations it has not been fashionable to associate Virginia with democratic movements. Also, Virginians themselves were divided on the subject and possessed no tendency, then or now, to glorify individuals with pious generalities. Bacon was a people's leader, the first we know, but nobody knows where he was leading them. Most probably he did not know.

The effect on Virginia of the young aristocrat's leadership of the yeomanry was to clarify, for all time, the lines between those who were to rule and those who were to be ruled. Philip Ludwell was one who called Bacon's followers "the rabble." Though this was not totally true—considering Giles Bland and many landowners with Bacon—it does reveal that in a then powerful section of America the word rabble could be used effectively in dismissing those opposed to a ruling class. It reveals that by 1676 a caste had formed that could perpetuate itself in power by repudiating "the people."

In other sections of the country recognition of castes was to be less honest, more guileful, but no less effective. However, in Virginia, and through Virginia in the thirteen states of the South, the principle of rule by the privileged was established with imperious forthrightness. Since the leaders were under no compulsion to mouth demagogic phrases about democracy, they were not forced to make deals with urban political machines nor with what we today call pressure groups. No group could pressure the rulers of an aristocratic republic. There was no way to get to them.

Nathaniel Bacon's rebellion had aired the grievances of the people and released their unified energies for that one violent summer while young Bacon led. In a backwash of spent adrenalin and faded hopes, the chastened yeomanry returned to their planting— at least free of the Indian menace—and surrendered the rule of Virginia to the few. Spurred to direct action only once, and that briefly and without clear purpose, the yeomanry were finished when the strange, dark star fell.

As a loosely defined class the yeomanry continued in Virginia (though migrations out of the state were heavy), and individuals continued to rise from the yeomanry into the ruling class. The first Thomas Jefferson in Virginia, the President's great-grandfather, was at the time a modest yeoman working a small holding near The Falls. In 1679, he fell afoul of the shrewd young Byrd's acquisitiveness, over a matter of 167 acres, and no one would have predicted that his grandson (the great Jefferson's father) would be on the way up when Byrd's grandson was on the way down. The Virginians' had a song about *The Wheel of Fortune*, and it spun very fast in the colony. But it spun no more for classes: they were fixed in time.

Most of the laws, which the people's representatives had jammed through in that heady 1676 session of the Assembly, were gradually repudiated as emotions subsided and the Indians provided no fresh exacerbations. The planter oligarchy, more solidly entrenched after the challenge to their power, grown more articulate in design and knowledgeable in operating the machinery of control, received the tactical advantage of being disembarrassed of their gaudy symbol of oppression, Sir William Berkeley.

His maddened acts of vengeance in the aftermath of the rebellion focused all the resentment and attention on the old tyrant. Even the Crown suspected that the governor had allowed things to get out of hand when a civil war could flame up across the colony, and the governor's personal soundness was made suspect by his senseless killings. A commission was sent from Charles II to investigate the past happenings and appraise the present situation.

The three commissioners became so obviously hostile to Berkeley's course that the Lady Frances vented on them a rather winsome act of spite. When they were driven away from Green Spring, she contrived to place them not in the governor's coach, but in the public hack with the hangman as driver. Her bewildered old husband took a more serious view. He decided to make a trip to his homeland and present his case personally to Charles II. The complex, controversial figure was never to be seen in Virginia again.

When he arrived in England, one of those friends who delight in bearing ill tidings reported a remark made about him by Charles II. "That old fool," the King said, "has killed more people in that naked land than I did over the execution of my father."

Monarchy was all that was left to the sixty-nine-year-old former courtier whose life had gone down the drain in the hot wilderness of the Crown's first colonial empire. When the monarch turned against him, nothing was left. Sir William Berkeley, dilettante-playwright and husband of a young beauty, who had enjoyed in a colony a splendor of privilege which comes to few men, was to his despotically irrational end a man of conviction. When he was denied by his King, who personified his conviction, the tired, tough old heart broke. Sir William, without ever presenting his side, died within a year of his terrible young adversary.

The rival aristocrats had played out their symbolic roles as in some heroic drama and, quite unwittingly, fixed the mold of the colony over which they had fought. No more cavaliers need come. From then on, Virginia would produce its own home-grown, self-made aristocrats. The nucleus was already there, fixed in power by the old despot, and this ruling caste would perpetuate itself through intermarriages. With Bacon's death the air was cleared of unrest and peoples' minds of uncertainties: Virginia was established, for all time, as an aristocratic republic.

Bacon's solid positive contribution was to clear the Tidewater of Indian menaces. Though a physical frontier would continue in Virginia for another century, as settlers migrated ever further westward away from the ever-widening monopolistic holdings of the big planters, in tidewater Virginia the Age of the Frontier ended, for all practical purposes, with Bacon's rebellion and the aftermath. The structure of the society, emerging out of the wilderness, was completed. Virginia Laydon, born in Jamestown in 1608, could have lived through it all in a normal span of years.

9

The little group of powers, who had been established in control by Sir William, were of necessity flexibly open to new members. As planters acquired land and built substantial establishments in the fashion, showed themselves to be well mannered and discreet, subscribed to the code and (as they said) "lived bravely," places were made for them. Usually the newcomers were brought along by gradual stages, advanced in power and place as they demonstrated themselves "to be worthy of honors." Such was the post-Bacon course of Benjamin Harrison II.

Not big enough to attract attention during the Rebellion, his holdings fortunately outside the periphery of Bacon's destructive march, he was beginning to assume some importance as the colony quieted down and the newly entrenched powers were alert for new recruits to swell their forces.

Of all those who had been loyal to Governor Berkeley, none was more handsomely rewarded than the Philip Ludwell who did in Giles Bland of Berkeley Hundred. He won the hand of the widowed, still beautiful Lady Frances, and with the hand the fine estate of Green Spring. He must have been a stout supporter of ambitious Benjamin Harrison, since their families were joined through the marriage of Ludwell's son and Harrison's daughter, and the young planter had the advantage of living across the river not far from Jamestown.

Two years after the rebellion was over, Harrison had done well enough to be given the profitable and honorable steppingstone of sheriff of his county. The oligarchy, working on the proposition that only those who had demonstrated the capacity to manage their own affairs should be trusted with the affairs of others, gave only to those, who had already done well, the posts that led to the real power and the glory. Harrison performed his new duties ably and honestly and, having revealed his fitness for position, was sent the following year (1680) to the House of Burgesses from Surry County. He was then thirty-five years old and the House, freed both of the royal toadies of Berkeley's reign and the assertive yeomanry of Bacon's hour, was assuming the substantial character that would continue for a century.

Once in the government, Harrison showed himself to be an astute politician. Neither flashy nor grasping, he brought to his understanding of political values and the practicalities of maneuver the same clear-eyed shrewdness that he brought to the business of planting. Just as he had identified his course with the emerging class of big planters, so he formed personal alliances with the powers emerging within the class. After serving five terms over a period of eighteen years, Harrison was established among the political rulers even before he was tapped for the Council at fifty-three. As councilors were the recognized royalty of Virginia's untitled nobility, Benjamin Harrison II had gone as far as there was to go.

He had won the top position himself in a life of steady, unobtrusive acquisition. Building soundly from the first five hundred acres, and then his river-front store, he paid quitrent on 2,750 acres in several working plantations, in addition to land settled on his sons. Though huge land grants were given to Charles II's pets, and the whole tendency was toward much larger holdings than the modest operations of the pre-cavalier days, by Harrison's day, counting only property, he was in the upper brackets.

The unostentatious accumulator always spread his operations beyond the conspicuous category of "land and niggers." He had for his own operations only twenty-one tithables, though he probably bought slaves and indentures to help his sons get an early start. What he had was horses and mules, cattle and hogs and sheep, boats and his store—and cash. Though he also seemed to have tended less to conspicuous consumption than some of his more lavish-minded friends, he made the standard investments in silver and books and furnishings from England. He wanted of all things to do well by his children, and this he most certainly accomplished.

Benjamin Harrison II does not come across time with any high color: there are no stories about him at all though there was an occasional not wholly complimentary reference to his political power. Yet, in hewing steadfastly to the single, clear course which established his children in the ruling caste of Virginia, he was probably more typical of the planters who arose in the frontier age than those who lent themselves to legend. After all, there are no really colorful stories about the first William Byrd, the first two Richard Lees, except for the second Lee's fanatical devotion to royalty. These were sober, conservative men of ambition, and the frontier times in which they had grown up placed great demands on time and energy.

Many men came well endowed to the colony, cut a figure for a spell, perhaps left some influence on styles and the arts of living. But few arose like Harrison to found a line that continued for generations in a public service which formed the background for the later Virginia Dynasty. Those who did could not have indulged themselves too much in high life. For Harrison, conforming to what was to become a Virginia tradition, the family was the thing.

No reasonable assumptions have to be made about the forces which formed the futures of his children. They were trained for the large responsibility—to their estate, their class, their country (Virginia). They were born too late to remember the frontier. They were the swing generation in Virginia's evolution. Born into the ruling class in the existing order of an aristocratic republic, they matured as aristocrats with an inherited sense of privilege, a position of rule, and a dedication to sustain the existing order.

Though their father had not reached the pinnacle of the Council during their early years, he was so solidly established with the ruling class that the children never knew any intimates outside it. One daughter married Philip Ludwell's son, himself a councilor, and from their union came an ancestor of Robert E. Lee. Another married "Commissary" Blair, commissioner of the Church to Virginia (unofficial bishop, as the Church never established Virginia as a diocese), founder and first president of William and Mary College, and long president of the Council. Benjamin Harrison III married young the daughter of another Councillor, Colonel Lewis Burwell, who had done extremely well in land and indenture speculation.

The elder Harrison lived on until 1712, full of honors and the patriarch of a most powerful clan, interlocked by marriage or friendship with the mighty. It is not likely that he dwelt on the olden times of the frontier days. He was a busy man, his head crowded with the details of the physical world and the tangible power. The wisdoms of acquisition, and not of reflection, were what he passed on to his children. The seeds fell on most fertile soil. Benjamin Harrison III and his younger brothers, Nathaniel and Henry, increased their inheritance proportionately as their father had built from five hundred acres and a good name.

Reversing the English procedure, Benjamin, the oldest son, left the homeplace, and established his line of the family on the north side of the river at Berkeley Hundred. He might have been sensible of the ghosts of Giles Bland and Captain Thorpe and poor Willi Tracy, and all those buried in unmarked graves in the plantation patented by John Smythe (for young Harrison held an interest in Virginia history), but the source of his attraction was that three mile river front with a landing where "the big boats could ride."

At a very early age he looked beyond his father's wharf store and beyond tobacco. The maturation in young Benjamin Harrison of the early adventurers' dream went beyond anything that the Berkeley Hundred founder, the scholarly Mr. Smythe of Nibley, could even have imagined. For Harrison was building a private domain, a dynastic center for generations of rulers, some of whom would defy the British king.

# THE AGE OF THE ARISTOCRAT

❀  ❀

## CHAPTER V

# PORTRAIT OF A PLANTER —
## *AS A MAN OF BUSINESS*

1

No one seems to know the exact date when Benjamin Harrison III settled at Berkeley Hundred, which his father bought from the Blands in 1691. As the younger Harrison's life was short and his acquisitions vast (more than twenty thousand acres and one hundred slaves), the probabilities are that he planted there soon after his family acquired the property. As he was born in 1673, this would place him on the large tract in his late teens—a thoroughly responsible age in his day.

Among the reasons for placing him at Berkeley in the early 1690s, with his eye on that river landing, was his established position in shipping by 1697. That year, when only twenty-four, Benjamin Harrison exported a cargo on a ship that landed with false papers in Scotland, where prices could be obtained that were higher than in the restricted British market. That same year he journeyed to England on a ship of which he was half owner, to plead the planters' interests before the Committee on Trade and Plantations, *and* to maneuver for the post of Attorney-General of the Colony. He must have started young to come that far on his own. In sterner times the purpose of training was not to postpone a child's assumption of responsibility but to hasten it. The early growth was particularly developed on plantations.

On his father's plantation in Surry County, where young Harrison

[ 103 ]

had been trained from the earliest age in the details of managing the complex operations, his growth would be fast because all the influences in his life were focused in the plantation and toward the goal of plantation mastership.

At his father's river store—that combination of wharf, warehouse and trading post—he learned his ciphering and practical balancing of books while, in effect, learning the business. Being responsive to trading and shipping, he absorbed what amounted to an intuitive knowledge of world-barter much as children growing up in the country absorb, without being actually taught, the simple wisdoms of the earth.

The knowledge of planting he also acquired in the same way, by observing and doing under tutelage. He had to know how tobacco plants needed to be guarded from suckers and worms and weeds, how the tobacco stem had to be cut in a single strong stroke downward and sliced off at the bottom, how the leaves were hung and graded as they cured in the sheds, and how the sizes were arranged for packing in hogsheads. It was not intended that young Harrison should ever work in the hot fields or roll a hogshead to the boat, but he must be able to judge tobacco and know when others were working properly.

He developed an eye for animals and could act as his own vet if necessary; he learned the simple home remedies for sickness—to purge and bring on vomiting—and would, as most planters, act as doctor for his people. All these were the details of operations.

Most of all, and fundamentally, he learned the management of people. With all else, as chattel-slavery became the system of labor (the slave population tripled from two thousand to six thousand in the thirty years from 1670 to 1700), the young planter must know how to rule subjects if his operations were to be efficient.

The Negroes in the first large shipments did not come (as in the next century) to established slave systems, with small colonies of their own people already acclimated and adjusted. The plantation of the legend, the idyll, was some years away, and the system, newly introduced in Harrison's time, was in an experimental stage. First there was the language barrier. Many of the Negroes fresh from Africa, finding themselves settled as slaves on some clearing, immediately took to the woods. Others, who had been chieftains and the like in their own tribes, were arrogant and pugnacious. Most of them, quite naturally, did not want to work. As there was no inducement for any of them to work, it took some doing to develop a happy management-labor relationship with the hostile captives.

Despite the later abolitionists' tales of cruelty, from the beginning and to the end, the intelligent care of property discouraged the use of physical force as a means of getting work out of slaves. It was always ineffective, and employed only by stupid brutes who could think of no other methods; these were usually overseers who were, after all, not impairing their own property. When slaves were beaten, it was to punish them for running away or for other offenses, in harsh times when physical punishment was generally meted out for most offenses adjudged to be criminal, and flogging was by no means the most severe indignity suffered by citizens.

Of course, in situations where individuals hold the power of life and death over others, the domineering and sadistic can make life miserable for those under them. But planters who treated slaves badly, or took improper care of them, were regarded with contempt. Mean masters were not restricted to slaveowners. Employers of white indenturers had, by cruelty and hard use, almost caused uprisings, and hundreds of white men had run away from harsh masters. The whites, however, ran more purposefully. They knew the language and the country and, as soon as they had made their way out of the owner's region, they could travel to one of the other colonies (usually North Carolina) and make a new start on their own.

Mastery through physical force or bullying was not the answer to getting work out of people, whatever their color status. The planters were no more humane than their fellows, but they were eminently practical. Also, as their power made them more aware of the need for personal dignity, they felt it demeaned them to strike or insult persons under their protection.

Children were taught from an early age not to take advantage of those in an inferior position. As a father wrote one of his children ". . . carry yourself so that everybody may respect you. Be calm and obliging to all the servants, and when you speak, do it mildly, even to the poorest slave. If any of the servants commit small faults that are of no consequence, you hide them. . . ."

Such typical advice expresses the attitude of the master, and though its purpose be essentially for the self-discipline of his children, it implies at least an awareness of others in a unique condition. Certainly it is not an attitude that would condone vicious behavior toward slaves.

On the plantation a young master such as Benjamin Harrison would first learn self-control, and he would take pride in it as he was brought along to assume control over others of his fellow men. Along with learning self-control and developing a sense of his own dignity, Harrison learned to control the slaves and the white artisans who were to cultivate his private domain. This was acquired while doing—a habit of authority—so that there was no transition between preparation and (as we say) entering into life. He grew up in and was conditioned by the domain where he would rule.

About the education of young Harrison, and all planters' children of that era, it is impossible to learn anything definite. The scattered free schools of the time seem to have been charity affairs, endowed by legacies of the well-to-do for the education of the less fortunate. Contemporaries of Harrison were known Latin scholars and his father's contemporary, Richard Lee II, enjoyed wide repute for his scholarship in Latin, Greek and Hebrew. It can only be assumed that the rudiments of education—reading, writing and arithmetic (possibly Latin)—were absorbed, as was everything else through environment.

Literate children were usually the sons and daughters of literate parents. Perhaps the parish clergy gave some help in Latin, perhaps tutors were hired, though it was in the next generation that tutors became commonplace fixtures in plantation life. Since all the young men of the ruling class were trained in politics and were expected to take active part at the county level in their twenties, perhaps elder statesmen also imparted phases of education to their potential successors.

This guesswork is limited to Harrison's swing generation, the first born to rule. As this generation matured, the stress they put on formal education—tutors and college—could indicate that they felt a lack of cultural background, or perhaps were convinced that a classical background was a requisite of a ruling class. Always their stress on education was classical. They never introduced a course in anything like, say, plantation management.

Whatever his preparation in letters, Benjamin Harrison III—

young planter and prototype of the youth in the new class—was prepared to assume the duties of a very responsible adult when he settled himself in the house on the old clearing at Berkeley Hundred.

2

In his private world, still more primeval than cleared, young Harrison was remote from the unrest and occasional tumults among the people. Since the end of the Stuart Kings (1687), oppressions from the Crown had grown lighter, and under William and Mary the royal governors could never attain the power held by old Berkeley. The Council was too strong and jealous of its own power. From the Council down, as from the apex of a pyramid outward, the Colony was governed —without police or even a single instance of vigilantes—by a chain of control at county levels, with every public office held by a member, however humble, of the oligarchy.

Except for the skillful aspirants to power, the bulk of the population was blocked off from advancement, and this caused a shifting and unsettledness as families and individuals groped to discover their own level. The legend that divides Virginia's population into patrician and plebeian ("poor white") still persists after all proofs to the contrary. Virginia developed a very fine middle class, with all the traditional characteristics (except acquisitiveness) of the planter class. They were later to form the body of Lee's army, to which they contributed Stonewall Jackson, but at the end of the seventeenth century they had found neither their economic or social position.

The self-respecting, modestly ambitious families were, except for those who migrated out of the state, to find their way in one of three courses: as cities began to grow, some moved into town as artisans and clerks, merchants and lawyers, or simply as workers; as the western part of the state was opened, some moved beyond the big planters' domination; those who stuck it out in Tidewater abandoned the money crop and became in time the "Virginia farmer" as differentiated from the planter. They were good people. When young Harrison emerged into personal power at the turn of the century, these courses had not been defined, and there was great unrest outside his periphery.

Some dispossessed yeomen and freed indenturers were finding their personal courses in the rough, adventuresome life of the frontier. Some of the more practical became cattlemen in the unsettled land beyond the rivers and employed the historically abandoned colonial "cowboy." Even tougher than the cowboys were the men who ran the mule teams of the Indian traders, like William Byrd, deep into the Southern wilderness. As blasphemous and hard-bitten fatalists as ever risked their lives daily for sustenance, they had a kind of rude mastery of their world. Then, too, the "rangers" offered careers to the brave who added competence and discipline to their personal freedom from the planters' dominion. The rangers were the first professional frontiersmen in America.

The colonists needed to be protected from three menaces—Indians, England's enemies, and slave insurrections. In lieu of a standing army, each county maintained a militia of practically all its able-bodied men, who met monthly and stood at call for any emergency. The bulk of the militia were the yeomanry who got most of their meat from shooting game, so no need existed for "target practice." But the colonists, feeling the need for some permanent force, had by 1682 gradually legalized a group of companies of professional soldiers of the woods who patrolled the frontiers. They not only guarded against Indian attack, they also developed a practical knowledge of the unexplored wilderness and prepared the way for later settlements. Though equally ignored by history and the Virginia myths, the Virginia Rangers were the precursors of all working frontiersmen in America and their lives represented a paid escape from the dominating powers.

Yet, when rangers, Indian traders and frontier cattlemen hit Jamestown (or, by 1699, Williamsburg) and visited their families in the counties, they could scarcely have added a stabilizing influence to those segments of population shifting restlessly to find a center. Worse than the violent characters who had found their individual way were the shiftless and raffish who, by the oligarchy, were all identified with the "people" and intensified the confusion of the recently displaced. This turbulent element, composed of dispossessed yeomanry and those freed indenturers who were really unfitted for the struggle, first became drifters and then petty criminals.

To them were added criminals and undesirable elements which the British government at times tried to unload on Virginia. Though the stout protests of the Jamestown Council checked that purblind measure of colonization, hundreds or perhaps thousands of the men and women sent in during that experiment had survived. Debased to begin with—thieves and whores and gin-dums—they brought their habits with them to a new environment which was less designed to absorb them, and contributed to the unsettled and vicious life outside the river principalities.

Plantation masters were not the only producers of mulattoes. British female graduates of Newgate were delivered of bastards by Negro fathers, and many a non-landowning white man left descendants of a passing lust shared with a black woman. Altogether, the various elements combined to create a tumultuous background which the refined myths have never associated with Colonial Virginia.

Outside the solidly respectable who slowly found their own way in Virginia (and the continuous stream of migrants out of the state), there were among the casuals those who gradually drifted away from Tidewater to less settled sections. Some formed in little settlements along the North Carolina border where, away from taxes and the long arm of the oligarchy, they rudely subsisted off corn and hogmeat, with additions to their diet from field and stream. Later branches built wild baronies (in unconscious imitation of the plantation masters) in the mountain fastnesses and achieved something of a romantic fame as the untamed denizens of "The Blue Ridge Mountains of Virginia." The unstable elements, then, also found their courses out of Tidewater and, needless to say, some were absorbed.

Yet, the myth is sound, in terms of historical forces, to neglect them as an influence on Virginia. That these thousands of people can be dismissed as a historical force attests to the might of the dream that could be sustained by a few families (hardly more than two dozen in young Harrison's early time) who could control a British colony and design its destiny into the present.

3

Removed from all this unrest and potential danger by his natively born faith in the control of the few, young Harrison was undistracted as he devoted his early blooming talents to his own plantation and to his own class. The struggles within the ruling class have been equally neglected by the myth, but those involving Harrison's own family were enough to require his constant and alert attention.

All was not sweetness and light among members of the oligarchy and never was. Within the group a ceaseless maneuvering went on for position. There were few really big plums, where posts of rank carried large financial rewards, either through cash incomes or tangible privilege. For these places the manipulations were conducted in a high-level atmosphere of inner-group loyalties and rivalries, with exchanges of favors and blocking of favors.

There was a tacit agreement, however, that no faction would expose the peculations of another as long as the private gain was made at the expense of the public domain. This system by which those in power maintained a united front was a practical aspect of their British-gentry model. At that time, English government officials were corrupt and rapacious, and the Virginians actually operated with more personal restraint and larger public responsibility than the originals. Yet it was a risky business for Royal Crown colonists, and collusive acts always occurred between members of a loyal inner group.

By the time Benjamin Harrison III was settled at Berkeley Hundred, the formerly controversial Bland property had been disposed of, and adjoining Westover had been purchased in 1688 by William Byrd I, the most successful of the traders with the Indians, who maintained his outpost at The Falls. Along with the twelve hundred acres of riverfront property which Byrd settled at Westover in 1690, he acquired an additional thirty-three hundred acres of adjoining high ground back from the river. In that land-hungry period, shrewd planters like Byrd and the Harrisons always tried to draw their holdings into several solid tracts and not have scattered properties all over the wilderness.

However, when Byrd acquired the property, he was not ready to plant those thirty-three hundred adjoining acres, though by law all patents must be planted within four years or revert to the colony "in escheat." Likewise, when quitrents were not paid, a patent was declared in escheat. It happened that Byrd, growing in power with the years, was then escheator. The acquisitive never cease their small savings, and this landowner who acquired twenty-six thousand acres in

Tidewater Virginia neither planted the property nor paid quitrents on the thirty-three hundred acres, nor did the escheator declare his own property to be in escheat.

Byrd's evasion of the law here illustrates both the united front of the whole and the exchange of favors among the loyal inner groups. All new patents in Virginia were issued through the Council, so the councilors simply ignored his fat acres lying idle east of Harrison's Berkeley. But, as the land was in escheat by law, a new patent had to be issued when Byrd was ready to plant it around the turn of the century. Benjamin Harrison's younger brother, Nathaniel, who had enlarged their father's south-side holdings and was a Burgess at twenty-two, then patented Byrd's land in his own name. After a decent interval, transfer of ownership was made to William Byrd I, fellow councilor of the elder Harrison.

Later, Nathaniel Harrison received the earthly reward of becoming auditor general, while Byrd's son became receiver general. These posts paid their holders 5 per cent of all receipts. Since all this was open knowledge in the oligarchy, it is clear why the rivalries became intense and even bitter, and why the tight inner loyalties were necessary.

When young Harrison went to England in 1697 to try to land the attorney generalship, his family alliances were as powerful as any in the colony. Both his father and father-in-law sat on the Council, as well as his brother-in-law, Philip Ludwell, who had married Benjamin's sister Hannah. At that time Jamestown, the old frontier capital, was being abandoned, and Harrison's father and kinsmen by marriage were on the powerful board that allotted land in the newly planned capital of Williamsburg.

An idealistic group wanted for the new capital a new college (successor to ill-fated Henricus), and their leader was Harrison's other brother-in-law, Dr. Blair, commissary of the Bishop of London and rector of Bruton Parish. Commissary Blair was working with Scotch obstinacy to overcome all obstacles to the founding of a college and it was through this dedicated purpose that the Harrison bloc aroused a ferocious enemy to oppose young Harrison's appointment as attorney general.

4

The enemy who was to plague the Harrison bloc was Colonel Daniel Parke, a swaggering and handsome gentleman out of a lusty era. Among the enterprising Harrisons and Byrds, this reckless gallant, though he owned large holdings in Virginia and the West Indies, was like a holdover from the Restoration bucks. Known to no one, probably not even himself, his debts were equally large, for Parke lived with lordly self-indulgence. Well connected in England and Virginia (a member of the Council), he married one of Ludwell's daughters and, hence, was by marriage connected with the Harrisons: his wife's brother was the husband of Benjamin's sister Hannah.

But this British-Virginian was a freebooter and joined no family clans. His two daughters were to marry William Byrd II and John Custis, whose son became the first husband and financial endower of Martha Washington. Parke's oblique relationship to "The Father of His Country" would have meant little to this brazen adulterer and aggressive duelist (with a rapier) who lived by his own anachronistic code of honor.

Like many others in Virginia in the early period, the individualistic Parke belonged more to the privileged world of Old Europe than to a New World evolving its new character. His morals were those of Charles the Second: anything is forgiven the ruling class except cowardice. Parke had courage in the tradition and he had style. In Virginia he represented an age that was passing while very definitely contributing to the character of the aristocracy.

He allied himself with Sir Edmund Andros, one of the transient governors of that period of the council's supremacy, rather than with the native landowners' oligarchy, to which he belonged. Andros was a limited career government servant who was sent to Virginia, after an awesome failure in New England, as part of King William's policy of appointing dependable timeservers whose loyalty to the Crown was unquestioned. For some reason Andros was outraged at the idea of a college being founded in a colony, and Parke—an old-guard aristocrat —supported the governor.

Convinced that Oxford and Cambridge provided adequately for those who deserved higher education, he subscribed to Governor

Berkeley's theory of educating the people. Sir William had said: "I thank God that there are no free schools of printing; for learning has brought disobedience, and heresy, and sects into the world, and printing has divulged them, and libels against the best government. God keep us from both."

There was nothing old-fashioned or unique about Berkeley's view. Parke and Andros could arouse as much support in England for opposition to a college as Commissary Blair could arouse for it. When Dr. Blair personally appealed to a British secretary on the grounds of saving the peoples' souls, Seymour shouted at the churchman, "Damn their souls! Let them plant tobacco."

Fighting British government officials was an old story to Dr. Blair. In his late thirties and early forties during the period of controversy, the pious and scholarly Scotsman had first locked horns with Andros's predecessor, Governor Nicholson.

Nicholson was an irascible eccentric. On a later tour in Virginia, he fell in love with one of the beautiful Burwell girls, a sister-in-law of Benjamin Harrison, and was quite beside himself when she refused to marry him. He threatened that if she married another he would cut the throats of three men—the groom, the minister performing the service, and the justice who issued the license. In his quarrels with Dr. Blair, this weird governor included Blair's wife (Harrison's sister Sarah) in his spites, though in so doing, he stirred up a foe who was restrained by none of her husband's Christian forbearance.

This Sarah Harrison was a most unusual lady for her day. Her face was handsome and willful, with a full mouth slightly turned up in a knowing smile and large eyes looking on the world with a malicious, secret humor. She knew her own mind, as they said, and she let Dr. Blair know it in the wedding ceremony.

When the Reverend Mr. Smith, reading from the Prayer Book, reached the line, "Wilt thou love him, comfort him, honor and obey ——" he was startled at her casual interruption of the sacrament.

"No obey," said Sarah Harrison.

After a flustered pause, Mr. Smith began all over at the beginning of the question. "Wilt thou have this man to thy wedded husband . . ." When he reached the line containing the word, "obey," again Sarah said with casual firmness, "No obey."

By then her groom's fellow clergyman was defeated. He continued on with the question, finishing with "keep thee only unto him, as long as ye both shall live?"

Having established her point, Sarah Harrison answered pleasantly enough, "I will."

Whether or not Sarah obeyed Dr. Blair is not known, but it is known that she remained as strong-minded and as individualistic as she showed herself to be in the ceremony. Sarah Harrison Blair became what is known as "a character," and apparently not one characterized by lovable qualities. Unlike her father, her Sister Hannah and her brothers, Sarah did not practice the planters' virtue of being "discreet."

When Governor Andros inherited Nicholson's feud over the college, he included Sarah Blair among the enemies; and when Colonel Parke allied himself with Andros, this gallant was moved to violence by the sharp lady.

It happened that Dr. Blair had been devoting several sermons to the evils of adultery. It was known that Parke admitted an illegitimate daughter in the West Indies, and had passed off in Virginia a lady not his wife as his "cousin," and the anachronistic beau thought (probably rightly) that his enemy was using the pulpit to get at him. On the pretense that Mrs. Blair was pre-empting his pew at Bruton Parish Church in Williamsburg, the handsome colonel strode down the aisle and furiously wrestled Mrs. Blair out of her pew and pushed the outraged lady away.

Dr. Blair managed to control his indignation at this insult to his wife and in his church, but that was the end of his cheek-turning. He quietly wrote his powerful connections in the Church of England and the British government, and soon Governor Andros was transferred from Virginia. After his departure, the dashing Colonel Parke went to England and joined the staff of Marlborough.

It is said that, as an aide-de-camp of the duke, he had the honor of bringing to Queen Anne the news of the victory of Blenheim. Through his British supporters he was appointed governor of the Leeward Islands, and was tortured to death at Antigua in the rebellion of 1710. He died game. While his captors heaped insult and physical abuse on him as they prolonged his suffering, Parke said, "Gentlemen, you have no sense of honor left, pray have some of humanity."

Long before he died, the notorious courtier had, while in England, arranged a slap of vengeance at the Blairs and their kin. He used his own power in England to block the appointment of Benjamin Harrison, Blair's brother-in-law, to the coveted post of attorney general for Virginia.

Such a setback in the course of interparty feuds was taken philosophically by young Harrison. This was the chance of the game. Undiscouraged, he obtained an appointment as clerk of the council and, in close contact with the powers, manipulated for a substitute post. By 1700, when he was twenty-seven, he was rewarded with the special assignment of acting attorney general for the prosecution of criminals on trial, with the title of "His Majesty's Council at Law." That he had never studied law made no difference. All the county courts were run by gentlemen who learned their law—as they learned everything else—as they went.

The road opened to the well-paying posts of honor, Harrison returned to his shipping and planting with the conviction that time and industry (he was a very hard worker) would advance him. He went up very fast. Within five years of his special appointment, he became treasurer of the colony, while already Speaker of the House of Burgesses. As the Council was by then becoming virtually hereditary, he could not move up while his father still sat in that august body.

5

When Benjamin Harrison III, the master of Berkeley Hundred, joined his brother Nathaniel in the House of Burgesses, the statehouse was then in the new capital of Williamsburg (named for the reigning king), and to these young men of the age of the aristocrat the old frontier capital of Jamestown was little more than a relic of a time gone—a time of their father's youth and of their long-dead grandfather's unknown beginnings in Virginia.

Jamestown had been largely rebuilt after Bacon's fire of 1676, but the complaints grew about its malarial, "insalubrious" climate and a movement began toward establishing a new site. The inevitable inertia encountered was overcome when another fire, accidental, again destroyed all except four or five buildings, and left the island strewn with brick rubbish. The town was not rebuilt after that fire, and in 1699 Jamestown was abandoned as a capital.

In time, vines and new trees grew over the highway, the back street, and the Public Green where young Bacon had defied old Berkeley in front of the statehouse. Even the foundations were obliterated, and eventually nothing was left to suggest all the dreams and heartaches, violent deaths and prolonged deaths, all the cavalcade of men and women who had lived out their brief hours on the hallowed ground. A private plantation or so was worked on the ghostly island and the only public use made of old James Towne was an occasional burial in the churchyard. (The Harrison boys' sister Sarah was soon to be buried there and much later, after a long life, the good Dr. Blair. Finally even the graveyard fell into neglect, and a sycamore tree grew through Sarah Blair's tombstone.)

Public interest centered in the new capital at the crossing of the road from Jamestown to Yorktown with the old Pocahontas Trail that ran right up the center of the Peninsula from the bay to The Falls, where William Byrd's trading post was expanding on the present site of Richmond.

Mindful of the physical disadvantages of their first capital, the government selected comparatively high ground (at least, not in a swamp), where fine wells were plentiful. Nor was the new capital allowed to grow helter-skelter as had Jamestown. Before the first building, the town was planned in detail as carefully as a blueprint is made for a house.

The town's area was close to three hundred acres, and a broad, tree-lined one-mile center street ran from Dr. Blair's new college, William and Mary, straight to the new capitol. Off one side a palace green led to the great mansion conceived for the colonial governor, and on another side was the wide public square—a site for fairs and stock shows and a park for the people. No lots were sold to speculators. All must be built on within two years, and the houses, whether brick or frame, must have brick chimneys and cellars.

Of course, all that did not happen overnight, though the new capital grew surprisingly fast. By the time Williamsburg was laid out, towns such as Yorktown and Hampton were growing, every county boasted around the courthouse a cluster of buildings which was called a town, and colonists had developed a need and a desire for a center, both commercial and social. Councilors, like the elder Harrison, built houses there for seasons at the capital; artisans set up shop for the yeomanry and dealt in specialties for planters; and taverns came with their "ordinary" licenses.

From the first, because of its gracious design and the handsomely indigenous architecture that developed, Williamsburg held a soft and pervasive charm, and to native-born Virginians who had never seen a city their new capital became a place of wonder and splendor.

When Benjamin Harrison III first went to Williamsburg, the new capital had not been established as the accustomed center, and aside from the time when political duties took him there, he devoted his hours primarily to Berkeley Hundred and his shipping. The year after he became Speaker of the Burgesses—in 1705, when he was thirty-two—Harrison's closest plantation neighbor changed, and the great operator met a great dandy.

The most elegant gentleman seen in Virginia since the departure of the "sparkish" Colonel Parke (in fact, the son-in-law of that courtier), the new neighbor was the son of William Byrd, and had reluctantly returned to the home acres from London on his father's death.

William Byrd I, after thirty-odd years of an almost unparallelled career devoted to the acquisition of wealth, honors and power in the colony, had died at the age of fifty-two. His cavalier wife having died before him, the master of Westover, after a modest legacy to his surviving daughter (one had died and one had disappeared), turned over all his property and a card to all his ranks to his oldest son, who had never liked Virginia enough to live there.

This natively gifted son, Colonel William Byrd II, has become something of a symbol of the legendary Virginia aristocrat. Yet, it could never be said of the younger Byrd, as it was of old Captain Matthews, the peoples' governor during the interregnum, that "he is a true lover of Virginia." In the final sense, he was not a true Virginian at all. This much-publicized colonial prince was neither formed by Virginia nor did his descendants later take part in forming the new republic. If William Byrd II had never lived, the social forces of Virginia would be unchanged. It was in style, in the learning and manners of the great world, that the younger Byrd personalized the final Old World influences on the hardening mold of the Virginia character.

A baby during Bacon's civil war, he had been sent for safety to his well-connected mother's family in England. Except for brief and reluctant intervals in Virginia, he had remained in London. Actually Byrd was the dilettante son of a merchant father who wanted to cut a figure among the fashionable intellectuals in the capital. For this role, he was well endowed.

His father paid his bills, his mother provided channels, and—thus enabled to devote himself to charm and culture—he, like many another clever provincial, endeared himself to a few powerfully placed men of learning. Though his brother-in-law, the historian Robert Beverley, said that Byrd was a most arrant social climber in London, skillful adulation could then (as now) win a place near the head of the table. Once established with a learned great, the eager climber knew what to do with his favor. He did have wit, charm and style, and he was truly learned. Except for his consciousness of social position and his grandiose self-indulgence, Byrd could have been a top-flight man of letters.

As it was, when his enterprising father died and America's first literary expatriate was forced to come home and look after the plantation that supported him, Byrd concentrated his energies immediately on obtaining a position of rank and cash. He was unfortunate at first, having made few friends in the colony at that time, but friends of his father saw to it that he was adequately taken care of. From the day that he settled in the house at Westover, his inherited position was as strong as Benjamin Harrison's (with whom Byrd was of an age) and that of the other younger members of the ruling class.

The specific difference between Byrd and all that his neighbor Harrison typified was that the heir to the emigrant's fortune did not belong to the evolutionary line of the Virginia character. Byrd was a sport, the last throwback to England. Necessity placed him in Virginia at the age of thirty-one, and his father's position placed him among the powers. Young Byrd outwardly adapted himself to his lot, but revealed his sense of exile in nostalgic letters to English friends and patrons. He also guarded the secret of his addiction to lusts of the flesh. Missing the licentious aspects of life in London (where parts of his allowance went to prostitutes), he kept himself within bounds on the whole by most definitely not placing his wife on that pedestal where Southern ladies were supposed to abide. Instead, he dutifully recorded that one of their episodes occurred upon the billiard table.

At that time, neither Harrison nor Byrd had built on Berkeley or Westover the great houses that have survived more than two centuries. The evolution of the aristocratic pattern was one step away from the enduring house as a dynastic center. Land was still the perpetuating center, and despite Benjamin Harrison's large concepts he did not conceive of a house as a center for perpetuity.

His Berkeley Hundred home was what was called "a Virginia house." It had been built in 1652 in the style of those first graciously lined and indigenous homes that Harrison's father had seen going up in Surry County when he was a boy. Above a brick basement fifty feet wide by twenty feet deep, the full first story was divided into three rooms, with an inside as well as the commonplace outside chimney. The division of the rooms was unequal in size, providing for the great hall which served as the main parlor-living room of the house. The top floor was steeply roofed with dormer windows. Relatively commodious and well-built, the house was neither pretentious nor designed for the ages.

Most of Harrison's construction was done on the outbuildings. There were only two small ones attached to the house-unit when he acquired the property, and at the time his family moved in most of the physical operations of running a house were performed by servants outside the center establishment. This required kitchen and laundry, meathouse and icehouse, an office and quarters for house servants. Beyond the house-unit were houses for overseers, field-hand quarters, barns and sheds and the small buildings where artisans worked. This made the home something like the big house of a village, though in Virginia the house of the main plantation was then called "home-house."

The great hall had sideboards stocked with the dishes for social life—punch bowls and decanters, tumblers and wineglasses, teapots, cups, saucers and spoons, though not dishes for meals. The dining room was by then fashionably set apart. The parlor had not yet become the social room. It was more of a family room and contained a standing bed and a trundle bed. Except for the great hall and the dining room, beds were everywhere—to accommodate the large families and the guests. When spontaneous drinking parties began to roll, some of the group became overnight guests quite suddenly, and the Harrisons were prepared for all the exigencies of entertaining.

They had a good house, though not deemed worthy of preserving. Around the time when William Byrd II became Benjamin Harrison's neighbor, the big planters were just beginning to envision great houses as the crowning glory of their baronies. The Governor's Mansion in Williamsburg perhaps inspired the idea of the splendor that was to come later. Then, too, as the planters began to buy slaves for the house as well as the fields, the families acquired the servants necessary to maintain a large establishment.

Benjamin Harrison had the servants before the great house. Along with his wharf and shipping enterprises, he worked eighty slaves at Berkeley plus twenty at his south-side holdings.

The broadly based sufficiency of his operations enabled his home plantation to run with such outward blandness that, on the surface, his life could appear to illustrate the idyll of the legend.

Place him in one of those typical paintings of a life in thrall. There, with family and friends, playing cricket of a warm afternoon, the group-figure would be frozen in time, as graceful and as lifeless as a pageant. The frame would contain the broad, shaded lawn, the background of the tidal river and a cloudless sky. To one side of the happy cricket players would stand a sleek, saddled horse, held by a brightly liveried Negro, and on the other side, to balance, little Ben Harrison IV, born in 1700, would be caught in some moment of childish grace with a fat Mammy beaming over him. Squarely in the center a Negro butler, with starched front, would stand smiling with a vast silver tray containing decanters and goblets. In the foreground the master, in silver knee breeches, blue silk-lined coat with silver buttons and linen neckpiece, would stand transfixed forever with a goblet in his hand while the sun, breaking through a willow tree, would fall like a nimbus upon his head.

Like the legendary image of the Old Massa, all these components existed, though scarcely in such idyllic arrangement. By the turn of the century, the saddled horse was a symbol of the gentry and racing was their favorite sport, but the horse would not be on the lawn and all planters did not ride. The Mammy would scarcely bring the child out to a grown folks' gathering, nor would the butler serve drinks during the company's exercise, and certainly Negroes did not always smile. Benjamin Harrison III did play cricket on afternoons when friends dropped in and suggested it, but this was not a daily occurrence and the game was usually played after the work was done.

Most of all, the composite picture would fail to suggest what existed beyond its frame—the wharf and warehouses, tobacco fields and sheds, sawmill and stock barns, and the countless small buildings where wool was carded, hides were tanned, bread was baked and hogsheads made. All that was outside the picture constituted the life of Benjamin Harrison far more than the idle hours passed on the shaded lawn.

The impression of leisure all the time was suggested by the *sense of leisure* attained by Harrison's total mastery of his own domain and, with that, a mastery of time. Life in all its aspects flowed in a constant stream, with no compartments of time for work, play, rest. As the core of his integrated domain, Harrison from the center of his house controlled all the activities in a flexible, timeless discipline.

It was not in his consciousness that work could be isolated into set periods, beginning and ending at arbitrary hours, and that at other set periods he should relax. He was always relaxed and responsibilities for a planter never ended. A slave could get ill at night, a ship arrive during dinner, and a hailstorm spread wreckage on Sunday. Like a general practitioner, he was always on call for duties; and, as a planter, he was always on call for social exchanges (some of which might include making decisions vital to the fate of the colony).

As nothing was done by the clock and only planting by the calendar, social engagements were never made in advance, and a time set apart for non-work, like a weekend, would have been incomprehensible. Friends and kinsmen visited him as the humor struck them, tarried briefly or indefinitely. Harrison was close to his two brothers, to the husbands of his sisters and to James Burwell, his wife's brother. Outside the family his intimates were neighbors—Byrd on one side and Colonel Hill of Shirley on the other; Colonel Randolph, a little farther west at Turkey Island; the Stith brothers, and Mr. Anderson, rector of Westover Church. It would never occur to any of these visitors that a host could excuse himself on the grounds of being "busy." He would have been regarded as a monster of ill-breeding and as some dangerous defective who allowed outside events to control the man.

Though no routine was fixed in Benjamin Harrison's fluid pattern (except for going to nearby Westover Church on Sunday morning), his mornings usually started early with a conference with his overseers and an inspection tour of his fields. Some planters began the day reading Greek or Hebrew, some with making love to their wives (as recorded in diaries); some ate a light breakfast and some ate heartily; none by record began the day with a hooker of rum or brandy, and all began the day very early—between five and six.

The long mornings were the least likely to be interrupted by visitors and if house guests were around, they amused themselves. After Harrison assured himself that his planting and subsidiary operations were moving as they should, he went to his wharf and shipyard, where masts for his boats were cut from nearby virgin timber. The buying of tobacco and selling of imports were closely under his own supervision, as was the shipping on the boats which he either owned or had interest in. He was more absorbed in sea commerce than any of the Harrisons and far more than most planters. His shipping of other planters' tobacco was so extensive that his plantation came in time to be popularly called "Harrison's Landing."

Harrison had put in something close to an eight-hour day when, around two o'clock, the family gathered for the midday dinner. Unless they were entertaining specially, wine was not likely to be served, though before a heavy meal the master might take a hot rum toddy in the winter or a cooled punch in the summer. This main meal was the time for casual visiting with intimates—such as his father from across the river, Byrd, his closest neighbor, one of his sisters or brothers with their spouses. This big meal was usually a family affair.

In the afternoons, unless his visitors tarried, Harrison settled down to his greatest time consumer—letters to London and what amounted to bookkeeping. London was Harrison's mercantile capital and communication with this center of his business interests was sustained entirely by mail. He, like other planters, engaged in constant wrangles with British factors, who regarded Virginia planters as existing entirely to be milched by English businessmen. Factors showed endless ingenuity in finding new charges for handling tobacco and imports, and, to be blunt, some of them cheated all except the most wary. Working with the greedy and guileful factors was the strongest test of a planter's steel.

This paper work, always with him, was not necessarily confined to the afternoons. If Harrison felt poorly, if the weather was too rainy, he could shift this chore to the morning. The heat would never house him: native-born Virginians were acclimated to the peculiarly damp, breathless and suffocating heat that comes to the peninsula; in fact, learning to live with it one third of the year contributed to their attitude of leisure. They never fought the heat any more than they fought time. They went along with both.

Harrison seems not to have formed any addiction to sports, such as hunting, riding for pleasure or horse racing. Since his brother-in-law, James Blair, the Bishop's commissioner, judged at a horse race, it is possible that Harrison attended such neighborhood events; but even his elastic pattern could not include much time for the distractions that characterized a later generation of gentry. He certainly did not need the exercise; his days were largely spent outdoors in any case; and, after a heavy meal (he was a hearty eater), it sufficed to stroll on his river-front lawn in the cool of the evening.

Harrison was a serious reader. He read with flexible continuity, finding time between the handling of affairs and entertaining, when the mood was on him.

The planter's reading was divided into three more or less equal parts—religion, entertainment and what we would call "self-improvement." Religious books were as popular then as now, though the approach to the subject was quite different. There were no guides to the application of religion to the business of living and no appeals to sinners to become "converted." Emotionalism in religion was held to be in bad taste and regarded with suspicion. (Even today in a traditional Virginia Episcopal Church the overpious is apt to be pointed out with the disapproving comment, "Look, he's got religion.") The planter's books were more philosophical about theology, concerning more the spiritual relationship of man to God, and an old favorite was "The Practice of Piety," which had been brought to Berkeley Hundred by its first colonists.

The entertainment sections consisted of plays and poetry. Cowley was a favorite, Shakespeare a standard, and the Elizabethan and Restoration playwrights were popular. No library would be complete without the Greek and Latin "Classics," even in translation, though whether these were truly entertainment or self-improvement would depend on the individual.

This self-improvement covered a wide range and included much reading for pleasure. Needless to say, the books were not hints on how to get ahead in the world, since the planter already had. There were practical books on law and medicine (Byrd owned more than one hundred volumes on medicine) for practical reasons. The planter always doctored his own people, usually himself and his family. While there were practicing physicians in the colony—the first bona fide M.D. came in 1608—most of the gentry regarded them without enthusiasm.

Beverley said that among Virginians "their Distempers are not many, and their Cures so generally known, that there is not Mystery enough to make a Trade of Physick there, as the Learned do in other Countries, to the great oppression of Mankind."

Law prepared the planter for the day when he sat on the courts or acted as attorney for the colony, as Benjamin Harrison. Essentially all self-improvement was a preparation for the fulfillment of the responsibilities of their position. They were great believers in history (Benjamin Harrison was preparing a History of Virginia); they read widely on travel and the natural sciences, and of course a standard was "The Polite Gentleman."

As it applies to Benjamin Harrison personally, not as a prototype, one item is significant. Though he and his wife visited and received back and forth with family and friends, it is noticeable that he never tarried long when he visited; sometimes he wouldn't even stay for a meal. Also, when minor routs began at his house, Harrison went along with the party rather than instigated it. Harrison's brothers and their wives, his sisters and their husbands, were (except for Dr. Blair) in their mid-thirties, and when several of them arrived at Berkeley on the same afternoon that a couple of neighbors dropped in, a game of cricket would be followed by a round of claret or punch. Before long it would be time for supper, and then someone would call for a fiddler, and the dancing would begin. When some of these parties really got rolling, the group might move on to another house; but a night party initiated elsewhere never ended up at Ben Harrison's.

A good companion and gracious host (Byrd mentions being "very merry" at Berkeley, sitting before a fire after the midday meal), there was nothing of the gay blade in disciplined Benjamin Harrison III. Only once does a contemporary note that he was "particularly gallant" to a lady. While he was well liked for his social graces and conservative character, Harrison was essentially respected for his acumen as a planter and a politician. He was highly regarded for the devotion and sagacity he brought to public affairs.

Much has been made of the dedication to public service of these early members of Virginia's ruling class, and much should be made of their basic responsibility to the society. But the skillful and steadfast determination with which the planters sought lucrative offices makes it clear that their primary motivation was self-advancement. Except for a few, planting grew tedious, and except for the widely based operators, like Harrison, tobacco became inadequate support for the scale on which they wished to live. To their credit, most of the early political powers renounced large-scale peculations and almost all of them performed at least adequately in their posts. The performance of duty, however, was certainly not their only reason for seeking the posts.

The scope of Benjamin Harrison III's operations placed him beyond the need of dipping into the public trough. Yet, rather than make public-spirited idealists out of the acquisitive men of his era, it is simpler to say that they were men of their own time and place, capable of executing a bold concept which combined ruling the whole while independently operating their private baronies. For whatever motivations Harrison took various offices, the son, like his father, served with an intelligent conscientiousness that made him by definition the true aristocrat. As such he passed on to *his* son the obligation to public service in exchange for the privilege of being in its ruling class.

6

For his young son, Benjamin Harrison provided a school at Berkeley, to which planters in the neighborhood sent their boys of Ben's age. The school probably consisted of no more than one of the small buildings in the plantation "village," where a transient tutor prepared the young gentlemen for William and Mary. At least it was a start to some system in educational preparation. This was fortunate for the fourth Benjamin Harrison, since responsibility came to him when he was still a child.

Benjamin Harrison III had suffered from gout from at least his thirty-sixth year. In early March of 1710, when he was thirty-seven, he was afflicted with a sharp attack. Within five days he was about again, and when some friends dropped in one afternoon, joined them in a game of cricket. However, he soon grew tired and was forced to stop before the game was over. A week after that day, though obviously not well, he again joined in cricket, that time on the lawn of his neighbor at Westover. Byrd observed that his friend grew very red after playing the game.

Harrison went to bed immediately after this, and was found seriously ill the following morning before daybreak. While observers seemed to connect the gout with his final illness, it seems more likely on the basis of his symptoms that he suffered from hypertension and had a stroke.

The whole clan—blood kin and in-laws—gathered with neighbors and friends, to make of the house at Berkeley Hundred something of an impromptu hospital without doctors. Since each plantation master served as his own physician and apothecary, everyone suggested remedies and presumably most of them were tried. For the first few days, Harrison showed some improvement, though his fever never passed entirely.

On the fourth day, in midmorning, his brother and two of his brothers-in-law, Commissary Blair and James Burwell, felt safe to break their vigil and strolled to Westover, where they had a glass of sack and shot billiards with Byrd. The vigils were hard. Three of the men would sit up all night, to be on call. Probably they took turns dozing, but they remained dressed, and the watches were tiring.

On the thirtieth of March, Benjamin Harrison took a turn for the worse and even his unprofessional attendants could see that he had entered a phase of grave danger. Within a week, his brother-in-law, Blair, despaired of his life.

On Sunday, April ninth, the dying man said he would like a partridge, and good neighbor Byrd sent him a brace. Though he ate one bird, when his family came home from church, he was sinking fast. A friend, coming Sunday night to inquire, found him "past all hope" and the family gathered in deep gloom. At four o'clock the following morning, he died.

Planter families from all over eastern Virginia drove in coaches to Berkeley, and on the morning of the funeral the house was crowded with guests at a wine-drinking and cake-munching party which lacked only the noise to make a "wake" out of the affair. There were no professional undertakers in the American colonies then: the first, a woman, came in 1768. The earliest "undertakers" were upholsterers and/or cabinetmakers. Since families could not make an ostentatious display for their dead with costly boxes, the style was to make the display in the pre-burial party. Funerals and weddings were the only affairs at which guns could legally be fired.

At Berkeley the family and guests mingled until around one o'clock the unembalmed corpse began to move in the coffin. Then the ship, *Harrison*, began firing a gun every half minute, and the company took the short walk to the Westover Church graveyard.

The rector, Mr. Anderson, after reading from the Prayer Book, apparently became carried away with memories of hours shared with his neighbor, and his sermon became a eulogy. Friend Byrd, though bemoaning the loss of a good neighbor, and feeling that "the country has lost a very usefull man," grew irritated at the panegyric and resented Mr. Anderson's references to Harrison as "this great man." By the time the funeral service was read, when the coffin was lowered into the grave, poor Mrs. Harrison had begun to tremble violently.

After the service, Elizabeth Harrison's sisters and sisters-in-law stayed with her, for she was in deep melancholy at the loss of a young husband, who had left her with two children and an unsettled estate. Benjamin Harrison III had not made a will.

When he was dying, he told his wife before witnesses of certain dispositions he wanted made with the property; but these last directions merely covered current debts and created ready cash. In doing this, Harrison's purpose seems to have been to concentrate operations at the center of Berkeley Hundred.

According to his instructions, the widow sold off some five thousand acres in two grants on the south side of the river near the original Harrison homeplace, and twenty slaves there. Mrs. Harrison had some court trouble in disposing of the property, as well as in settling title to the twenty thousand acres and eighty slaves remaining, but she was helped by her husband's brother Nathaniel, then thirty-five years old, and of great and growing wealth.

The sale of the south-side property and slaves evidently established the family in a fluid cash position, and Elizabeth Harrison had in her own right the (then) not inconsiderable sum of two hundred pounds a year. Nothing is known definitely about the operation of the plantation until Benjamin Harrison IV, ten years old at his father's death, gradually assumed control. With a tightly integrated plantation unit such as Harrison erected, presumably Mrs. Harrison could entrust the actual work to managers and overseers, with the guidance, supervision and help on details of the closely allied male contingent of the whole clan. She had two brothers and two brothers-in-law, and her husband's brother-in-law, Commissary Blair, was one of those men of almost terrifying energy who was forever looking for good works to do.

Dr. Blair and his wife, Sarah Harrison, had no children, and for such a dignitary as the Bishop's commissioner—also president of the college and president of the lordly council—home could have been no haven with that "character" of a wife who often hit the bottle. The plain-faced vigorous Scotsman spread his beneficences through all his family where they were most needed, as, for instance, in the home of his young nephew, Benjamin Harrison, IV.

Elizabeth Harrison was born before the fragile belle of later legend had even been imagined. Thirty-three at the time her husband died, she had grown up in one of those houses overrun with family and guests, before the day of the large staffs of trained servants. In fact, she was of the generation of young women who trained the house people as the young planters trained the field hands. Like the planters, Elizabeth Harrison trained herself for management as she trained others to be managed.

When she married and settled at Berkeley Hundred, the bride accepted as her full responsibility the running of her establishment as her husband ran the plantation. Observers noticed when wives were not good managers, and no such observation was made about Elizabeth Harrison. The jump from being responsible for her home to accepting the responsibility for the plantation would not have been great, though she might have been in trouble without the help of her male kin. With their support, Mrs. Harrison was able to turn over the plantation to her son in the condition in which she received it. As far as records show, the widow, in addition to her own legacy, received no financial help beyond the four hundred pounds her son inherited from his grandfather, Benjamin Harrison II, when the patriarch died in 1712.

Outliving his oldest son, the founder of the Harrison fortune in his span of sixty-seven years, had seen the change from the era of the yeomanry into the age of the aristocrat illustrated dramatically in his own family.

He began life with a five-hundred-acre grant and his mother's estate was so modest that she had left to his daughter, Hannah Harrison Ludwell (ancestress of the Lees), only "the horse colt that sucks on the black mare."

This second Benjamin Harrison, not retaining large holdings himself, either in land or slaves, founded for his three sons estates which they increased to more than fifty thousand acres and more than three hundred slaves among them, in addition to making fortunes in cash.

Henry and Nathaniel, remaining on the south side in the vicinity of the Surry County home place, operated mills and shops as did their brother, Benjamin, traded on a large scale in wharf stores, and Nathaniel ran the bakery for the making of hard biscuit which he sold to ships. Nathaniel inherited his father's seat on the Council, became "colonel" of the county militia, and acquired among his large holdings Martin's Brandon—the river plantation patented in 1616 by the one member of the original 1607 Jamestown council who survived in Virginia. (Today, simply as Brandon, the house built by Nathaniel's son on the magnificent site is one of the famous James River mansions.)

The youngest brother, Henry, also a councilor, accumulated a separate fortune which, as he died childless in 1732, he left to his nephew, Benjamin Harrison IV of Berkeley Hundred. Benjamin III, Nathaniel and Henry, and sisters Hannah Harrison Ludwell and Sarah Harrison Blair, had all been born when their father was on his way up—accumulating around the core of his wharf store, he was a Burgess waiting patiently for and working skillfully toward his place on the Council.

When Benjamin Harrison IV, after losing his father, began to prepare himself for the assumption of his responsibilities, two of his grandfathers had been councilors, his uncles on both sides were then councilors (one of them, Commissary Blair, the president), he was under the protection of neighbors such as William Byrd II and Colonel Randolph, and belonged in a group whose power was greater than existed in the colony when his father was born.

Because this Benjamin Harrison was not to live to much more of an age than had his father, the lifetimes of the third and fourth Harrisons together would coincide with the single span of that swing generation—the third generation in Virginia and the first born into a ruling class. Their neighbor, William Byrd II, who lived out his three score and ten, chronologically spanned that generation which two of the shorter-lived Harrisons comprised. In effect, Benjamin Harrison the third and the fourth can be regarded as comprising a single era in terms of the evolutionary cycles of the aristocratic rule in Virginia. For purposes of definition the father might be called "The Shipper," and the fourth "The Grandee."

## CHAPTER VI

# PORTRAIT OF A PLANTER –

## *AS A GRANDEE*

1

*Benjamin Harrison* IV differed sharply in detail from his grandfather, father and uncles. In that third evolutionary generation, which the two Harrisons, III and IV, spanned, the dream of the private principality was completed with the erection of the baronial mansion to serve as the symbol and center for the new dynasties. The fourth Benjamin Harrison was both a product of and a builder of this completing phase.

In line with the concentration on splendor which characterized his time, Harrison spread his attention from the scattered small industrial-commercial enterprises that had contributed to the solidarity of his family's wealth into the area of "conspicuous consumption"— land and slaves.

The ten-year period from his eighteenth through his twenty-seventh year was the time of the greatest slave influx into the Colony— eleven thousand—and slaves accounted for one third of the total population, then approaching one hundred thousand. Virginians, already gravely disturbed by the growing population of black slaves, attacked the "un-Christian traffic of making merchandise of our fellow creatures."

Harrison went with the more typical majority in expansion, and in this he was perhaps influenced by his father-in-law, Robert Carter, called "King." The richest man in Virginia, owner of three hundred thirty thousand acres, one thousand slaves, and large sums of cash, Carter conceived of founding separate baronies for each of his sons, breaking with the English custom of leaving younger sons to shift for themselves. Harrison was twenty-two when he married Anne Carter and, as with his forebears, responded early to environmental conditions.

As Benjamin and Anne Harrison were to have ten children, his large family also would have encouraged Harrison to follow his father-in-law's example. Finally, through bequests Carter made his daughter and the fortune Harrison received from his Uncle Henry, he came into greater wealth—in land, slaves, cash—than even his enterprising father could have accumulated by his own efforts. To an extent, he was freed from the money-making activities that had absorbed his father and uncles.

This is not to imply that, as the second half of the swing generation, Benjamin Harrison IV neglected the inherited estates. Far from it. While the earlier Harrisons had been occupied essentially with building a single integrated plantation center, with outlying tracts and appendages, this Harrison of the period of grandeur, starting life with the successful center entity established, was occupied with accumulations on a vaster scale.

He acquired large holdings on both sides of the James River, and worked eight absentee-operated plantations. Ensconced in his great house (with the name significantly changed from "home-house" to "manor house"), Benjamin Harrison IV entered more into the role of the traditional planter than had his commercial, cash-minded predecessors. Harrison had the cash: his task was to invest it soundly in land and slaves for generations to come.

The significance of this turn is that the Virginia planter now assumed that the money was *there*; it no longer needed to be *earned*. In future generations, this led to an attitude of superiority toward money. The consequences were frequently disastrous to individual planter families, but on the whole, the Virginians' indifference to money-standards contributed to some of the more pleasing aspects of plantation society. In time, myths grew around this attitude, and from those myths, impoverished Virginians take pride in their indifference to money in a belief that they reflect, in less heroic times, their ancestors' noble scorn of sordid cash.

To Benjamin Harrison IV, there was nothing sordid about cash. Freed of the necessity of earning it, he was burdened with the responsibility of administration and increase for his family. As a most successful administrator and increaser, he gave less time than any of the early Harrisons to politics. He inherited none of his grandfather's zest for political maneuver nor any of his forebears' need to win the posts of power. His own family, intertwined through marriage with other families, was already solidly established in the ruling class and his father-in-law was the richest man in Virginia—who built, along with at least five dynastic mansions, his own quite lovely church.

Although he neither needed position nor had an interest in politics, Benjamin Harrison IV accepted his class responsibilities as a member of the House of Burgesses, and indirectly served his group by making of his home-house at Berkeley a symbol of its rule, as fortresslike castles had symbolized the rule of the feudal barons.

During the formative years of Benjamin Harrison's youth—from 1710, when he was ten, to the age of twenty-two—Virginia was again under the influence of a strong governor, the first successful autocrat and man of parts since the resplendent Sir William Berkeley.

Colonel Alexander Spotswood, son of a British colonial army doctor, had been a professional soldier who rose from ensign at the age of seventeen to lieutenant colonel when he was thirty-four. At this point, perhaps influenced by his early years in foreign posts, he shifted his career into England's expanding Colonial civil service, and he must have been well connected to receive Virginia as his first assignment.

Exactly one century after Lord Delaware and his hard-bitten colonizers had begun the regime that established England's first colony, the British, totally disregarding the people who had won the land and evolved a new life, sent a new governor with the policy of operating a colonial system strictly for the benefit of the home country. In that hundred years the British government had not learned (as it was not to learn in the next two hundred) that a people distant from them existed for any other reason whatsoever than for the enrichment of Britishers. Under the influence of the newly powerful merchant class, the Crown even repealed the Acts passed by the Virginia Assembly for the founding of "ports and towns," and bravely begun cities had to be abandoned. On the scene, Governor Nicholson had resented that Virginia inhabitants thought of themselves as Virginians, and Governor Spotswood resented the very idea of colonials regarding themselves as capable of making their own laws.

In this he was not stupid. He simply subscribed wholeheartedly to the prevailing British attitude. Technically all the land in Virginia belonged to the Crown, and the payment of the land taxes in the form of a quitrent legally established the landowners as renters. This legality has confused later-day Virginians into claiming, with proud backward glances at the past, that *their* family's land was "a king's grant." All land was, legally, a king's grant, and this distinction was no proud thing to the landowners, especially the small planters struggling on a borderline self-sufficiency. Spotswood accepted the technicality of the King's ownership in all literalness and expected his "subjects" to share his regard for the supreme authority of the Crown as the unalterable and beneficent nature of things. Any questioning of this was both heinous and vulgar, and the thing that Colonel Spotswood most detested—in addition to self-assertion of "the Common People"—was vulgarity.

Yet, within the limits of the callous and selfishly shortsighted British policy which he represented, Governor Spotswood was an able, vigorous administrator and insofar as the Virginians' interest did not conflict with the Crown's, he sincerely sought to stabilize a weak economy based on tobacco prices. The fluctuations of these prices from low to lower complicated the whole economy because, in the absence of currency, tobacco was used in barter. As with all colonial inequities, this system struck most heavily at the small planters.

Forced to live on credit against the tobacco crop, the poor planters fell behind when prices dropped and, once in debt, they could rarely catch up again. When families became dispossessed of their holdings and joined the "vulgar rabble" of the landless freed indenturers, their existence was made more precarious by the absence of currency. What they needed was cash and not tobacco. Much of the petty stealing among the dispossessed in Virginia was done in desperation. Branded as a criminal and publicly humiliated in the stocks outside the jail, the individual who had stolen in hunger lost his self-respect and drifted into the criminal element forming around the towns and taverns.

Governor Spotswood tried to alleviate the currency problem by legalizing the Dutch and Spanish coins which the people cut up into pieces. But the British government, unmoved by any measure which concerned only the welfare of the colonists, feared that having their own currency might tend to remove the people from total dependence on England.

Spotswood then innovated a scheme for a substitute currency, with the sugar-coating of an appeal to British financial interests. He got the Virginia Assembly to pass an act which required tobacco to be inspected at the government warehouses, where it could be graded for quality and weighed for quantity. Certificates of its value could then serve the small planters as legal tender. Believing strongly (and rightly) that properly graded tobacco would provide at least some stability in the economy, the governor obtained the support of the Church in Virginia. The poorly paid clergy, nearly all of whom were at that time imports from England, welcomed an act which assured them of their salaries in a uniform quality of tobacco and not whatever the vestry palmed off. But the British government, advised by speculators in tobacco, failed to perceive any benefits to itself in a colony's stability and annulled the act which Spotswood regarded as his crowning achievement.

Then the Church turned against him for his interference in the appointment of rectors and Spotswood became the third governor to lock horns with young Benjamin Harrison's uncle, Dr. James Blair. The Bishop's commissary had not lost with time either his grimness in battle nor his guile in the in-fighting, and eventually Colonel Spotswood would yield the field to that "old combustion"—as he called the wiry Scotsman.

Where Colonel Spotswood enjoyed the vigorous support of his home government was in his efforts to break the big planters' illicit tobacco trade which evaded the law requiring them to sell only to England. Planters big enough, either singly or in combination, to consume a ship's entire cargo, or those like the Harrisons who owned or chartered boats, packed tobacco in barrels labeled beef or pork, even hid tobacco under corn, and shipped it to Curaçao and

St. Thomas for the higher prices and lower export taxes. Having not the slightest intention of existing solely for the benefit of British merchants and their monarch, the big planters proved hard to get at, and they continued an elastic opposition to the governor —most of them going along when it suited their purpose and fighting openly when it did not.

Large as these failures loomed in the future of Virginia's relations with England, whittling away as they did at the life line to the mother country, they were Spotswood's only defeats in a constructive administration, and his regime (1710-1722) was characterized and remembered far more for the rich coloring he brought to the raw capital at Williamsburg.

The personality of the strong-willed and regal-minded autocrat offered many positive aspects to the fledgling bourbons. Virginians had by then been fighting somebody for so long that struggle was accepted as the natural order, like the heat, and (with a few exceptions) the aristocrats' conflict of interest with the governor in nowise affected their regard for him personally nor their appreciation of his flair for splendor. Spotswood liked to do well for himself and this the Virginians approved of—so long as they were not plundered as they had been by Sir William Berkeley. The former army colonel was totally unlike the aristocratic old courtier.

Berkeley had come to Virginia for a personal domain, like the planters with whom he formed his coterie, and became in effect a Virginian—the first ruler of the ruling class which formed under his aegis. Spotswood came as a colonial-service careerist, and his interest in establishing the colony's total welfare was that of a professional with a job to be done well—though he, too, became a Virginia convert, and settled in the colony after his period as governor.

Spotswood was more in the mold of that other professional soldier, High Marshall Dale, who had come a century before to secure the colony's existence. Since Dale's days of unsung personal glory, other groups had formed a whole colonial system along the Atlantic, the nucleus of a separate nation. The French had formed a colony to the north and explored the continent behind them, along the Mississippi; a still powerful Spain controlled vast territories from Florida to the south; and, as a physical part of America, the little Virginia colony existed amid what amounted to international alignments. While the Virginians were largely unaware of this, Spotswood, who had lived and soldiered on three continents, was not. His job was complicated and large, and his financial rewards were not great.

The stupid British system forced the acting governor to divide a two-thousand-pound annual salary with a "permanent" governor, some political favorite who was not required to visit the colony or even to read a letter from it in order to receive a stipend drawn from taxes on planters' tobacco. However, perquisites increased Spotswood's salary by another six hundred pounds or so, his mansion was provided him, and he did well enough for a careerist with none of Berkeley's greed. It was ultimately through this mansion and all it implied that Colonel Spotswood most affected Virginia.

Whereas Berkeley had built Green Spring as a private estate, Spotswood worked on the governor's house in the new capital of Williamsburg as a symbol of Empire. He had good taste, unlimited money (though the House of Burgesses complained at the expense), and it was his expansions and elaborations that caused the governor's house to be popularly called "The Palace." It was the first great house in Virginia and, both in impetus and architecturally, its influence was profound.

Historically Spotswood is best known for a drinking hegira which romance has blown up into the legendary episode of "The Knights of the Golden Horseshoe." It happened in August of 1716, the month when the summer begins to grow wearisome in Virginia. The former soldier, then forty, had been six years away from campaigns. With a number of aristocratic boon companions, rangers and Indian guides, servants and a cavalry regiment of pack horses, the governor set out on a leisurely riding trip of "exploration."

The party of hard-riding gentlemen pushed neither their horses nor themselves. They stopped early each day, so that a camp could be comfortably made in the woods beside some stream. While plenty of daylight remained, the cooks prepared an elaborate dinner and the gentlemen had at the rum and brandy. Alexander Spotswood liked to do well not only for himself, but also for his friends.

In just under three weeks, loosely following the course of the Rapidan River, the hearties rode the 150 miles to the Blue Ridge Mountains. There they looked down on the incredible wonder of the

Shenandoah Valley, where herds of buffalo grazed in the great meadows spread between the forests.

They did nothing directly toward settling the Valley, and their tales of its beauty did not immediately encourage Tidewater Virginians to forsake their own damp heat—though the trip did influence the settlement of the pleasant, rolling Piedmont of middle Virginia, between Tidewater and the Blue Ridge. It was some fifteen years after Spotswood claimed the Shenandoah Valley for the King that Germans and Scotch-Irish began coming down from the north in what became that long surge southward and southwest through the Cumberland Gap into Kentucky. The Daniel Boones and Sam Houstons went westward in that surge into and from the Valley, and in time fugitives from Tidewater brought their own culture into the Valley.

All that was in the future when Spotswood and his friends first rode down the western slope of the Blue Ridge, but something of a lost gallantry, of an old pageantry, colored the Valley's history from this first recorded exploration by Englishmen.

Back in Williamsburg, in the lovely, mellow fall, back at his desk and faced with the problems of empire, Spotswood remembered those carefree days with his drinking companions in an unexplored wilderness, and sentimentally decided to commemorate the adventure. He had shod their horses for the trip, and to each member of the party he sent a small golden horseshoe set with diamonds (whether paid for out of his own pocket or the public purse is not known.) Time and retelling did the rest to establish into legend the trip of the mounted band to the Blue Ridge, and all Shenandoah Valley history begins with Spotswood's "Knights of the Golden Horseshoe."

2

Just about the time of this (then) more or less private party, in the middle of Spotswood's vigorous regime, Benjamin Harrison IV entered William and Mary, to become the family's first college man. "The College" then consisted of the so-called Wren Building, with numerous small outbuildings for servants, cooking and storage, and the like. Since Sir Christopher Wren was then surveyor (or architect) for the British government and the college was a government building, undoubtedly the great architect with his associates worked on the design of the handsome red brick main building. Young Benjamin Harrison, judging by his own later building, must have been impressed by its classic beauty, as he was by all the fine architecture in Williamsburg.

One mile down the broad Duke of Gloucester Street, which Spotswood had straightened from the original horsepath, the student looked at the new Capitol—"as noble, beautiful, and commodious a pile as any of its kind,"—so a professor newly arrived from England described it.

The founders of William and Mary very deliberately placed the college at the seat of government and the center of commerce so that the students, instead of being isolated from the business of life, should grow up in the midst of it. This decision obviously stemmed from the planters' own training for life in which they grew up with deepening responsibilities on the plantation. It was also the self-aware purpose of the ruling class to train their successors in government and politics right at the scene.

To the students, the Duke of Gloucester Street was like an extension of their large, open college grounds. Midway down the broad street, The Palace Green, cutting off to one side, led to Spotswood's "Palace," then reaching its full splendor. The three-story red brick building, topped with cupola, was flanked by beautifully balanced smaller buildings which formed an impressive forecourt, entered through handsome iron gates. At the back, a private canal flowed through formal gardens, lawns and orchards. The young Harrison student absorbed the details of this magnificent building, and all others in the growing town.

Bruton Church was, according to the same new professor who instructed Harrison in philosophy and mathematics, "a large, strong piece of brickwork in the form of a cross, nicely regular and convenient, and adorned as the best churches in London." The new magazine for public arms on the Market Square was an interesting octagonal-shaped structure and a cosmopolitan atmosphere was given by the new theater which faced the Palace Green. William Levingston, its proprietor, also taught dancing to Harrison and other students at the college. On the Duke of Gloucester Street, on the two main parallel streets and the side streets, houses, shops and taverns were going up steadily.

Technically a tavern was a public place where drinks were served (like the later-day saloon), ordinaries were where food was served, and inns had lodging accommodations. In Virginia the names were used interchangeably, as the functions frequently overlapped. The Raleigh Tavern, built later, was praised for its table as much as its rack punch, rum spiked with the fiery arrack. Essentially, however, the taverns were public clubs where men gathered to read papers, study the ads for "runaways," chat over a mug of ale and a rented pipe. Shops were not stores as we know them, but the establishments of artisans and artificers, such as tailors and bootmakers, silversmiths and wigmakers, and so on. A store was still practically a warehouse, literally a storage place for goods that were *to be* sold.

Young Harrison's grandfather's house was then occupied by one of his uncles, and the Ludwells, his aunt and uncle-in-law and a girl cousin, lived in a fine city home there. The boy probably dined with members of his family during the Court Season, and visited the Capitol with his uncles. There he may have stood silently on the outskirts of the groups that gathered in the Capitol Yard to talk politics and horse racing and tobacco, to barter land and slaves, and gossip about the frailties of their friends—great names and abstract powers at our distance in time, but old shoes to the youth who heard of one being spurned by a tavern wench and of another whose beds stank.

Harrison and his friends went too much about the town for their sharply observing professor, the Reverend Mr. Hugh Jones, who complained of "the liberty allowed the scholars . . . and the opportunity they have of rambling abroad." This twenty-five-year old Oxford clergyman was a fortunate find for William and Mary in its humble beginnings. Intelligent, learned and ambitious, active and creative, he held, on a base of firm personal convictions, a broadly realistic sense of values about the way of the world. A devout Anglican, his advice to young clergy (written when he was little more than thirty) could serve as a model in any age.

"They . . . should be persons that have read and seen something more of the world than what is requisite for an English parish . . . as can converse and know more than bare philosophy and speculative ethics . . . have studied men and business as well as books . . . be good scholars without becoming cynics, and . . . good Christians without becoming stoics . . . give up a small matter rather than create disturbance and mischief . . . yet . . . not condescend too far nor part with a material right. . . ." If these precepts were followed, the clergy in Virginia would "meet with the love, reputation, respect, and encouragement that such good men may deserve and expect. . . ."

Hugh Jones most definitely expected these intangible emoluments and won them by his abilities and by his gravitation to, as he said, "persons of the greatest figure." As a result of his rapprochement with Governor Spotswood, Jones was, in less than two years, appointed chaplain of the House of Burgesses. However, though he wanted to get on and was skillful at doing so, the young professor, who came to Virginia for opportunity and stayed because he loved it, brought a concentration of his gifts and wide interests to the little college of one hundred students and eight professors.

Jones assumed his duties at the time Benjamin Harrison entered as a student. There could have been little love lost between the student and the master, since the college president was Harrison's uncle by marriage, and Jones (through his alliance with Spotswood) became a bitter enemy of Dr. James Blair. Yet, no personal feelings would have affected Jones in his duties nor young Harrison in his student life.

Benjamin Harrison came with his personal servant (or servants), and with the sense of responsibility for his wealth and position well advanced. His early maturation—as well as the presence of his powerful kinspeople in Williamsburg—placed friendship with any professor, however brilliant and well-connected, outside the realm of his serious calculations. He came to Williamsburg and to college to prepare himself for the final assumption of his responsibilities, and he was typical of the Virginia planter of that period in that intellectual abstractions failed to interest him.

This lack of intellectualism has been used against the planter class as an indication of mental sloth, cultural poverty and indifference to learning. This is a superficial and ill-natured judgment. Many planters were learned men (especially young Harrison's neighbor Byrd) and most substantial planters placed great stress on education. But the planter—living comfortably with his religion, finding his climate delightful and his life a joy—lacked the tormented conscience of the New Englander who, during the snowbound months in small low-ceilinged rooms, turned to introspective brooding, which, being of a frugal people, he turned into written prose and thus gained for his region a reputation for culture.

The planters were outwardly interested people. They read and they discussed books and plays and poetry, and some even reflected, but they possessed no urge to communicate by the written word. The nature of their social life produced in them a gift for the spoken word, and in this unfortunately underrated accomplishment they excelled. It made of them skillful orators and debaters, and later (also unfortunately) forceful demagogues. They had, nearly all of them, the outward-going character that is based on the exchange between personalities, the living warmth of reaching and being reached by other people.

The generations succeeding Harrison were (as history knows) capable of great abstract concepts, but always, even in Jefferson's case, they had a practical end for society. And practicality, in young Benjamin Harrison's terms, did not include intellectual abstractions.

Young Harrison entered the college when learned Dr. Blair and his associates, under control of the Crown, were struggling to adapt to their needs the curriculum of post-medieval universities. Entering students were supposed to have learned Greek and Latin fundamentals, called "grammar," and college studies concerned the nature of the physical world, mathematics, and that all-embracing subject they called "philosophy." At William and Mary this included logic, ethics and metaphysics. Though the energetic and dedicated Blair had some good men on his staff, the problems of founding a college where none had existed before were complicated by the Crown's control (which passed after Harrison's time there), by the division into four schools, and by the diversity of pre-college education.

No systematized preparatory-school system existed in Virginia because the planters instructed their own children according to their individual tastes, and no interest was felt in mass education. For the poor who really wanted an education, there was a scattering of "endowed" (charity) schools, designed to achieve basic literacy—reading and writing. Parents with a little money could send their children to a few "public schools," which anybody who paid could attend. The more well-to-do had a choice of several "private schools," more restricted and with higher tuition. The very rich like Benjamin Harrison were taught by tutors, either privately or with a few neighbors. Some boys were sent to school in England, and some stayed there for college or law, though this number was not as large as usually supposed. During the colonial period, forty-eight went to Oxford and Cambridge, thirty-eight to Edinburgh (where they had a Virginia Club), and something less than a hundred to the various Inns and Temples where law was learned.

Because of the irregularity of and disparity in preparation for college, from the very first, William and Mary placed the emphasis on the "Grammar School," or lower school, organized like an English public school where students came as young as ten. Indicative of the planters' awareness of the need to produce superior men, was the specific injunction to the master of the lower school "to let no blockhead or lazy fellow in his studies be elected," or advanced.

Energy and attention were diverted to the Indian School, as part of the Virginians' persistence in that vain and unrealistic purpose of converting savages into useful Anglicans. Even good churchman Jones said the attempt was hopeless, and Jefferson later said the purpose could be better served "by maintaining a perpetual mission among the Indians."

After observing the British for a century the denizens of the woods simply preferred their own savage ways and lived almost entirely to themselves. Except for some of those rough drivers of the traders' mule trains who lived in unblessed cohabitation with Indian women, no record of intermarriage in Virginia existed after John Rolfe's wedding with the "princess."

In their primitive state, though numerically too weak to make war in Tidewater Virginia, the Indian bowmen still liked to paint their faces hideously enough to scare any enemy, and while they proved unresponsive to the formalized Episcopal liturgy, they had priests who led them violently in their less inhibited rites. Their heaven consisted literally of "a happy hunting ground," though not so called by them. Along with their own matchcoats of fur and their more dressy ones of feathers, they had taken to making something of a matchcoat out of discarded British greatcoats, which they regarded as very fine indeed.

There was nothing in common between them and the white students at William and Mary and efforts at conversion failed to produce a single Indian priest. Later a Brafferton Building was built, but in

Harrison's day there was only a house. There the master for Indians lived with the few young red men during their bewildered interlude in civilization, before they skulked happily back to the brush. Doubtless, the master of Berkeley made no acquaintances in this school.

Harrison, prepared in Greek and Latin at his father's tutor school, entered directly into the college—in turn divided into two parts. The Philosophy School would seem to be equivalent of our undergraduate college, and the Divinity School was something of a cross between a general graduate school and seminary. There is no real approximation between our clearly defined curricula ,and the one-building college Benjamin Harrison attended. In the Philosophy School he studied, under Hugh Jones and one other professor, rhetoric, logic and ethics, physics, metaphysics and mathematics. He followed these studies in very loose "courses," compared to today's rigid curricula, with no such time divisions as semesters and no fixed years for graduation. In fact, it is not known how long he attended. Harrison probably resided in the Wren Building two or three years—certainly more than one, though hardly four.

It is unlikely that he learned much to help him either in the mastery of life or in the appreciation of life's distilled aspects in art. It is more likely that his uncle, the learned president, the professors and trustees, learned more about curricula from him and his companions. At least, the college steadily improved after his time, while he went on as if the experience never happened.

Matured before his arrival, Harrison took the interlude much as did the Indians—with one exception. Under the influence of the Williamsburg architecture, he went home to build one of the first of the home-houses that became the great houses of Virginia.

3

There is no arbitrary date to indicate when Benjamin Harrison took over the full control of Berkeley from his mother. He had worked gradually into the administration and, as he would legally come into the estate at twenty-one, he probably began to assume control after the hiatus of Williamsburg. Certainly there was no abrupt change in his life nor in the management of plantation affairs when he reached his majority. That he was regarded by then as a young man of substance ("discreet") is indicated by his acceptance as a suitor for "King" Carter's daughter.

Robert Carter was originally called "King" in derision of the vast arrogance with which he wore his power. There is no denying the size of his pride of spirit and vanity of the flesh; his was a really kinglike imperiousness. But this Carter (who was to be an ancestor of Robert E. Lee) was large in all ways. He was built on a heroic scale, and in an acquisitive society he was the most acquisitive. He was also as large of mind as he was of will and—while like many rich men, he regarded himself as the final authority on all subjects—his ideas were original, sound, and wide-ranging. He compiled a huge library, was an early and passionate advocate of education, and William and Mary made long strides when Carter was rector (a position similar to chairman of the Board of Visitors). He would have been a personality of great force even without his almost illimitable power; with it, he must have been somewhat awesome.

His father had come to Virginia during the cavalier influx of the 1660s and settled in the Northern Neck, that pleasant peninsular bounded by the Rappahannock and Potomac Rivers and abutting on Chesapeake Bay. It was the demesne of the Lees and the Washingtons, fertile country for plantations and veined with waterways. The first Carter prospered as a planter there, rose steadily in colony politics, and provided his son with the foundation on which to erect his own domain.

Robert Carter (who was born in Virginia, 1663, and educated in England) was in a position to receive the fat assignment of acting as agent for the proprietors of the Northern Neck territory. This proprietorship was the solution to all the confusion wrought by Charles the Second, when he blandly gave to seven favorites the land already partly occupied. Because some of the landowners were such willful powers as Richard Lee II, the distant claimants could get no cash rewards from the King's favor. One by one they sold out their rights, until Lord Fairfax became the sole frustrated proprietor. Then Richard Lee broke the impasse by agreeing to pay quitrents to Fairfax, an act which acknowledged the proprietor as the liege of the land. Lee had his own subtle reasons for doing this.

The unoccupied land of Fairfax could then be leased directly from the proprietor, thus destroying the century-old system of granting land by headrights—one hundred acres for each person settling or each slave or indenture bought. With the precedent broken in the Northern Neck, the government soon abandoned the old system and land went on public sale at the Williamsburg land office. The original reason for the head-right system was, in the colonizing period, to attract settlers and not speculators; the reason for Lee's maneuver was to throw open the land to the rich, who could acquire by purchase, and tighten the control of the ruling class.

For Robert Carter the practical result of Lee's quiet *coup* was that he, as agent for the Fairfaxes, drew in commissions large sums of cash in a currency-poor colony, and with the cash and access to purchase, he acquired land and slaves on a scale unimagined before his day, at the same time amassing ten thousand pounds in cash. All this wealth and the overbearing self-awareness of power enabled Robert Carter to achieve a position of pre-eminence for his family. Typical of his contemporaries, he was founding a ruling-class dynasty. Though this, too, might have been an expression of pride, it also expressed a conviction and contributed to the molding of the Virginia society as an aristocratic republic.

This overwhelming figure—with four sons to groom for places in the master class—had to be favorably impressed with Benjamin Harrison to accept him as a son-in-law. This is no implication that young Harrison came courting hat in hand. No one was more powerfully placed through family connections than he, and his first cousin was married to Richard Lee's son. She was the daughter of Hannah Harrison Ludwell who had lived in Williamsburg when Harrison was in college, and her husband, Thomas Lee, was at least one baron to whom Carter was just another man—big, yes, but no bigger than a Lee. The important point is that Benjamin Harrison was not overly impressed by the "King," but that Mr. Carter was favorably impressed by him.

4

The size of Robert Carter's bequest to his daughter, Anne, is not known. It came ten years before Harrison's legacy from his own Uncle Henry, and the amount must have been considerable, for soon after his marriage the twenty-two-year-old husband began planning the baronial mansion. Though Benjamin Harrison enjoyed a large income from Berkeley and shipbuilding, even before his expansion into other plantations, those manorial houses were erected at tremendous cost.

Mann Page, who married Anne Harrison's sister, Judith Carter, built Rosewell in Gloucester County, the largest and greatest house in all Virginia, and his family was impoverished for two generations by the expense and ultimately was forced to sell. (Since then the interior has been gutted by fire, but even today the bare walls suggest the grandeur that was Rosewell.) Young Harrison's neighbor, Byrd, with his cozy inheritance, ran into debt for several reasons, one of which was the cost of building the classically lined Westover.

Those houses could not be paid for in ungraded tobacco. Much of the material was bought in and shipped from England. Most of the skilled artisans (there were never enough) could demand cash, and the whole building was an isolated operation. Until recently, the legend persisted that each planter was his own architect. With all the protean accomplishments of a successful planter, there is no reason (beyond myth) to assume that several dozen busy country gentlemen should all in one generation develop spontaneously a talent for architecture. That so much was made of Jefferson's architectural gifts in a succeeding generation would indicate the rarity of this talent.

The probability is that each planter, stimulated by Spotswood's Williamsburg and influenced by the prevailing books on the subject, did develop his own general concept of a house and employ a journey-man architect (called a "master workman") to work out the details. It is known that the planters, like young Harrison, owned contempo-rary books on home-building (with drawn models) and that architects without fame, sometime even called "joyners," worked in the colony. As the planters were highly practical, as well as very busy men, it would follow that Benjamin and Anne Harrison pored over books and visited Williamsburg in their four-horse carriage until they con-ceived their idea of a house, and then employed one of the talented young men who had graduated from the artisan class. One of the best of the early architects was known to have come to Virginia as an in-dentured servant of high skill.

There was certainly no master architect in Virginia. Of all the great houses that were erected over a period of ten or twenty years, no two looked alike. Each expressed the individuality of the planter and

none had white columns. But, whatever unrecorded journeyman architect made a physical reality of the young Harrisons' dreams, he
was a sound student in his field and advanced in ideas. It is sad that
he and his fellows are lost to posterity as a result of the aristocratic
concept that demeaned all work, even the most creative, except planting. These unknowns, who probably hobnobbed at the taverns with
the casuals and the dispossessed, were really small-time Michelangelos
creating for colonial de' Medicis.

Whatever their status and whatever the extent of the planters'
control, all the houses were indigenous to the climate and adapted to
the social life. In viewing from today what seems to be luxurious
wastefulness expressed in high ceilings and wide passages, it must be
remembered that in their time the houses were eminently functional
—and, with servants, still are. The passages gave cross ventilation in
the summer and the high ceilings made the heat more bearable. While
all this space made winter heating more of a problem, the winters
were short and servants attended the fires built of plantation timber.

All the houses were designed for families with innumerable house
servants, which all great families had by 1725. Every purely functional activity in the supply and operation of the house was placed
outside. These outbuildings consisted of kitchen, meathouse, icehouse,
laundry, tutors' house (which served also as playroom), and servants'
quarters, sometimes the planter's office. At Berkeley, as at most of the
great houses, these outbuildings formed a forecourt (sometimes enclosed by a wall) which comprised the house-unit. The stables and
coach house, with quarters for hostlers and coachmen, were always
placed well beyond the house-unit, so that the family could escape
the odors and the summer flies.

Within the general court were the "necessaries," handsomely
built brick affairs with windows, a fireplace and as many as four seats.
They were usually approached by an arbor, which afforded some
secrecy for the trip—though in that time there was less finickiness
about bodily functions (fewer jokes, too). To avoid a trip to the necessary, very elegant chamber pots were used, and these came under
the province of servants. As the servants also cared for the fires, each
room was equipped with a fireplace, and logs of such size were used
in the main rooms that two men would stagger in with a single one.

Those features were common to all the great houses. As the first of the Hanoverians had then sat his gross person upon the throne, that period of academic grace and grandeur became known as "Georgian," though nothing could have been more remote from the character of German George. Of all the Georgian houses built in that period in Virginia, that at Berkeley Hundred is one about which no guesswork is needed to establish the exact date of building. In a wall-panel stone, the initials of "B" and "A," for Benjamin and Anne, are inscribed above the date, 1726.

When the Harrisons' neighbors built on either side, at Shirley and Westover, the new houses were erected near the site of the old, close to the river. From the living room at Shirley, you look right into the water. At Westover, the classically beautiful house is back about fifty yards on a broad lawn, so that the river, shaded lawn and house form an open court of slumbrous tranquillity. Both lawns, though Westover's suggests the lordliness of life there, are essentially intimate, and flanked with walled formal gardens.

At Berkeley, with a three-mile river front, the Harrisons abandoned the old site closer to the river and built on a slight elevation nearly a quarter of a mile back, which gave to their foreground (it was not all lawn) a vast and impressive sweep. During the Civil War all of McClellan's Army—one hundred thousand men with animals, guns and wagons—camped there between the house and the river.

At Berkeley, as at all the James River mansions, there were actually two entrances.

The arriving visitor would travel from the public road one and a half miles along the private driveway—passing the tobacco fields and sheds, the villages of quarters and shops—and, entering the gateway in the brick wall that enclosed the house-unit, would approach *a* front door, white-painted in panels under a glass transom. For the family, and neighbors strolling over from adjacent lawns, *the* front door would open on the river side where all outdoor life was enjoyed.

Similar doors opened at both ends of a wide hall which bisected most houses of the period, and by the time the Berkeley house was built that hall had come to be more of a passage, as we know it, though the space was furnished and served as a reception place for non-intimates.

In place of the former all-purpose "great hall," there were two huge square rooms on one side of the center hall, which the Harrisons called "The Great Room—North" and "The Great Room—South." These rooms were connected by doors on either side of a massive center fireplace. The connecting doors, which were later removed and replaced by arches, could be opened to throw the two rooms into one grand salon. The rooms were magnificently paneled in wood, with elaborate decorative woodwork.

On the other side of the hall, the room facing the river was a formal dining room, with two mahogany tea tables (probably serving tables) in addition to the mahogany dinner table. The front room on that side, nearest the front entrance door, seems to have served as combination of intimate family room, study and the master's spare bedroom. It contained a single bed, with no trundles or cribs, a desk and two tables, an easy chair and six mahogany chairs, and the walls were decorated with a dozen prints. Probably Benjamin Harrison conducted there the planter's interminable correspondence, retired there to escape the noise of his ten children, and perhaps took naps there after his prodigious meals.

There is also the possibility that Benjamin Harrison, like other planters, wanted a bedroom near the front door to protect his family against physical danger. Though the Tidewater Indians were to war no more, the planters did not know this and the menace was kept alive in their minds by the fearsome raids continuing on the frontiers. At Berkeley, as at most river houses built in that period, there was a brick, underground escape passage. For all the splendor of the house-unit, the plantation was still an isolated clearing in the forest, and the great trees shading the lawn were primeval timber.

With the exception of the combination study-family room, all bedrooms were on the upper floors. Besides the master bedroom and the nursery (so-called by the Harrisons), the other bedrooms accommodated the older children according to sex, with provisions for shifting around when guests overflowed the house. As an influx of guests was a somewhat permanent condition, the children existed in a state of transience, and no child at Berkeley (and few anywhere) enjoyed the luxury of his own room. Yet, expecting no such thing, the children grew up in an atmosphere that prepared them to accept hospitality as part of the excitement of life.

The main house and all the outbuildings were of brick, probably made on the plantation or in a Virginia kiln. There has been considerable controversial speculation over whether or not the bricks in the great houses were imported. Supporters of the importing theory base their argument on the uneven size and soft substance of the handmade plantation brick. Homemade bricks for barns and out-buildings were of an inferior quality, but planters were not building for the ages in the outbuildings nor using the fine masonry that required even bricks. As there was fine clay in Tidewater, it seems likely that brick masons were imported who, building the bricks with more care, baked them long enough to obtain the hard consistency required for the great houses that were to stand permanently.

At Berkeley, the walls, three feet thick, were laid in English bond below the water table and Flemish bond above. A full brick basement served as wine cellar, storage space and for other uses. Above the two upper stories was a dormer-windowed, lower-ceilinged top story; technically, it was a three-story house. The unknown journeyman architect enclosed the top story with the first heroic pediment roof in Virginia, which he presumably copied from a bookplate of James Gibbs's church at Derby, England. The window sashes were also unusual, being four lights (panes) wide with twelve lights to each of the two sashes.

The house at Berkeley was, in brief, an advanced representation of the greatest architectural flowering ever in an American colony. When Anne and Benjamin moved into their new house around 1726, the design of the baronial life of the Virginia planter was completed. They were, as far as they knew, as integrated in time as the country life of the British aristocracy on which they modeled themselves. The young couple, very happy personally, quite unknowingly were setting the stage for what, from a distance, would be called "the golden age."

5

While the Harrisons were settling in their somewhat overwhelming new house, their next-door neighbor, William Byrd II, returned from a ten-year hegira in England, bringing with him a new wife. The elegant master of Westover had been one of the planters who got on the wrong side of Governor Spotswood, and stayed there. In 1716, things were so bad that Byrd went to London to try and enlist well-placed friends in his behalf. As his volatile wife died soon after arrival, he stayed on to try to find a rich lady. His financial affairs were in a poor way.

Byrd, as an administrator of his inherited estate, was adequate and no more. At Westover, the Byrds had never operated such scattered enterprises as supported the planting of the Harrisons at Berkeley and Brandon. William Byrd I had underwritten his land-buying and planting with a most successful Indian-trading business, but his English-born wife had wished to protect her son from the rude, isolated life at The Falls. Though the younger Byrd maintained the trading post with managers, he was unfamiliar with the details of those mule-team caravans with their fierce, wildly uncouth and hard-swearing riders of the wilderness trails. Thus, he lacked the practical experience in trading which the Harrison boys gained at the old wharf store.

Byrd's income came largely from planting and land speculation, and it was primarily over the latter that he fell afoul of Alexander Spotswood. From Byrd's father's time, the members of the Council had played loosely with the land laws for their own enrichment. Philip Ludwell was accused of adding a cipher to a two-thousand-acre land grant, and not one fellow councilor blinked when he received twenty thousand acres; and it was common practice to evade the requirement of planting land by having a ten-shilling house built in a half-acre clearing and turning a few hogs loose in the woods. Spotswood determined to end these abuses, and he criticized the methods by which Byrd, as receiver general, collected quitrents from the land-owners. The governor in no sense impugned Byrd's honesty; he simply demanded a new and efficient system of collecting the revenues due the King. Byrd, feeling that his honor was involved, took the criticism personally and began a fight with Spotswood which he could not win. To avoid a showdown, he sold his office for five hundred pounds and went to London where, as an individual, he could continue his battle with the governor.

Deprived of the revenues from his receiver generalship and with his plantations operating without him, Byrd's affairs were further complicated by a deal in which pride ruled his judgment. Byrd's pride had been hurt by the settlement of the estate of his father-in-law, that dueling gallant, Colonel Daniel Parke. While his first wife had been, as he said, "fobbed off with One Thousand pounds," her sister (married to John Custis, Martha Washington's father-in-law) received all of

The main house at Berkeley Hundred as it appears today and (below) a view of the interior of the Great Room — South. Berkeley is one of the few Georgian houses of its period which can be exactly dated: carved in a wall panel are the initials "B" and "A" for Benjamin Harrison IV and Anne Carter Harrison and the date, 1726.

A Virginia tobacco wharf very like that at Harrison's Landing; tobacco was the original source of the family's great wealth. Below, an engraving from De Bry's "The Great Voyages," depicting the Jamestown Massacre of 1622, in which nearly a third of the colonists perished.

The elegant William Byrd II, builder (about 1730) of Westover, the plantation house which, together with the Carters' Shirley, flanked Berkeley on the James River. Sir William Berkeley (*right*), Royal Governor of Virginia and suppressor of Bacon's Rebellion, about whom Charles II is reported to have said: "That old fool has killed more people in that naked land than I ever did over the execution of my father."

Two drawings from *Harper's Weekly* showing General McClellan arriving on the bank of the James River and *(below)* Union transports landing reinforcements and stores at Harrison's Landing. Berkeley

— the plantation house can be discerned in the lower drawing — was used as a base by McClellan and Lincoln himself came here to interview the General on the prosecution of the war.

Colonial Williamsburg

It was in the superb Wren Building, original structure of William and Mary College, that Harrison men, beginning with Benjamin Harrison IV, heard lectures on mathematics, logic, ethics, and metaphysics. Historic St. John's Episcopal Church, Richmond (below) was the scene of much impassioned Colonial oratory, some of it distasteful to the aristocratic owners of Berkeley.

Colonial Studio, Richmond

A view of Virginia's beautiful capitol in Richmond, designed by Thomas Jefferson. Richmond replaced Williamsburg as capital in 1780 and it was to this city that Benjamin Harrison V came in 1781 to serve three terms as the state's first post-Revolutionary Governor.

William Henry Harrison, Berkeley born, adopted son of the frontier whose victory over Tecumseh at Tippecanoe was the propaganda weapon that helped win for him the Presidency of the United States in 1840. Thousands of campaign handkerchiefs like the one below were distributed, "revealing the likeness of the stalwart Indian conqueror in a field of blue, and on a white border were touching pictures of Harrison's imaginary log-cabin birthplace and the Signer's son in shirt sleeves at a plough behind a team of horses that looked like elongated Percherons."

Parke's lands in Virginia and England; and, more insulting, Parke's valuable properties in the West Indies were left to an illegitimate daughter. However, Mrs. Custis was also given the obligation of paying off Parke's debts and her husband, shrewder than Byrd, at Byrd's request transferred the Virginia and English properties to him in exchange for Byrd's assumption of the debts.

The whole transaction was a gentleman's agreement (nothing was put in writing) and Byrd at first was pleased as his factor, the redoubtable Micajah Perry, assured him that the properties amounted to more than the debts. Perry miscalculated. Parke's debts heavily outweighed the amounts Byrd could get from the properties, and he was harried by the unprofitable details of settling the estate.

With the exception of one year, 1720-21, Byrd spent ten years in London, enjoying fashionable society and the fleshpots, while seeking an heiress and/or a lucrative colonial post. A dilettante in the world of fashion, Byrd had no interest in returning to Virginia. Then in 1726 he finally landed a well-endowed lady who endeared herself to him by her knowledge of Greek. The marriage was something in the nature of an elopement because the Colonial dandy had been thwarted once before by a disapproving parent, and his lady's mother, whom he called "Medusa," wanted none of him in her family.

After his new wife had given him a daughter, and Commissary Blair had disposed of his enemy, Spotswood, in Virginia, the fifty-two-year-old beau accepted the inevitable and returned to his home place. In "this silent country," as he called it, Byrd lived out his declining years as family man and country gentleman, relieving the tedium with extraordinarily good writing. His works are largely unappreciated because of the limited appeals of the subject matter and perhaps because he wrote outside any regional line of literary men.

Along with his social and cultural gifts, William Byrd also enjoyed the boon of good spirits, and wasted no time in repining. Instead, observing the new glory of the Berkeley home-house, and the house-building all around him, the lively-natured Byrd devoted his hours to building his own lovely mansion, which he stocked with the finest library in the Colonies—four thousand volumes in English, Latin, Greek, Hebrew and French.

Byrd was not widely acquainted in Virginia. He knew few people outside the ruling class, with not all of whom he was popular, and his social life with his new wife (as well as his home life) was quieter than in his younger days with the high-spirited daughter of Colonel Parke. He resumed his old friendships, especially with the large family at Berkeley—"Harrison's Fair family," as he said—and his younger children of his second family played with the children of Benjamin and Anne Harrison. Between Byrd and Harrison, who had been a boy when Byrd went to England, there was too much age disparity for them to become cronies, though Byrd was a close personal friend of Benjamin's mother, a cousin of Byrd's first wife, and Harrison's oldest son enjoyed the run of Westover.

With Byrd's return and Westover occupied again, the old plantation neighborhood was established as of Harrison's first memories, and a family flavor was added when his wife's brother, John Carter, married into the Hill family on the other adjoining plantation at Shirley. For this sufficient community, there beside the tidal river, life seemed to flow in changeless time. Writing back to England of the James River planters' life, Byrd said:

"Like one of the patriarchs I have my flocks and my herds, my bond-men and bond-women, and every sort of trade amongst my own servants, so that I live in a kind of independence on everyone but providence. . . . My doors are open to everybody . . . and a half-crown will rest undisturbed in my pocket for many moons together . . . we sit securely under our vines and fig-trees . . . (and) can rest securely in our beds with all doors and windows open, and yet find everything exactly in place the next morning. We can travel all over the country by night and by day, unguarded and unarmed. . . ."

Though Byrd might have been trying to sell himself on "the advantages of a pure air," his description evoked the aura of the perfected plantation life in the age of the aristocrat. This period held the most timeless quality, the essence of that "life in thrall," of any time in Virginia's history. The planters' mastery of their age on earth was complete in an era when, on the surface, there was not even threat of internal conflict or the whisper of change.

6

Beneath the surface, tensions were building that would soon involve Virginia in international situations, with epochal changes, but this underground stirring did not then touch the tranquillity of the plantation. In fact, one of the most significant quiet happenings, which presaged future conflict and change, was accepted by the planters only as an indication of the permanence of their rule in immutable pattern.

After a nonentity followed Spotswood for a few years, Virginia, in 1727, got a governor who was to have the longest continuous rule in the colony's history—twenty-two years. William Gooch (later created a baronet for his services in Virginia), was forty-four years old at the time he came, and, like Spotswood, a former professional soldier, colonial-service careerist, devout Christian and faithful subject of the King. There the resemblance ended. Though Gooch also was sent to Virginia as the King's representative, to operate the colony for the benefit of England, he lacked Spotswood's strong-willed and rigid autocraticism. Instead, Gooch was of amiable disposition, deeply courteous, and of a fair-minded flexibility. These qualities enabled the governor, in adjusting to Virginia as he found it, to experience a personality change that foreshadowed the changes to come.

When he arrived with his wife and son at the Palace in Williamsburg, the new governor expected to take up where Spotswood had left off—curbing the illicit trade in tobacco and establishing the State (England) over the Church (local) by overruling the vestries in appointment of rectors. Unlike Spotswood, Gooch perceived that the churches were reasonable in their position and (also unlike his predecessor) he found it expedient to muffle Commissary Blair with an excess of courtesy rather than to arouse the bristly Council president and thereby become embroiled with the whole Council over a detail of principle. His concession won him instant approbation. Aided by this approval, Gooch slowly made his own significant personal change: while unquestioning in his loyalty to his King and home country, he began to view the illicit tobacco trade from the planters' standpoint.

Being on the scene, Gooch was able to do what the British government was incapable of doing. He saw that Virginians were not an abstraction of "colonials" who existed solely to be exploited. Once this obvious fact was recognized by a dedicated representative of the King, future relationship between England and *all* the Colonies became endangered.

For while Virginians evaded the laws on tobacco commerce,

New Englanders defied the law which prohibited colonial manufacturing. The reason for the prohibition of manufacturing in the Colonies was to force the colonials to buy from British merchants, needless to say, to their enrichment. And the reason that New England, and not Virginia, broke the laws on manufacturing, was because New England had no money crop—no tobacco. They had to manufacture, or starve. Thus Virginia, in adhering to one law while breaking another, became totally agricultural, while the law evasion of the Northern colonies led them into what was to become the industrial pattern of the future. With no eye on the future, each region did what it must for survival despite the laws of England.

That Gooch was aware of the compromise, whereby, in effect, planters foreswore manufacturing in exchange for illicit tobacco trade, is indicated by the good man's efforts—once he went over to the Virginians' side—to prove them innocent of manufacturing. The British government had discovered that a man in Yorktown was making pottery, and secretaries upbraided the colonial governor for allowing this illegal manufacturing. Gooch, after covering himself by proclaiming the unworthiness of the "manufacturer's" earthenware as of a quality too inferior possibly to compete with British products, at last breathed a sigh of relief over this isolated infraction when he wrote, "The poor potter at Yorktown is dead."

As for the four iron mines that were being worked in Virginia, he was forced to explain that they ran only pig iron, "and as that is sent to Great Britain to be forged and manufactured, these are rather beneficial to the British Trade than inconsistent with it." In brief, William Gooch had become an apologist for the colony he was supposed to exploit.

It is human that Benjamin Harrison and the other planters viewed his change of heart only as a symptom of their power and not as the prelude to a break with the mother country. In the same way, at Berkeley and all the other great houses then being erected, the families—discussing local affairs—viewed at a distance the attacks of the Indians in the Shenandoah Valley and the alliance of the French and Indians in warfare along the Ohio (then a part of Virginia). Those western areas were more remote to most Tidewater planters than India is to us. At least, India can be brought into our consciousness for political reasons. To Tidewater Virginians at the time of Benjamin Harrison IV, "beyond the mountains" was unrelated to the politics of their small dominion.

To Gooch, a European, this was not so. As Spotswood, with his drive to westward explorations, had to consider international alignments, so Gooch had to contend with them in a paradise which considered itself forever self-sufficient. However, it was the rising generation in Virginia that the agreeable governor was to affect. Those already mature when he arrived regarded his interest in Virginians simply as compliance with their ruling class, and the future to Benjamin and Anne Harrison meant no more than a duty to establish their children in positions to continue the idyllic present indefinitely.

By coach, chariot or chaise (Harrison owned all three), Benjamin and Anne Harrison broke the sameness of life in their private world by trips to Williamsburg, where they saw new faces, ate in public places, and danced at the Governor's Palace. The world beyond their capital was remote—centered in London, where they shopped and sometimes visited, but closer to their consciousnesses than the capitals of other colonies in America.

## 7

Byrd had said that they were independent of everyone but Providence, and it was an act of Providence that ended the idyll for Benjamin Harrison IV.

Thunderstorms in Virginia have a frightening violence. When the heat builds up and the electricity begins to shoot from the sky, people and animals, barns and houses, are in danger, and many a great home was destroyed by fire caused by lightning. In the summer of Harrison's forty-fourth year, a typical electric storm lashed Tidewater Virginia.

Benjamin Harrison was not alarmed by the storm, only mindful of the rain driving through the open windows on his imported furniture. Since no house servant was handy, the master went upstairs to close a bedroom window. He had been playing at the time with two of his daughters, and took them along, one in his arms. Perhaps he was telling them there was nothing to fear as he approached the window, manipulating with his free hand to get leverage. In the instant that he stood there, a bolt of lightning struck, and Harrison and his two little girls were killed instantly.

This sudden death dramatically completed the seventy-one years of the third evolutionary generation the builder of Berkeley mansion shared with his father. Byrd, born one year after Benjamin Harrison III, also died in the year that the fourth Harrison was killed—a neat seventy-year span.

Unlike his father, the fourth Benjamin Harrison left a very complete will, made the year before. A devout Anglican, he began with a long preamble: ". . . I give and bequeath my soul to Almighty God who first gave it its being, in sure and certain hope of a joyfull resurrection through the Death and Passion of my blessed Savior Jesus Christ, my body to the earth from which it was first taken, to be decently buried on Berkeley Plantation near by little dear son Henry's grave. . . ."

Then, following the example of his father-in-law, Robert (King) Carter, he broke with the English tradition of primogeniture, which gave everything to the first-born son and sent the younger sons into trade and to the Colonies. Settling on the first son the six plantations that comprised Berkeley, with all the slaves and stock and equipment, and the goods in the Manor House, Benjamin Harrison IV divided among his four other sons the eight separate working plantations, with their slaves and stock, plus additional tracts of land, lots in Petersburg and a mill. His daughters were given, after the custom, cash sums and personal slaves—house-people and body servants.

With all his family provided for, as he hoped, this second-half member of the swing generation left the center of the power and the glory, the self-sufficient home-plantation, for the full flowering of the line in his first-born son, eighteen years old at the time.

The year before had died the father of eleven-year-old George Washington, who was to become a personal friend and compatriot of the fifth Benjamin Harrison on a stage incomparably larger than Tidewater Virginia. They belonged to that rising generation which, firmly entrenched in power in an evolved social structure, were to use the self-sufficient plantation dominions as a basis for operation on an international scale.

❀ ❀

## CHAPTER VII

# PORTRAIT OF A PLANTER –
## *AS A MAN OF DESTINY*

1

*Benjamin Harrison* V, the perfected product of an aristocracy devoted to producing the superior individual, grew up into his majority under the good governorship of affable William Gooch. The first of any line in America to be born in a baronial mansion (presumably in 1726, after his parents had moved into the new Berkeley Manor House), the fifth Benjamin Harrison matured as the plantation idyll became aware of a world beyond itself. Freed of all need to earn money on estates which, by then, seemed largely to run themselves, this Harrison of the continental stage used his background and position to support a public career as hazardous as those of the early adventurers to Berkeley Hundred.

An eighteen-year-old student at William and Mary when his father was killed by lightning, Ben Harrison possessed the good looks and the personal style that befitted his rank. He looked aristocratic. Very tall and powerfully built, he carried himself like a prince. His features were clearly defined, with a well-shaped mouth above a strong pointed chin. His expression was animated and self-assured, with dark eyes looking out at the world in bright, bold confidence. He was casually proud, with neither assumed modesty or haughtiness, and his attractive face reflected the good humor that was perhaps his chief characteristic. Possessing the easy temper of some large men, he loved laughter and amiable companions, and was himself a quick man with a joke.

In his youth, before heavy eating filled out his huge frame, he moved well as a result of his outdoor life, riding, and lessons in fencing and dancing, and had a figure for the elegant clothes then fashionable. Virginians had become very clothes conscious (newcomers were advised to turn themselves out well), and Harrison's taste ran to long, ruffed, silver-buttoned silk coats in brilliant shades of yellow, blue and purple. Silk knee breeches above trim stockings were of a lighter shade, and the elaborate lace shirt front and collar were set off by a long waistcoat which matched the coat. His wig was blue-tinted white, the silken hairs brushed straight back from a snug fit at forehead and temples. The big, young master of Berkeley Plantation was an impressive figure as he strolled along the streets of the capital and joined his elder kinsmen on the porch of the Coffee House near the Capitol, where he became inoculated with the practical lessons of politics.

He spoke in the accent of middle eastern England (the educated Londoner was the Virginia model) that in Harrison's day was being softened and transmuted into what became the Virginia accent. With never any of the molasses drawl of the Lower South, the true Virginia accent is seventeenth-century English spoken with a liquid, slow, slurring sound, in which no final "r" is pronounced. "Mother," "suffer" and "river" become "mothuh," "suffuh" and "riv-vuh." (The fugitives from Tidewater, who found sanctuaries in isolated baronies in the Blue Ridge Mountains, and were never exposed either to outsiders or Negroes, spoke Elizabethan English into this century.)

"You-all" was invented as a necessary plural of the singular "you" and, though often spoken by the indolent or ignorant as to sound like "y'awl," it was never applied to a single person by anybody except foreigners trying to be funny—"foreigners" meaning non-Virginians. Curious regionalisms developed, such as a "y" sound inserted after a beginning consonant, so that Ben Harrison pronounced his mother's maiden name of Carter, with "rs" silent, something like Cyahtuh. He referred to his garden at Berkeley as "gyahd'n," spoken slowly with no syllable value.

The custom of his class required that consideration of others and tactfulness in dealing with them which comprise the soul of courtesy. By the time of the fifth Benjamin Harrison's youth, the planter families had developed the *noblesse oblige* that extended their responsibility from their own entrenched class to the whole society they ruled. The paternalism that grew from living in a slave community spread into a broad concept of paternalism, which came to characterize the Virginian's theory and practice of government.

This courtesy had by Harrison's time become so fundamental that the Virginians would excuse almost anything before rudeness. The social crimes that were most inexcusable extended from lack of courtesy—such as suspiciousness, which impugned one's own honor, and cheating which, revered by some as sharp trading, betrayed the whole code of honor that found its expression in consideration. George Washington's later shock at Benedict Arnold's betrayal went deep because the Virginians' code of honor was repudiated when his own consideration was taken advantage of by one who professed to subscribe. As a boy of fourteen, while Ben Harrison was a student at William and Mary, George Washington wrote down a code of manners that, applicable to all his planter contemporaries, illustrated the stress on consideration and the acute awareness of class distinction. Among the long list of rules, Washington wrote:

"Every action done in company ought to be done with some sign of respect to those present. . . . When in company put not your hands to any part of the body not usually discoverable. . . . Sing not to yourself with a humming noise, nor drum with your fingers or feet. . . . To one that is your equal, or not much inferior, you are to give the chief place in your lodging, and he to whom tis offered ought at the first to refuse it, but at the second (invitation) to accept, though not without acknowledging his own unworthiness. . . . If any one comes to speak to you while you are sitting, stand up though he be your inferior, and when you present seats let it be to every one according to his degree. . . . Persons of low degree ought not to use many ceremonies to lords and others of high degree, but respect and highly honor them, and those of high degree ought to treat them (those of low degree) with affability and courtesy, without arrogance. . . ."

The Washington boy pondered in great detail over the niceties of removing the hat. He said that it was "ill manners" to bid one more eminent than yourself to replace his hat and also in bad taste not to bid one less eminent to replace his; likewise, the person bid to "be covered" should do so, though not with unseemly haste.

These mottoes could have been written by Benjamin Harrison if he had needed the self-disciplinary exercises of the methodical Washington, but gregarious young Harrison was not concerned with building himself into a great character, and with his fellows he acted more intuitively out of a naturally happy nature.

About the time of his father's death, the caste system was becoming rigidified in Harrison's relatively populous Tidewater. There the disrupted yeomanry were finding identities as farmers and respectable townspeople, and forming, without self-awareness, Virginia's stalwart middle class. Though not aware of a class by definition, the people were aware of their own differentiation of level in a caste system in which they existed, literally, in the middle. They had their own pride and courtesy, their formalized values and customs, and a voice in the government through representatives in the House of Burgesses who sat alongside those aristocrats (like Benjamin Harrison, a Burgess at twenty-two) being trained for the higher positions. Patrick Henry was to become one of their representatives who, by means of personal force and the opportunity of emergency, rose politically to high estate, though his personal intimates among the bourbons were few indeed.

The building of cities, despite the frowns of the British merchants, opened opportunities to sons who simply were not cut out to be farmers. The shops around the Public Warehouse in a city gave the outlying farm families a chance to *buy* goods when they sold their money crop, tobacco, instead of operating on the credit system with shipping planters like the Harrisons. The big planters were sound, from their viewpoint, in distrusting cities: they made the small planters less dependent.

In 1737, when William Byrd II had been desperate for cash after building the Westover Manor House, he conceived of a shrewd idea. Instead of selling his land around the public warehouse at The Falls as farm acreage, he would found a city at this growing trading center and sell it in lots as city real estate. With this mercenary motive, the city of Richmond was founded. However, the aristocratic legend, to which Byrd contributed his European elegance, is so persuasive that mercantile Richmond, beginning life as a frontier trading post, identifies its founding with the lofty gestures of the aristocracy, and "Father Byrd" holds the place in Powhatan's former stronghold that Spotswood's "Knights of the Golden Horseshoe" hold in the Shenandoah Valley.

The small planters of the day regarded the new city with a more practical attitude. Tobacco hogsheads were rolled along the road to the public warehouse by oxen. A projection like an axle was built into both ends of the hogsheads, and shafts from these projections were attached to the oxen. Heavy wooden (and sometimes iron) tires were placed around the hogsheads to provide the actual rolling surface for use on what were called "the rolling roads." The small planters, or farmers, had a song about the new city at The Falls which showed what it meant to them:

> *Gwine down to Richmond town,*
> *Gwine down to Richmond town,*
> *Gwine down to Richmond town,*
> *To carry my 'baccer down. . . .*

Along with the positive value of Richmond, and the establishment of Petersburg in the same period, the growth of Williamsburg and spontaneously developed small shipping ports, like Hanovertown and other cities that have vanished with the mutations of time, the non-plantation population also received help in stabilizing the evolving, respectable middle-class through a negative measure—the elimination of the disruptive criminal element sent from England.

Early in the century the British government overrode the objections and laws of the colony, and began sending in habitual criminals to cut down to England's population of undesirables. Hardened in viciousness, depravity and lawlessness, these imports statistically increased the crimes of murder and robbery, influenced the weak and unsettled the displaced. Their effect reached a point where Virginians, as in the evasion of the British tobacco laws, were forced to solve the problem in their own way.

It happened that England at the time was again warring with Spain and calling on all the Colonies for a quota for the army. The House of Burgesses passed a law which, carefully exempting all useful citizens of whatever degree, conscripted for Virginia's quota "all able-bodied citizens . . . who follow no usefull calling or employment," *i.e.*, criminals. So successful was the prosecution of this law that governors from other Southern colonies sent agents to fill their quotas with Virginia's conscripts. While this practical remedy permanently removed a disturbing element and allowed the self-respecting population to become disassociated from England's refuse, it hacked away at that life line to Britain and gave Virginians a most profound distaste for irresponsible legislation from the outside.

2

The whole colony, then, was formalized and, within itself and its limitations, more stable when Benjamin Harrison V came home from William and Mary to the Manor House of Berkeley around the age of twenty-one. His mother was then dead and he was sole master of the six working plantations that comprised Berkeley, of "Harrison's Landing" and its shipbuilding facilities, of slaves and artisans. But, with his father's landholdings divided among four other brothers and slaves given to his sisters, he was back to the estate with which his father had begun, with the slave population reduced on the home plantation.

In all divisions of slaves, Benjamin Harrison's father specifically forbade the splitting of families. Though Negro families had been formed quite informally, they were respected as families, and the planters had developed a sense of duty about indoctrinating slaves in Christianity. There was a diversity of opinion about baptizing children who were property, and the Negroes themselves came in time to prefer the religious faiths (Methodist, Presbyterian and Baptist) of the middle class who broke with the Anglican Church, but they were more responsive than the Indians even to the ritualized liturgy of the Episcopalians. Incidentally, Indians cherished a deep and abiding hate of the Negroes because of their adaptiveness to a servile state. Indians could not be successfully employed as chattels: they would die first.

How much white blood had entered the Negro race in Virginia by the day of the fifth Benjamin Harrison could, of course, never be known. All planters denied secret miscegenation, but obviously some, most likely the unmarried boys in some families, made night trips to the "Quarters"—and thus saved the cash their Northern neighbors spent on prostitutes.

Since most men at some age in their lives regarded the privilege of sexually using an unlimited number of women as their own earthly paradise, and as many employers did so use the women within their power, it seems idle for anyone to deny that one of the less savory aspects of human slavery was the privilege of sexually using fellow mortals. That, historically, males debase the mortal dignity of fellow creatures through the sexual act does not negate or even minimize the spiritual crime of the plantation boys who used black women. This, too, increased their imperious sense of mastery, ultimately to their harm.

When Benjamin Harrison inherited the Berkeley Plantation, there were already mulattoes among his own slaves, though it seems unlikely that anyone could ever discover who produced them. Overseers had their own rights over the bodies of black women and doubtless exercised them, and for a fact visiting youths sometimes explored the areas beyond the house unit of their host. While nobody will ever know who begat whom among bright-skinned Negroes, it seems likely that the begetting must have contributed to that confusion about the christening of chattels.

This is not remotely to imply that the fifth Benjamin Harrison took carnal interest in female slaves. It is only to place the conditions prevailing among slaves and free at the time of his ascendancy to the manor house in which he was born. Because of his father's departure from the actual terms of legal primogeniture, young Harrison came up in a generation whose members were the guinea pigs in what proved a dangerous experiment.

Though his personal wealth by inheritance was large, the division of the total property removed *each* son from the vast financial power while giving the *first* son the responsibility connected with a vast estate. This break with the model of the British ruling class proved, from the viewpoint of founding a new ruling class, to be a mistake. The mistake did not become apparent in the generation of Benjamin Harrison V because of the *then* self-sustaining plantation with, as his father had it in his will, "my flocks of cattle, hogs, horses and sheep," the tobacco and food produce, the mills and wharf, the store and ships. But somebody had to be the manager, as Harrison's neighbor, the third William Byrd, discovered. This wastrel son of the grandee lost everything his enterprising grandfather had won, and became probably the first American to dramatize that saga of "shirt sleeves to shirt sleeves in three generations."

Harrison, nothing of a wastrel, found the obligations of his class to be almost as costly, as he completed his family tradition of achieving typically in his own time and place. The product of a most adaptive line, Harrison spread his personal horizons beyond the plantations and the colony, as Virginia was forced by international alignments to spread its political horizons beyond its immediate borders. Nearly a century before, Benjamin Harrison II, young Ben's great-grandfather, had his vision widened beyond the frontier neighborhood by the coming of the cavaliers. When good-natured Benjamin Harrison V was in his early-maturing teens, the agent of change was the coming of the French—with guns in their hands and with Indian allies.

3

The backdoor attack of the French, designed to limit the British colonies to their Atlantic coastal strip east of the Alleghenies, caused Virginians to become aware (as Spotswood and Gooch had long been) of their involvement in world power struggles. At first the awareness was limited to the immediate threat from the French on their western borders.

Benjamin Harrison was from the beginning, more interested in politics than in planting and by the time he entered the House of Burgesses in 1748 the territorial troubles with France were becoming a concern to the more enlightened planters in their alternate role of government leaders. From our perspective it is obvious that the question of rights could only be settled by armed might, and it was obvious then to the new governor, Dinwiddie, who, after a brief interim of local governors, succeeded Sir William Gooch.

After the Spanish, the French had been settled on the continent longer than anyone except Virginians, having founded Quebec the year after Jamestown. At the geographically southern extreme from Canada, they founded New Orleans in 1718, and soon the French revealed, through their exploratory expeditions, their purpose of settling the valleys of the Ohio River and the Mississippi. East of the Mississippi their areas would loosely include the present states of Michigan and Wisconsin, Ohio, Indiana, Illinois, West Virginia, Kentucky, Tennessee, Mississippi and Louisiana. It happened that Virginia claimed much of this land. As it also happened that the various colonies regarded one another's problems with self-absorbed disinterest, the French threat became almost exclusively a Virginia affair.

The French were more guileful than the Virginians in making allies of the Indians. Where the British made no bones about their intention to colonize territory, the French made friendly "treaties," and, whereas the Indians saw the British establishing permanent white communities, they saw the French as individual traders, trappers, explorers and the like, who intermingled with the aborigines and cohabited with their women.

The raids of the French red allies on Virginia frontier families did little to arouse the colony's government, partly because the usually able Gooch, who clearly recognized the menace of France, was unaccountably supine. Of course, he was no longer young and, doubtless grown tired from his long stretch (twenty-two years) in office, the courteous gentleman was not seeking new troubles. However, when Dinwiddie assumed the governorship in 1751, he had a personal motive for resisting French claims.

He belonged to the Ohio Company, a land-development enterprise formed by the big planters of Virginia and Maryland. The redoubtable Thomas Lee was the first president and two of his sons (Harrison's cousins) were members, as was Benjamin Harrison's brother-in-law, Robert Carter II. Robert Dinwiddie had long known these gentlemen. At fifty-eight, this Scotsman had spent thirteen years in the Colonies as the Crown's surveyor general of the southern district, and during the ten years preceding his appointment as governor he had made his residence in Virginia.

Besides his interest in the Ohio Company, Dinwiddie, in his capacity as governor, was sincerely concerned about the French encroachments. He was a strong administrator, of real vision, and knew the country at first hand. Both for the colony and for England's future, he wanted the French driven out of the land claimed by

Virginia. Dinwiddie's execution of the plans conceived in his official capacity was given force and spirit by his private pecuniary interests. The happy blend of idealism and practicality in a man of energy was to bring on a world war that resulted in France's exclusion from North America and would lead, through the Colonies' intensified awareness, to the colonial revolt that founded the United States.

Through the New England emphasis in the writing of American history, the figure of Dinwiddie does not loom large in the events foreshadowing the Colonies' independence, but one of his actions—revealing an astute ability to judge character—brought into prominence a twenty-one-year-old surveyor named George Washington, and started that indomitable young man of ambition on the road that all history knows.

It was actually the first trip of young Washington ("the Gent I sent," as Dinwiddie said it) to the French-claimed wilderness that served to open the hostilities. Washington left Williamsburg in October, 1753, with a small party and a few Indians and returned in mid-January, after having exhibited the most remarkable physical strength and endurance, and that rare trait of fearlessness—where being literally without fear is distinguished from having courage. (In later fighting, when he first heard "the bullets whistle," he wrote "there is something charming in the sound.") Though his negotiations with the French authorities had been predestined to bootlessness, the governor's purpose had been accomplished: notice was served on the French that they were trespassers and they were warned to vacate. Virginia's governor was honorably ready to begin what some called "Dinwiddie's War."

The governor encountered unexpected trouble in getting appropriations through the Assembly, since Benjamin Harrison and fellow Virginians shared all the Colonies' distrust of a standing army. Dinwiddie sent one small ill-equipped force to build a fort at the vital forks of the Ohio, at the present site of Pittsburgh, while Washington was ordered to recruit, equip and train another. It was one of those civilian-operated armed expeditions that are doomed from the first. The small force at Pittsburgh lost the fort to the French, who built Fort Duquesne there, and Washington led his extemporaneous band to its unglamorous surrender at Fort Necessity. He was but twenty-two, and, as young planters learned everything, he was learning warfare by practicing it.

Washington's small action began the concentration of events that led to full-scale war between England and France over the colonial empire. Called the Seven Years' War (1756-1763), it embroiled most of Europe, with Frederick's Prussia coming in with England, and Spain and Austria joining France. To the Colonies, England sent its lobster-coated regulars under trained officers to combine forces with the local militias. Colonel Washington became commander of the Virginia militia (the First Virginia Regiment), and his motley irregulars trained, marched and fought with the British pros under very regular General Edward Braddock.

Despite his good record as a soldier, the major general was to repeat the same fundamental mistake the British professionals made a century and a half before at Jamestown: he failed to adapt his methods to the country. Accustomed to the impersonal obedience of the British regulars, Braddock was outraged at the individualistic self-assertion of the Virginians. When, flouting all army regulations, the convivial colonials hit the bottle, the general vented his outrage on them with two hundred lashes. The punishment, far from whipping the men into a common mold, only instilled in them a personal hatred of the whole establishment.

Even the native-born Washington was baffled and depressed by the tough-bitten characters from the new frontiers of the Shenandoah Valley. Since most of the Indian ravages had fallen on their families, these men of violence formed a good part of the Virginia militia, and Washington (along with the British) experienced his first contact with that personal republicanism which was later to be called "frontier democracy." At the time of the abortive fighting between the British-Virginia forces and the French and Indians, their sense of inviolable personal independence was expressed by walking away from "the army," defying rules of discipline and threatening to blow Washington's brains out when he punished them. In brief, the combined expeditionary force that marched northward to Fort Duquesne under Braddock was anything except a happy military family.

Again Washington was to know defeat, larger and more disastrous, in which General Braddock was killed when his troops were caught in an ambuscade. Again Washington was to show fearlessness, rallying his Virginians as if unaware that two horses had been shot from under him and his uniform was slashed by bullets making their "charming sound." He also showed tremendous personal force in leadership, and his rallying of the troops saved the expedition from annihilation. Washington came out of the fiasco personally with an enlarged and lustrous reputation. In Virginia he became one of the young men for the oligarchy to watch.

Another force was formed, under Forbes, and over Washington's protests Braddock's mistake was repeated in detail, and so was the result. Still a third force was formed, but by then the Indians had had enough. They deserted the French, who abandoned the fort at the river forks where all the fighting had begun. The British forces in Canada captured Quebec and from Georgia northward, from the Atlantic to the Mississippi, the continent belonged to the British—with a large slice of the West claimed by Virginia.

Washington returned to Williamsburg, still under thirty, a hero and a burgess. He accepted his acclaim with the impressive calm that came to characterize the big man and, while his tide was running in, sensibly courted a rich widow of New Kent County in Tidewater. When Washington married Martha Dandridge Custis, he entered the alliance of powerful families to which Benjamin Harrison belonged.

Benjamin Harrison's wife was beautiful Elizabeth Bassett, and her brother was married to the sister of Martha Washington. In other words, Harrison's brother-in-law was also the brother-in-law of Washington's wife. Though the connection might seem remote in terms of kinship, in terms of the family unit that formed the center of the ruling class, the imposing and impassive young war hero and the politically adroit and cheerfully self-possessed master of Berkeley were in the same family.

## 4

Fifteen years a burgess at thirty-seven, Benjamin Harrison was a capital veteran when the Seven Years War ended. The older members of the oligarchy had quickly found the bent of his talents, and Harrison became a man of the committees. While others harangued across the green-covered table in the House of Burgesses wing,

Harrison lounged at ease in the small rooms where a few men worked at the serious business of preparing bills to be presented.

To the give-and-take of committee work, he brought a bluff equanimity, a forthrightness that gained force by his good nature. With his uncomplex nervous system insulated within his huge frame, Harrison smiled through wrangles that caused his friends to shout and sulk and grow damp under the tailored wigs. When business got snarled in personality clashes, Harrison broke the tension with a spontaneous line of bawdy humor. For a man who seemed to move so indolently, he was very quick verbally, especially in turns of humor. However, when business reached the point of decision, he was immovable in his firmness, and supported his position with a soundly practical intelligence.

The decisions which concerned the master of Berkeley were incomparably more delicate and complicated than the essentially provincial affairs which concerned the Harrisons before him, for the Virginia leaders were now deeply involved in the explosive problem of their relations with England. Until the war, though the Virginia Assembly constantly strove to improve the colony's conditions under British control and made practical evasions of penalizing restrictions, in principle the people unquestioningly accepted their status. Regarding London as the source of their laws and the hub of their world, they looked to England for their protection. Fiercely self-aware as Virginians, they were still British and their colony an integral part of a world power. During the war, native-born Virginians, who had never seen England, got their first look at Britishers in the mass and disliked what they saw.

The regular army officers were overbearing with the local militia officers, contemptuously dismissed their advice (as they had Washington's), and exhibited a rudeness which the Virginians found most unpleasant. Though largely unnoticed at the time in Williamsburg, the dislike went the deepest amongst the people west of Tidewater— those without traditional associations or economic ties with England. But all, regardless of status and talents, resented being looked down upon for being "colonials." Even the privates, poor debased creatures of the harsh British military system and not much above the level of galley slaves, were superior to the natives.

In all the Colonies, the British made a similarly unhappy impression. The colonists not only resented them, but closely examined the foreigners' attitude of superiority and measured it against their performance. Colonists found little to justify the superiority. Significantly for the future they found the worst failures in the military performance of the British Regulars. Dependence on England for physical protection had been one of the strongest bonds with the mother country and colonists had regarded the British Army as invincible. Suddenly they discovered with disenchantment that on their own ground their protectors were a bunch of feckless, rule-bound snobs. All they seemed to have to be snobbish about was that they were English, not Colonials.

This differentiation was implanted in people's minds *simultaneously* with their loss of respect for the protectors on whom they had been dependent and with a newly blooming confidence in their own military prowess. That their loss of respect for England's army was unsound, and their own self-confidence amounted to an unjustified afflatus, did not in the least lessen the psychological impact of these convictions. Once the colonists began to feel independent of a nation they had come to dislike, the break with England was only a matter of time—and, of course, the usual incidents.

A Hanoverian king, as every American school child is taught, provided the incidents. What every American school child should know about all wars is that incidents should not be confused with causes.

In Virginia, the causes dated back to the callous venality of Charles II one hundred years before. However, when the leaders, broadening their scope from the colony to the world, began to study the nature of the relationship underlying the causes, they were not then looking for incidents.

No prescience of revolution touched thickening Benjamin Harrison as, after a long wine-accompanied midday meal, he strolled with his wife in the slow-falling dusk of his tranquil domain, and saw the British Union Jack fluttering on the masts of one of his ships. His was the best of all possible worlds, and all that was needed for flawless perfection was a straightening out of the relations with England.

He was one of the class which a visitor described as "jealous of their liberties, impatient of restraint, and can scarcely bear the thought of being controlled by any superior power." That was true enough. But despite his own imperiousness, cheerful Harrison believed that matters could be worked out with England so that he would be free of intruding control.

As with all Harrisons, he was typical of his time. His mind was sound, well-informed and logical, rather than brilliant. He was a factualist. Secure in the apparently self-sustaining splendor of Berkeley Plantation, he was certainly not looking for incidents that could disrupt his paradise. The trouble was that he could find no way to stop them.

5

George III, the first Hanoverian to speak English without a German accent and so proud to be "a Briton," has acquired a hard name in history. In those simplified interpretations of the past, which personalize clashing forces, the "pompous king" is a handy villain. On the other side there is the impression of the happily virtuous Americans, lovable in their bucolic innocence, aroused to the "spirit of independence" by the unjust acts of a tyrant. George did love to play at king and he was not too bright; he suffered periodic spells of madness; but he was no more tyrannical than his ministers, the members of Parliament, the merchants and the landlords, and the Board of Trade that ruled on colonial affairs. After all, they should have known better, and it was the whole British government that grievously misjudged the temper of a people.

Britain had gone heavily in debt during the Seven Years' War; its people were taxed almost to the limit, and its powerful landlords taxed up to 30 per cent. In looking for new revenue, the natural place to turn was to the Colonies, who for so long had stood still to be milked for the benefit of Englishmen. The milking, however, had never been done by direct taxes. Aside from the nominal quitrents on land, import and export duties scarcely paid for the custom's service, and from England's viewpoint it was only fit that the Colonies should contribute to the cost of the war through direct taxation, as Englishmen were taxed. This seemed reasonable from their viewpoint.

The taxation came when the people, suddenly aware of their special identity as colonials, were also aware of their long exploitation. In Virginia arbitrary acts in George's early reign had aroused a brooding resentment even before the taxation. After Virginia had instigated the war to clear the French from the West and had much of the war fought on her soil—suffering loss in life and property— the king offhandedly dismissed Virginia's claims to the new land and established new provinces to absorb it.

In claiming this land Virginia, under the aegis of and with the support of its British governors, had sent out privately financed ex- peditions to explore and stake claims on the spot, and countless families had crossed the mountains to establish holdings. (Augusta County, in the Shenandoah Valley, advertised property for sale with a Mississippi river front). Under the King's proclamation, all these families must uproot themselves, abandon their homes, vacate the territory and recross the mountains.

Benjamin Harrison and his colleagues in the Assembly flatly refused to execute the order. But the accompanying order which for- bade new settlers, even traders and trappers, was out of their hands. The governor executed land patents and Dinwiddie's successor, so- ciable Francis Fauquier, perforce could issue no new patents. The territory the Virginians had won was denied the colony.

In winning that territory, Virginia had suffered a serious disloca- tion of its economy. In wartime it had not been possible to pay people distant from Tidewater in tobacco, and since England forbade a currency system, the colony was forced to issue paper money with no guaranty except its promise to pay. About £750,000 of paper money was issued, and to fulfill the promise the Assembly had al- ready introduced direct taxes of its own. As of 1763, when the war officially ended, Virginia had contributed in proportion more heavily than England and gotten nothing for her pains except new problems.

Among the details arising from the economic problems was a curious small affair which, actually marking the turn in the tide of the people's temper, served to introduce to the public Virginia's first rabble-rouser. Lanky, lean-visaged Patrick Henry, then twenty- seven years old, had been lackadaisically learning some law on the side while he kept store in Hanover County—that gently rolling and fertile farm country north of Richmond, famous especially for its tomatoes and watermelon. Law was about the only means to attain the large success for ambitious men outside the plantation oligarchy, for law opened a way to the Assembly, and there was no real power in Virginia outside the capital. In fact, the oligarchy brought *all* great men into government.

"Great" is used loosely for Patrick Henry, though there is no question that he was the precursor of the Revolution in Virginia. His father was an educated Scotsman who had come to Virginia to improve his fortune, settled in pleasant Hanover County, and married into the representative Winston family. Patrick Henry's Winston uncle was one of the persuasive orators of his day and his speechmaking appeared to be all that impressed the gangling, rather coarse-featured nephew.

In school Henry was an indifferent student, in the private learning common in his time his studies were superficial, and he seemed to prefer to spend his time not only in hunting and fishing but in the company of those of the humbler sort who did nothing else. However, among these people of the general public, Patrick Henry revealed a curious penchant for observing his fellow men and an astonishing power of analysis of their character. It was this power, and a natural affinity for the nonprivileged, that gave Henry his advanced and accurate gauge of the temper of the people.

One of the minor complications over Virginia's paper money gave him the opportunity to exploit this gift in public, and transformed the indolent, woods-minded storekeeper into the revolution's most hair-raising spellbinder. The case, called "The Parsons' Cause," was one of those little noted incidents in the rapidly deteriorating relations between Virginia and England.

The ferocious Dr. Blair had finally died after fifty-three years as the Bishop's Commissary and had been buried on the Jamestown island where he first arrived in the country he made his own. As the sycamore that grew through his wife's grave separated his from hers, a legend arose that "they were separated in death as in life." The dauntless Scot's posts were divided between two men: Commissary Dawson assumed the ecclesiastical duties, and the college presidency went to William Stith, William Randolph's grandson, and friend and neighbor of Benjamin Harrison. Without the personally strong and powerfully connected clergyman, the Church in Virginia fell afoul of a small, well-organized group of Oxford clergy fresh from England.

By that time the Virginia Church had many native-born clergy and many older clergymen who had become Virginians, and they operated the Church under strong lay control according to the conditions of the country. One reason for the strong lay control was that planters' resistance to acknowledge any superior authority, even in the Church. The new Oxford group, conditioned by the authoritarianism of a bishop-controlled Church, immediately wanted to transform the Virginia Church (which had no bishop) into the likeness of the English Church. On a religious level these English clergy were paralleling mistakes made by the British military in refusing to accept differences caused by local conditions.

These clergymen used the problem of paper money to make an issue for their cause. Twice the Assembly had passed a one-year law (Tobacco Act) permitting all salaries, debts, taxes and whatever to be paid in paper money instead of the legal tender of tobacco, at the rate of two-pence per pound of tobacco. The laws were passed for only one year because it took about that time for the British government to repeal a local law. Two thirds of the clergy and practically everyone else accepted this necessity of temporarily going off the tobacco-standard but, as tobacco prices unexpectedly rose above two pence in the second year off, the Oxford unit seized this issue and sued for the salary difference between what they received and what tobacco was worth that year. Their case was carried all the way to London. There the Board of Trade found for the principle of the clergy bloc by repealing the already lapsed Tobacco Act.

Virginians had grown guileful in evading British rulings. The vestries blandly announced that England had repealed the Tobacco Act in 1761 and, as the one-year Act itself expired in 1759, the British ruling could have no application to something that no longer existed. Since no repeal of colony law had ever been retroactive, the vestries were confident that no exception would be made.

Several clergymen sued in the courts but, though trivial damages were awarded in a few cases, in only one—that of the Reverend Mr. Maury—did the court find for the actual principle. At the next term of court in Hanover County, when a jury met on a writ of inquiry to determine the amount of damages, the defendants' attorney, John Lewis, resigned in the conviction that the case was hopeless. On his resignation, the defendants gave the apparently hopeless case to the obscure young lawyer, Patrick Henry.

As with Bacon the Rebel nearly a century before, it is impossible to know Henry's motives when he addressed the court. Never a deep student of law (or of anything except people), he was strictly a jury lawyer. No jury in Virginia had ever heard his like before, nor had Patrick Henry ever before displayed the power of oratory over the minds of men as he did in that December, 1763.

Instead of making a routine plea over the case, he erupted into surprising verbal pyrotechnics and attacked the whole system which permitted the arbitrary acts of a distant king. The sturdy members of the court stiffened when he shouted, "that a king, by annulling and disallowing the laws of so salutary a nature, from being the father of his people degenerates into a Tyrant and forfeits all rights to his subjects' obedience."

There were some uneasy murmurs of "treason," but the members of the court, carried away by Henry's impassioned outburst, allowed him to finish. When they recovered from the spell he cast, they awarded Mr. Maury one penny, and the young Hanover County lawyer suddenly became a figure.

The Reverend Mr. Maury wrote in a confidential letter that Henry apologized to him after the trial and said, according to Maury, "that his sole view in engaging in the cause, and saying what he had, was to render himself popular." If the deflated clergyman was telling the truth, Henry showed himself to be a most acute appraiser of the forming temper of the Virginia people, a temper that allowed treasonable words to win popularity. When, in his new status as a public figure, Patrick Henry went two years later to the Virginia Assembly, he was already a revolutionary—probably at that time the only one in Virginia.

Though Henry was disliked and distrusted by the old parties in the oligarchy, it is significant that, in reading the hearts of the people, his arguments were based upon studies of the analyses of the relations with Britain made by Benjamin Harrison and a group of his friends. One of them, Richard Bland (descendant of the merchant family who had once occupied Berkeley Plantation and Westover, and kinsman of Giles Bland "the Rebel"), has been curiously neglected by history. The original arguments of the colonial status derived from his measured and temperate pamphlet in which he stated that Virginia was "not a dependent of England" but *co-existed with England in the British Empire.*

This articulation of self-awareness of status indicated a profoundly changing attitude which before had been based merely on resentments. While there was nothing revolutionary in the attitude, in the sense of seeking independence, there was the most portentous type of rebelliousness—analytical and articulate, going to the heart of the matter—and this rebelliousness stirred in the ruling class.

At Berkeley Plantation, where Benjamin Harrison's friends gathered, the host was no longer the good-looking, sleek-cheeked young patrician who personified the triumph of the aristocrat. He had become quite large, grown broad in the face and a trifle jowly, and the jaunty expression had changed into one of humorous benevolence. He looked a man of substance, who enjoyed living.

There were still parties, for big Ben Harrison loved to dance, and there was still hospitality on a grand scale. By record, he bought whiskey by the gallon, brandy by the keg, rum by thirty-gallon casks, and Madeira by the hogshead. Only port was bought by cases of bottles, and the old Jamestown favorite, claret, seemed to have fallen into disfavor.

At the Romanesque meals and the three-day routs was a different cross-section of guests from that of his father's day. With the improved condition of roads throughout the colony, and with each planter owning his own coach or carriage, visitors could come from much greater distances and there were more facilities for putting them up in the great house with its two dependent wings. Where in his father's day, the guests were usually family and neighbors, by the fifth Harrison's time there were so many crossed bloodlines through intermarriage within the small planter class that the individuals comprising a whole family no longer formed a close unit.

In the great clan to which Harrison belonged, there was feuding between the Carters and the Lees, and Ben, who enjoyed drinking and gossiping with his political-minded cousin, Richard Henry Lee, equally enjoyed thwarting his reserved and learned kinsman in politics. The stately Lee, revealing early both his independence of mind and "irregularity," had ferreted out some large-scale peculations of the speaker of the house during the complications over paper money and tried to expose the friends who had benefited. Benjamin Harrison was too inculcated with caste loyalty to approve of such shenanigans.

Since everyone in the ruling class was kin to somebody else in it, the Virginia government was something like a large family, with all of a family's spites and jealousies, as well as the binding intimacies between some individuals. These closer personal alliances were being formed on the basis of political convictions when Harrison's friends met to discuss their relationship with England. On this fertile soil for rebelliousness, the British carelessly tossed the seeds with a measure called The Stamp Act.

6

The Stamp Act was the first measure of direct taxation (or, as the colonials called it, "internal taxes") imposed on the Colonies. In effect, this imposed a tax on every transaction that involved paper— deeds and titles, wills and mortgages, licenses of all kinds, newspapers and pamphlets, and even such items of the poor man's solace as the playing card. The list was endless. Such taxes were commonplace in England. The crux of the issue was that the American colonists were no longer English, and the Stamp Act, remarkably maladroit, provided the separate colonies with their first common grievance. It was the first tax that struck across all classes in all colonies, and for once the colonials howled the same words in a chorus of protests.

In Virginia, Benjamin Harrison and his kinsmen and friends formed a committee of eight in Williamsburg (October, 1764) to compose a formal, *reasoned* protest. The president was the King's attorney, fat, heavy-jowled and kindly Peyton Randolph, Harrison's brother-in-law (he had married Ben's sister Betty). Harrison's uncle, Landon Carter, was a member, as was his distinguished-looking cousin, Richard Henry Lee, the best speaker of the group. Another member was George Wythe, the scholarly and greatly loved law professor of Thomas Jefferson. Their reasoned protest was historic— and historically distorted.

Their protest introduced the principle that a people could not be taxed without their *consent*. There was nothing about "taxation without representation." Virginia could not be represented in Parliament, and that was beside the point. What they were establishing was a principle of self-rule in matters of their internal affairs. Carried to its logical implications of self-government (not independence), the principle of the eight Virginians of the planter oligarchy demanded what Canada and Australia were later granted in a Commonwealth of Nations.

While Harrison and his colleagues did not conceive the ultimate implications of their protest, the implications were inherent in the principle of self-management they evolved to deal specifically with the Stamp Act.

In London, however, their agent could not arouse the slightest interest among members of Parliament, and the other colonies were equally indifferent to the protest. In fact, Pennsylvania's agent, Ben Franklin, accepted defeat and wrote home that as the sun had gone down, "let us make as good a night of it as we can."

The Virginia Assembly did not accept defeat, though there was at first nothing of what would be called a revolutionary spirit. Benjamin Harrison and his group were politically enlightened conservatives. A man of property, with inherited responsibilities, the typical Harrison brought to government a flexibly analytical mind, forward-looking in the interests of his country while conditioned by the position of his plantation, family and class.

The aim of his group was to nudge the immovable older members of the oligarchy who, habituated to privilege in the *status quo*, preferred to accept the tax rather than disturb man's happiest estate. Into this decorous family affair, where Harrison's middle generation respectfully argued with their uncles, entered an uncouth radical in the plainly dressed, slouchy figure of their new Burgess, Patrick Henry. With no crested coach to join the procession that crowded the capital's sandy, rutted streets, the hunter had ridden to Williamsburg on horseback.

In a time of indecision, the electric voice of the twenty-nine-year-old sometime lawyer suddenly blared like a bugle through the high-vaulted wing of the House of Burgesses in the Capitol. There was no court reporter to record his words, but up to a point it is generally agreed that he likened George III to other tyrants, and the burden of his eruptive words ran, "Tarquin and Caesar each had his Brutus, Charles the First his Cromwell, and George the Third . . ."

At this point legend enters. Evidently the cries of "treason" from the old guard were louder and more authoritative than the murmurs of the simple burghers in the Parsons' Cause, for Henry broke off. Then he extricated himself by a lame finish, "George the Third may profit by their example." Some versions claim that he threw out one final defiance and shouted, "If this be treason, make the most of it." Other versions claim that he quieted down after his deft extrication.

In any event, the echoes of his bugling voice hung in the chambers like the reverberation of a bomb, and the well-mannered family affair was never to be the same. A radical element had entered as a counterbalance to the reactionaries. Harrison's group, hitherto a respectful progressive element, now found themselves holding a middle ground.

For Patrick Henry, along with all his spell-binding, offered a radical program. He offered a set of "Resolves" that would in effect declare for self-government then and there. There were more than one hundred members of the Assembly, and he won support from those Burgesses representing the less stratified regions beyond Tidewater. Suddenly it became the duty of Harrison's group to affect a compromise in the Resolves. Yet though a compromise version, the four published Resolves represent the first rousing statement of principle in the Colonies' struggle with England.

The heart of the Resolves stated: "That His Majesty's liege people of this most ancient colony have uninterruptedly enjoyed the right of being thus governed by their own assembly in the article of their taxes . . . that the inhabitants of this colony are not bound to yield obedience to any law or ordinance whatever, designed to impose any taxation whatsoever upon them, other than the laws or ordinances of the General Assembly aforesaid. . . ." This was the declaration of the principle of self-government within a commonwealth, though the issue then was internal taxes.

When the Resolves were published and circulated through the Colonies, the stamp distributor said that he would not attempt to levy the tax "without the assent of the Assembly of Virginia." The British governor of Massachusetts said, "Nothing extravagant appeared in

the papers till an account was received of the Virginia Resolves."
Then the other colonies grew excited and called a Colonial Convention to meet in New York.

Ironically, the Virginians could not attend because Governor
Fauquier dissolved the Assembly for its rebelliousness. This action
of Francis Fauquier was not typical of his most friendly and understanding relationship with Virginia. No governor was ever more
liked. A rarely perfected product of the eighteenth century, he was a
scholar, with a particular absorption in science, who loved music
and the theater and gay companions. One of the courtliest of gentlemen, he lived with a Renaissance magnificence, was addicted to high-
stake gambling, and still brought to his duties a clear head and a
finely balanced intelligence. In dissolving the Assembly, Fauquier
simply believed that Henry had gone too far—as did most of the
Governor's Virginia friends. Perhaps, too, his sensitivity was offended by Henry's crudities and lack of elegance.

Without Virginia the Colonial Convention sent to London an
emasculated version of the Virginia Resolves, stressing the principle
of consent in taxation. By then George III's ministers (and more
importantly the merchants) realized that they had unaccountably
stirred up the natives, and they repealed the Stamp Act. However,
in the purblindness of political inertia, the government stressed that
not for a moment had it conceded the principle of taxation. To
prove its point, and still hunting for revenue, the British tried some
"external" taxes, on imports, and finally came up with a tax on
such articles as lead, tea, glass, wine and so on.

As a tax, this did not affect Virginia directly. It hurt the
sensitive pocketbooks of New England merchants and smugglers.


7


There had been rioting in Boston over the Stamp Act and to
administer the Townshend Acts (named for the misguided minister
who inspired it), the British set up a board of custom commissioners
to enforce collections and put an end to smuggling. Reacting to these
grievances, the Massachusetts House of Representatives revealed the
awareness of the new common sympathy that had developed among
the Colonies. It circularized a petition (February, 1768) that asked

their fellow colonials to join in common cause against the Townshend taxes.

By the time such documents went by boat to England, were harangued over by the British government, and the decisions returned to the Colonies, months passed. During this interim, an "incident" occurred in Boston.

So respectable was smuggling in New England that one of Boston's leading citizens, John Hancock, was one of the country's leading smugglers. When in June, of 1768, the revenue officers impounded one of his smuggling ships, proper Bostonian Hancock collected a mob to drive away the British officials and protect his property. Incited by its own violence, the mob began rioting in general and the British revenue collectors went scurrying for their lives. In angry retaliation, England sent in two regiments of regulars to protect the customs' officers and enforce the collections.

As tax enforcement had been resisted by less violent measures all along the Atlantic Coast, the Boston "cause," presented in the cold facts, would have had a dubious ring as a legitimate grievance, except for Massachusetts' revolutionary counterpart of Patrick Henry. Samuel Adams was a stocky, frustrated man in his middle forties who, despite financial backing from his father, had failed in all business enterprises, and, like Henry, found a cause as a radical in the early revolutionary movement. A genius at propaganda as was Henry with words, Sam Adams associated the Boston troubles with British "tyranny" and colonial "liberties."

By the time the Virginia Assembly met (May, 1769) to act on the circular of the Massachusetts House of Representatives, its members were in solid sympathy with what Peyton Randolph called "their attention to American liberty." "Liberty" then meant political liberties in the sense of freedom from oppression, not independence. Also by the time the Virginia Assembly met, the British government had instructed its colonial governors to dissolve any colonial assembly that supported the circularized appeal for a united stand against the Townshend tax. The British government should have seen the way the wind was blowing when the assembly of its original colony unanimously resolved, among other things, to support the Massachusetts circular.

By then pleasure-minded Francis Fauquier had died and his

successor, Lord Botetourt, was (out of respect to Virginia's unseemly intransigence) made a permanent governor, as opposed to a deputy, and a genuine baron to boot. In his fifties and no careerist, amiable Lord Botetourt was not fitted by nature for controversy. He loved everybody and wanted everybody to love him, as the Virginians certainly did. Whenever Virginians liked a governor they named a county after him: hence, Botetourt (pronounced Bottie-tot), Fauquier, Dinwiddie, Goochland, and Spotsylvania for Spotswood, who had worked iron mines after his governorship in that area. But Botetourt had no choice except to wrap himself in his scarlet robes and announce to the tight-faced burgesses that their assembly was dissolved.

A few months later, in August, having followed the letter of the Crown's law, the affable governor called for a new election. There were only a few new faces, as by then the House of Burgesses was virtually as self-perpetuating as the Council. Benjamin Harrison was put to the expense of providing more rum for the voting-day picnic of Charles City County's freeholders and turning out at the poll himself. Voting was done vocally in the presence of the candidates, and few were the freeholders who wanted to vote against the plantation master and colonel of the county militia while looking him in the eye.

When Benjamin Harrison and the burgesses returned to the capital that fall, the big planters were as relieved as gracious Botetourt to be freed of problems for a while. After the daily sessions, Harrison and his friends gathered in the Raleigh Tavern to sample the arrack punch and the fancy victuals, and relax again in idle talk of things close to the heart. In November the planters returned to their manor houses to attend to the management of their estates, to look into the schooling of their children and prepare for Christmas.

But things would not remain quiet in Massachusetts. In March of the following year (1770) there occurred another "incident." The enlisted men of the British Army were, as the colonists knew from earlier experience, a sorry lot, and the regulars of the regiments occupying Boston confirmed the colonials' opinion by behaving like pigs. In turn, the Bostonians treated them with studied disrespect. Finally a civilian's insult to a soldier led to blows, the blows to a mob and, under the mob's provocation, an excited soldier fired into the encircling crowd. In group response other soldiers fired and eight civilians were left dead when the threatening mob dispersed.

It was an ugly episode from both sides, reflecting chiefly the unbearable tensions that had grown between the American people and the English people. But Sam Adams was at hand to turn the episode into the martyrdom of patriots. Calling the affair "The Boston Massacre," he engaged talented silversmith Paul Revere to make an engraving showing the innocent sons of liberty bleeding in the snow from the guns of the British oppressors. Prints were distributed from New Hampshire to Georgia, and again the Virginia planters were aroused to common cause by these terrible happenings in a sister colony.

Back to Williamsburg went Benjamin Harrison with little hope of another pleasant session in the capital. The troubles with England were getting out of hand, and the problems had spread from Virginia's soluble grievances to a colonial-wide turmoil. Gone were the times of his youth when Virginia was an insulated, self-sufficient dominion. Now the planters' colony was drawn into some amorphous force that threatened the perpetuity of their whole structure. There was disturbing talk of "independence" in Virginia's mellow air.

The spirit of independence did not, as is usually presented, sweep like a fresh breeze through the Colonies. It was an added starter to the growing awareness of the principles of self-government and it appeared unexpectedly and sporadically. As in the early days the extreme doctrine was usually proclaimed by loudmouths whom the men of substance regarded as irresponsible, the first stirrings toward independence came mostly as a disturbance to the responsible men of government.

When pacans to democracy were fashionable (as they were particularly during the intellectuals' *rapprochement* with Russia), it was stylish to stigmatize the Virginia conservatives as stuffy aristocrats who were insensitive to the striving for equality among mankind. There was nothing about democracy or equality in the revolutionaries' first agitations for independence. All of Patrick Henry's utterances, even as dressed up for school children, were directed toward the tyranny of a king. But the King had not been so tyrannous to

Benjamin Harrison and his fellow planters that they conceived of separation from the empire as a solution to an unsatisfactory situation.

Harrison had everything to risk and nothing to gain by independence. Far from being antirepublican in their aristocratic stuffiness, he and contemporaries showed an extraordinary sense of responsibility to their whole society in moving flexibly with the forces. After all, they were not the later-day "social-justice" apostles who talk a good game: they were men of rank and estate, rulers of a stable order, who were putting all they had personally on the line and exposing to a dangerous unknown the society for which they assumed responsibility.

8

From the time of Benjamin Harrison's return to Williamsburg in the spring of 1770, the new forces began to gather momentum. Patrick Henry and others began to use "liberty" as synonymous with independence, though still leaning on the older meaning of freedom from tyranny. Benjamin Harrison, then in his middle forties and over twenty years in the Assembly, had moved steadily from his part in the reasoned protest over the Stamp Act to the new conservative position which demanded, in effect, their autonomy in a commonwealth under the single rule of the Crown.

By then, a blockage to understanding had arisen between the British government and Virginians. England, as distinct from the British Empire, still regarded Virginia as an English appendage, and could not conceive that the Crown had come to mean quite separate things to the people of the mother country and to the colonials. While the Crown to Virginians was a symbol of the whole world empire, to the English it meant a personal king *and* the British Parliament.

When Virginians reached a point of political maturity which adjudged the representative Parliament of the mother country to be unqualified to rule in Virginia's internal affairs, the personal King came to mean to many, as Patrick Henry said, somebody "3,000 miles away" who committed "arbitrary acts" in the disinterest of the colony. The distant King failed to symbolize an abstract concept of "The

Crown" and became instead a personal symbol of what the radicals called "oppression and tyranny." This personalization of a symbol exerted no great appeal to the educated, landed classes in all the Colonies, who actually tried the sophistry of differentiating "The Crown" from the Parliament which *they* held to be oppressive. The appeal of a personal, oppressive king was strongest and most acceptable where the people were under the influence of a limitless frontier.

Although self-assertive individualism had developed in all Virginians, the people of the new frontiers (to whom even the Tidewater was too rigidified) lived by an undisciplined violence in their wild domains. Bending of the knee to anybody was foreign to their natures and understanding. Even the planter barons, with their fealty to the concept of the Crown, had become too imperious to accept treatment as second-class citizens and too remote from English life to feel a *personal* loyalty to a king in whose reign this unacceptable treatment occurred. Essentially, from the James River manor houses to the Cumberland Gap the Virginians had developed an individual will—or willfulness—to which a "divine-right" monarch was antithetical. Every man was a king.

These political considerations were evident in the subsurface emotional swell that accompanied the attempts to deal with Colonial problems in a legal framework. At the same time the new intellectualized concepts of "the rights of man" appeared in the mental climate. Though Benjamin Harrison and his kinsmen and friends did not evolve their theory of self-government with any notion of breaking with England and establishing a separate nation, their legal protest set in motion the incidents which released the emotional forces and produced men to articulate them in passion.

Restless Patrick Henry, forever moving from one house to another, found himself an attacker of the King in the eyes of the world and, like any intelligent man of ambition, stuck with a winning horse. Without financial stake in the planter class, he had nothing to lose in the event of physical upheaval. This is not to deny that he might have been stirred by the most patriotic motives. It is, however, a fact that he did not have to count consequences when his personal course in the Virginia Assembly, itself caught up in the headlong course of the Colonies, carried him to increasingly extreme positions. He was the most forceful and intemperate speaker of the growing radical element. Men did not remember what he said so much as they remembered being moved by his words.

Thomas Jefferson, only thirty in 1773, became the precocious political philosopher who hauntingly defined the new abstractions on the rights of man. Of course, he had read Locke, Rousseau, Voltaire and the rest, but it was out of the personal paradise of the Virginia planter that he conceived of "the pursuit of happiness" as a theory of government. The lean, sandy-haired Tom Jefferson, with the speculative eyes and cool personal dignity, has been obscured as a person by the grotesque distortions of his political philosophy. He was a slaveholder who lived in luxurious and insensitive self-indulgence on the heritage left by three generations of hard-working and constantly aspiring planters.

Compared with the Harrisons and other controlling families, the Jeffersons were late to arrive in the oligarchy. It was Tom's strong-bodied father who married into the planter class, a Randolph, and, finding Tidewater too settled, planted in the distant Piedmont in that beguiling country east of the Blue Ridge. Though Peter Jefferson did not accumulate on the scale of the big planters, he did more than just "all right."

Tom Jefferson had great respect for his father and apparently none for his mother (and what some Randolphs think of him is unprintable). However, as a realist and opportunist, the protean Jefferson was willing enough to use the position of his mother's family for his own advancement. Jefferson used all the advantages of his class rather than being spiritually of it. When he was at William and Mary, he availed himself of the extracurricular educational facilities at the Capitol as no student ever had. He haunted the lower floor of the Capitol, listening to the debates in the Burgesses and to the trials in the Court. His seeking mind and mannerly reserve made him attractive to older people, and he became a favorite at the Governor's Palace, where he absorbed—along with Fauquier's splendid pleasures —the governor's bland enlightenment.

When he entered the House in 1669, he already belonged to the future. Though he was a poor speaker, Jefferson was one of the toughest and most sagacious politicians who ever lived. In the sessions beginning in the spring of 1770, he put his incredible mind to work on the advanced philosophical theories behind Virginia's expanding movement against England. Not only a political theorist, he also used his political sagacity to advance his position among the new surgent powers in Williamsburg.

Benjamin Harrison, then forty-seven, had been placed among the "venerables" by his near quarter century at the capital and his family alignment with the older generation of the oligarchy. Neither political theorist nor rabble-rousing orator, the master of Berkeley Plantation was more typical than Henry or Jefferson of the men of estate who moved slowly in the decade from the Stamp Act protest to the formation of the extremely effective Committees of Correspondence between the Colonies. His cousin, Richard Henry Lee, originally a conservative, took a bigger jump and joined Henry and Jefferson in forming the potent committee. But Benjamin Harrison, though he participated in the activist committee, was operating from the manor house of a dynasty of which he was the titular head as his cousin was not, and he was weighted with personal responsibilities that Henry never had and Jefferson never fully assumed.

Jefferson had been a student at William and Mary (where in the planters' plan of education, he was at the seat of government and in the midst of affairs) when Harrison's group were groping toward their definition of self-government. Ben Harrison had been at the same college during that charming period of "life in thrall," when there were no clouds in the blue sky of the planters' idyll. Also, more practically, Harrison had a large family to provide for and, as he had given little time to planting and shipping, the fraying of his estate at the edges forced him to consider unpleasant details of economy along with pursuing his career in a government that was approaching revolution. That only seventeen years separated the two men is an indication of the speed of the swelling movement once it got rolling in Harrison's generation.

The men for independence, the Adamses as well as the Virginians, were receiving constant support and encouragement from two quite unpublicized orphans of the Virginia oligarchy. As younger sons of Thomas Lee, Arthur and William (brothers of Richard Henry Lee) had come into no landed estates and, of all things, had gone to England for opportunity. Better endowed financially than his brother, Arthur had studied at Eton and graduated in medicine; William pretty much on his own had become a moderately successful planters' representative in London. Far from being British-ized, both became among the first Americans to conceive of complete separation as the only solution and, operating more or less as spies in the enemy's camp, supplied the home leaders with ammunition.

Arthur Lee, who abandoned a medical career for pamphleteering, was also among the earliest to realize from his distant vantage point that the colonies must act in unison in common cause. "American liberty," he wrote, "must be entirely of American fabric." As much as any local patriots, these two Lees kept prodding the movement toward American union.

9

In the last month of 1773 the movement received impetus in the shape of another Boston "incident." Without the British pattern of ineptitude this incident would probably have retarded the forces of "liberty." One of the least noble affairs that ever served as a national legend, the "Boston Tea Party" was a mob-inspired action by commercial interests in unabashed competition with British commercial interests.

The British interests were represented by the somnolent East India Tea Company which, as a result of ennui—a business attitude not shared by aggressive American merchants—faced a future consisting of crowded warehouses and bankruptcy. In a sudden stroke of acumen, the tea company officers conceived of shifting their warehouses to America and, eliminating all middlemen—British jobbers, American wholesalers and retailers—underselling the American merchants. As with the Townshend Acts, most of the Atlantic coastal cities resisted this unfair competition in more or less dignified ways.

In Boston, however, having aroused a mob spirit, the merchants recruited a sort of brown-face Ku Klux Klan, and disguising themselves as Indians, dumped into the bay the tea arriving on the ships of the rival who could undersell Boston merchants. Even the redoubtable propagandist Sam Adams could not make other colonists swallow that incident as "a stroke for liberty," and in Boston his cousin, John Adams, deplored such hoodlumism.

The British government, however, then thoroughly bewildered by all the agitation among their dependents, could only muddle not "through" but on. To break the resistance of the mob spirit in Boston, the British ordered the port closed and threatened to turn the mercantile city into a graveyard. Along with causing this very real disaster, England threw in strictures on the civil government of Massachusetts and, as if warning Virginia to cease its support of a sister colony, donated all of its traditionally claimed land north of the Ohio River to the Province of Quebec.

Instead of driving Virginia and Massachusetts apart, the wholesale reprisals for the financial loss of British tea merchants caused the two most ancient colonies to form a binding union. There were able spokesmen in England for the American colonies, who defined as clearly as Americans could the constitutional rights of British citizens and who denounced the unrealism of the Parliament of six million Englishmen ruling the internal affairs of three million Americans three thousand miles away. But the government was in control of men who believed, as General Braddock had believed about individuals, that the Americans could be brought to heel by punishment.

In May, 1774, the Virginia Assembly resolved to hold a day of fasting and prayer for their sister colony, and what gave the resolution its portentousness was the object of the prayer—"to implore the divine Interposition for averting the heavy calamity which threatens destruction to our civil Rights and *the evils of civil War*" (not their italics), and "to give us (the colonies) one Heart and one Mind firmly to oppose by all just and proper means every injury to American rights. . . ." This clearly stated resolution for united action was an appeal to England for compromise as well as an incitement to indifferent Virginians. The implied threat of separation was a warning to England rather than a desired course, and also served to prepare the natives for eventualities.

Sweet-natured Lord Botetourt had by then died, his heart heavy with all the strife that divided his loyalties. In his place had come Lord Dunmore, with his wife, three daughters, and three sons who became students at William and Mary. He could think of nothing to do except dissolve the Assembly.

The members strolled the few blocks up shady Duke of Gloucester Street to the Raleigh Tavern. There, in an informal meeting, they decided the time had come for united action, and voted to call a continental congress. Two days later a horseman arrived in the capital with messages that local groups in Northern states had the same idea. So, in a tavern, eighty-nine members of the unofficially assembled House of Burgesses called for a state convention to select representatives to an American congress and to draft instructions for united action with their sister colonies.

Even then, Benjamin Harrison and his fellow moderates believed that a united front among the Colonies would bring the British government to its senses. The extremists did not believe it and did not want it, but they did nothing to disturb the majority. In fact, Jefferson said that he had a deep respect for those men of prudence. Though they could not be hurried as fast as the radicals might wish, the Harrison group were moving steadily toward increasingly stronger position, and time and circumstance would do the rest. The essential element was unanimity, in which each man of the group acted from sound conviction.

10

When the Convention met in Williamsburg in early August, there were no rousing appeals to emotion. Even Henry, who probably hated the plantation masters almost as fiercely as he hated the King, was unaccountably decorous. For the occasion he had gone so far as to turn himself out in a stylish coat and wore a brown wig fashionably tied in the back. Nor did the convention in any way make appeal to crowd support.

When the Boston merchants stirred up the mobs to pull their chestnuts out of the fire, Massachusetts introduced a pragmatic democracy in emergency that in time was to give political power to the numerical majority, a result quite apart from the intention of the colonial rich. As of 1773, the poor who were crowded into the cities of the North were in harder case than the Virginia poor on their farms, and the urbanites had built up legitimate grievances that had long gone ignored. It was easy enough for a skillful demagogue such as Sam Adams to incite a mob spirit against the British tyrants; the people, once formed into crowds, could have been incited against anything.

When the Virginians responded to their potential allies in a stand against England, the emergency was handled by the members of the oligarchy trained to govern. The separate methods by which Virginia and Massachusetts—two leading powers in resistance—dealt with the emergency made clear a most vital difference between the two sections, North and South. In the divergent approaches of these two powerful colonies to a common cause, all the *essential* differences were foreshadowed between the democratic North and the aristocratic South.

In electing its representatives to the Colonial Congress, the Virginia Convention crossed all lines to elect those men who had been most actively and intelligently engaged in clarifying Virginia's position of self-government to the obtuse and high-handed British. From the conservative side came Benjamin Harrison, his brother-in-law, Peyton Randolph; his friend, George Washington; his fellow committeeman, Edmund Pendleton, a real old-liner; and that Richard Bland who had first stated the colonial principle ten years before. From the radicals came Harrison's cousin, "Harmonious" Richard Henry Lee, and Lee's political crony, Patrick Henry. Young Jefferson, too ill to make the carriage trip from Albemarle County, somewhat brashly sent a written draft of instructions. While the instructions were not adopted, the paper was published, and, widely circulated, spread Jefferson's reputation throughout the Colonies as a philosophical author on the colonial position.

Benjamin Harrison and the other conservatives would have been deemed fairly radical a few years before. Though still not supporters of independence and believers instead in a relatively autonomous dominion within a world empire, they were, viewed within the context of their times and knowledge, progressive realists of genuine vision. Their problem was that the British government were short-sighted realists. They had blocked the westward expansion of the Virginians to their traditionally claimed land in a fear that, among other things, the Americans would gain a physical majority in population over England and an economic power that would render the Americans independent. Of course, their fears were justified. What they could not envision in London was the impossibility of stopping by edict the sweep of a continent or of retaining in a dependent status a people of more vigor, with more resources, and of potentially greater world power than themselves.

They had not then learned the American adage "if you can't beat them, join them." Harrison's Virginia group, as with similar groups from all the colonies, were inarticulately trying to get the British to follow this adage.

Packing in August for the long hot trip to Philadelphia in his coach—days on the muddy roads and nights at flea-ridden taverns—heavy Harrison longed for a settlement that would establish self-government while retaining the *status quo*. From his upstairs bedroom window, he looked out on his un-horizoned green land, on fertile fields baking under the sun, on shadowed forest and villages of artisans, on the three-mile river front with wharf and ships and shipyards, and his heart could not desire an upheaval that would threaten his counterpart in perpetuity of the British ruling class's landed estates.

It was the *British* he had tried to reach from 1770 to this spring of 1774, with resolves and in committees. If they weren't reached, the radicals would gain control and everything he knew would be changed.

Maybe he experienced a premonition that this class would be the ultimate loser (as it was), but his caste privilege saddled him with responsibilities for the whole, which now included masses of people from other colonies, whom he had never seen in his life.

His brothers came and offered him support in case of trouble, his lovely wife assured him that he was doing the right thing, and his children asked for presents from Philadelphia (whatever that was). His servants strapped his luggage to the coach, looking to see that the stableboys had the horses well groomed and harness glistening. Then, as his personal servant mounted the box beside the coachman, with weepings and wavings from his family and house-people, the big Virginian settled back on the cushions for the journey to meet Americans in a strange city.

✹ ✹ ✹ ✹

# THE GOLDEN AGE

❀ ❀

## CHAPTER VIII

# RELUCTANT REBELS

1

When Benjamin Harrison returned to Berkeley in September, 1774, the overpowering concern of the physically self-indulgent provincial was to take his ease among familiars. Philadelphia might be all right for people who liked cities, but the returning Virginia planters confessed that they were not among those who did. Shortly after his return home, when Benjamin Harrison went to visit some of his Carter cousins, the young Northern tutor of the Carter children reported the Philadelphia impressions of Harrison and his friends.

"They allow the City to be fine, neat and large," the tutor recorded, but "they complain a little of the small rooms, uniformity of the buildings, and several other like faults. They call the inhabitants grave and reserved; and the women remarkably homely, hard-favored and sour!"

Harrison personally offered to give a guinea for every handsome face found in Philadelphia, if anyone else would give a copper for every face that was not comely. But Harrison and his friends were impressed by the fat Pennsylvania countryside ("The Face of the Country," as it was called) and admired the methods of working of the land. As regards the first Continental Convention, then, the Virginia planters would seem to some extent like the cat who attended the coronation and saw only a mouse.

Certainly there was nothing in the attitude or the actions of the bulk of the delegates from the other colonies to disturb Harrison and the other men of property who essentially desired a conciliation with England on terms reasonable to the Colonies. From New York, New Jersey and Pennsylvania, Maryland and South Carolina, Harrison had met fine gentlemen of his own kind who saw eye to eye and were hoping to evolve sound measures toward a compromise short of this "independency" of radicals. Even two of the most radical, Virginia's own Richard Henry Lee and Massachusetts' John Adams, in answer to a point-blank question from George Washington, had assured Harrison's friend that independence from England was not their aim.

At the Convention, neither of Virginia's extremists, Lee and Patrick Henry, had distinguished themselves in carrying out the tasks allotted to them as Virginia's most widely known representatives outside the Dominion. Henry had caused a momentary reaction with a sample of his flushed oratory when he cried, "We are not Virginians and New Englanders, but we are Americans." However, away from the crowd-response and trapped alone with a pen, the blood-chilling jury lawyer lacked organization for his thoughts and lacked the education to substitute learning for creative vacuity. When the delegates settled down to business, the country lawyer, subdued in unwonted finery, had little to say.

Richard Henry Lee, after pleasing all with his polished and restrained oratory, did best at busying himself with his new crony, John Adams, and they probably hatched their own plots. But Lee enjoyed little influence in the Virginia delegation.

The Virginian's favored representative was Benjamin Harrison's brother-in-law, Peyton Randolph, and the plantation masters were gratified that he was elected president of the Congress and brought to the chair the kindly dignity of his huge presence. Their richest planter, Harrison's friend George Washington, observed with impassive impressiveness and let others do the talking. Harrison himself chiefly listened, and in private conferred with his friends and kinsmen on the delegation. Of this group, John Adams said, "These gentlemen from Virginia appear to be the most spirited and consistent of any."

They probably were. Having been spared all the troubles that had brought matters in Boston to open violence, the Virginians had nevertheless taken a strong position against British injustices as a matter of principle. Their support of Massachusetts—allying the two most populous colonies—expressed Virginia's attitude toward building a unity of resistance against England's oppression of colonial political liberties.

Even the Virginians were unified only on the *need* for a resistance that would produce a change in relations with the home government. That fundamental was about the only agreement possible between the business-minded delegates who represented the various colonies. They resolved to support one another (meaning, then, specifically Massachusetts) in their troubles and they reaffirmed the non-importation measures to strengthen the boycott on British merchandise. Aside from these unrevolutionary measures, the Continental Congress—or, really, convention—voted to meet again the following year. Then, mildly pleased with themselves, they went home to see what England would do.

As it happened, the British minister, Lord North, like so many colonial governors, had forgotten all about the dream of empire that had begun at Jamestown. His conception of empire was England and its sundry dependencies of inferiors fixed in perpetuity. Totally without comprehension of a nation in embryo across the ocean, North proceeded with an astonishing fatuity to threaten with a club in one hand, while offering a puny bone with the other, and gave never a thought to what kept the dog barking and snarling. North served unwittingly as the chief ally of the small colonial bloc of revolutionaries.

In Virginia, the Ministry's governor, Lord Dunmore, served even more effectively in nudging the reluctant rebels like Harrison toward the radicals and in deepening the sense of rebellion in those people distant from the demesne of (what a Northerner called) "the lords of the James."

In that period in England, to be a lord most nearly approximated heaven on earth, and Dunmore—earl of this and viscount of that and thrice a baron—evidently expected Virginians to regard him with the same awestruck reverence with which he regarded himself. Walking in haughtiness, even when trying to court popularity, he offered a flat contrast to his immediate predecessors—Francis Fauquier, the courtly cosmopolitan, and the sweet-natured Lord Botetourt. As a representative, in time of crisis, of a home government already regarded as tyrannical and disinterested in Virginia's welfare, Dunmore was type-casting for the would-be overlord who personified all that the people had come at best to resent and, in extreme cases, to find intolerable.

It was not the traditional Virginia rulers, like the typical Harrison, who, secure in their own privilege, had as yet found their grievances intolerable. Nor could they have been swayed by the demagogic Patrick Henry, whom they viewed with the same distaste they held for his Massachusetts counterpart, propagandist Sam Adams. Perhaps they sensed Henry's limitations.

After his explosive "I am an American," utterance in Philadelphia, when the troubles went from talk to the serious business of war, Henry became an advocate of Virginia for Virginians, and served as a model for the later state anthem, *Carry Me Back*. On the other hand, when the showdown came on a continental scale, Harrison was the last of the Virginians to leave Philadelphia.

Of the men in the colony who felt truly passionate about injustice, as a principle and as a fact, the most effectual in molding opinion was thirty-one-year-old Tom Jefferson. He, with the collaboration of the British government, was the unobtrusive influence on the Harrison-Randolph-Washington bloc.

2

This most literate of the Revolution's libertarians did not (as the impression seems to be) spring full blown from his own head as an apostle of independence and the avant garde of the rule of demos. Aware of his own aristocratic position and mindful of its responsibilities, as a theoretically humane member of the ruling class and as a philosopher in government, the reserved young Jefferson was originally motivated by a curiously personal loathing of despotism. With this went a repudiation of the divine right of kings on which despotism was based.

It is possible that had Britain responded to the colony's stand in 1774 and offered self-government in a limited (or nominal) monarchy, Jefferson might have accepted the offer—provided he had a hand in designing the self-government. For a certainty he looked with favor on, as he had been formed by, that political "moderation" which he had noted that Montesquieu defined as the characteristic of the "aristocratic republic." In Virginia's society of individualistic freeholders (landowners with voting franchise), any enlightened member of the oligarchy in planning an ideal state would conceive in terms of citizens. This concept, however, included nothing of the twentieth century's "The People, Yes!"

As an intellectual of his day, participating in government during political upheaval, Jefferson conceived of a limited, landowners' democracy, ruled by its superior individuals for the protection of its citizens against oppression of any kind. In effect, his state would have approximated the Virginia as he found it, only freed from any superior authority—the King and Parliament—with a centralized Federal control when the states confederated in a union.

In his revulsion toward any higher governmental authority, Jefferson reflected the instinctive aversion of Benjamin Harrison and his fellow planters to any restrictive authority. Jefferson differed from the plantation masters and their counterparts in other colonies (especially New York, New Jersey, Pennsylvania and South Carolina) in that the men of Harrison's background feared the mob more than they feared monarchy. This fear lay at the bottom of their preference for restraining British political powers while remaining in the Empire and continuing without change their extension of the British caste system.

The more ardent Jefferson, probing deeper into the nature of the relations, did not believe that compromise on the basic issues could be wrung from England without a united front, and, with the political insight that accompanied his "pursuit of knowledge" (his words), he was aware of the need of the support of all citizens. In indirect appeal to them, the vastly gifted young man turned out his most immortal phrases. Removed from the context of their time and circumstance, some of his phrases, re-dressed in modern connotations, have been used for ends never designed by Jefferson and under conditions never conceived by him.

During that last tranquil autumn which was to come to the James River barons, Jefferson felt none of the scorn which in his old age he declared he felt for the landed aristocracy. Indeed, in 1774 he was quite pleased to accustom himself to their style of living.

In his own patrimony he had received only five thousand acres in

the then westerly region of Albemarle County, and fifty slaves. By
1771 he had doubled his land holdings and more than doubled his
slaves with his marriage to a pretty young widow of Tidewater, in
the Berkeley neighborhood, who brought him a share of her wealthy
father's estate. With this material step up in the world, Jefferson—
albeit adding a wry cynicism on the authenticity of family armorial
bearings—requested a merchant friend to acquire for him in London
a coat of arms which "may be purchased as cheap as any other coat."

He had already as his own architect begun the costly life work
of building his stately and original manor house on the top of a
mountain, where he displayed a small conceit over his learning in
languages by giving the estate the Italian name of Monticello.
Though the institution of slavery repelled him, as did any form of
oppression, Jefferson, since he had slaves, made lavish use of them as
house servants and lived in a luxury more selfishly designed for the
personal comfort of the master than anything Benjamin Harrison
and the old-line aristocrats even dreamed of.

Yet, the presence of the blacks (and of the "bright-skinned" mulattoes he inherited from his father-in-law's estate) evidently bothered
his conscience. He not only spoiled them as servants but constructed
several passageways to the utility wings and house-peoples' quarters
so in all their movements the slaves were hidden from view.

These shadowed passageways, as well as an underground passage
with which Jefferson experimented in air-conditioning, gave rise to
later-day rumors of the fastidious gentleman's secret lechery with the
slaves. Young men at the age to slaver over such details of carnal-
ity would offer proof in the form of a letter existing in the library
of Jefferson's university. There was a letter, true enough—an easily
proven forgery of British propagandists used first to discredit George
Washington and then rewritten to smear Jefferson.

Though Virginia's young and astute political philosopher had
man's normal appetites (and in his youth was once so carried away
by them as to make a dishonorable proposal to the wife of an absent
friend), clearly his greater passions were of the mind. While his
pursuit of knowledge was diverted, by the period's exigencies, into
political science, he never lost his thirst for pure knowledge and the
natural sciences, and his pleasures were found in music, architecture,

his own writing, experiments in farming and ceaseless notations on every phenomenon under the sun.

Energy flowed in a steady, even stream from his wiry frame. Though he was not physically as powerful as Harrison or Washington, he was blessed with a sound body and almost illimitable endurance. He took good care of himself, walking and riding daily, and was a sparing eater in comparison to Harrison and other healthy planters. He wanted his mind clear and fresh all the time, and he was never bored. More sensitive than most people realized, his outward-turning mind was not given to brooding over those little barbs which can so easily fester and poison; but he did not suffer calumny in silence. He always wanted to get the record straight for posterity.

Jefferson seems an offbeat character in the company of the hearty Harrisons and Washingtons, with their love of the table, their gamy humor, and, in Washington's case, addiction to the hunting field. He could never have influenced them by direct appeal, and he could have only antagonized these middle-aged gentlemen of large affairs, if, like Patrick Henry, he had subjected them to the assaults of stormy rhetoric. He knew too well their distrust of any excess in the emotional realms. While Richard Henry Lee acted in proud indifference to the men of his class who regarded him as something of a renegade, Tom Jefferson, looking always to the end to be accomplished, never lost awareness of the need for unanimity at home before anything approaching unified action could be hoped for from the divergent and self-interested colonies.

It was he of all Virginians whose theories developed organically from the original concept of self-government, through the successive stages to the break, to the ultimate concept of a new republic—all effectuated by a practicality in politics which in itself was an outstanding achievement. Because of this logical progression, with an almost inhuman adaptability to each phase as it developed, he did not try to stir up those members of the oligarchy who had returned from Philadelphia in the fall of 1774. They needed time, time and events, and right then, after their many absences from their plantations, they needed most of all to look to the administration of their complicated estates.

3

While a visitor to Berkeley commented that all the conversation concerned the troubled times, the plantation master's thoughts were turning to his troubled affairs. No titular Harrison clan-head had ever so diverted his attention from planting and mercantile enterprises as had Benjamin Harrison V. As his father's friend, William Byrd, had discovered about his inherited Indian trading, the commercial adjuncts of planting did not run themselves.

Several years before Harrison had sold on the stocks for £1,100 sterling a double-decked, 110 ton vessel, with a capacity of 380 hogshead of tobacco. That was cash come and gone, without the continuity of income that his father and grandfather established by shipping cargoes in their own vessels. By 1774 easygoing, self-assured Ben Harrison was becoming aware of his failure in the commercial aspects of his planting-shipbuilding center, and admitted his limitations in a most significant way. While all preceding Harrisons had learned these commercial aspects, as they learned their ABC's and riding and use of authority, on their family's plantation, the fifth Benjamin Harrison planned to send his first-born son, then nineteen, to Philadelphia to learn business in a mercantile house.

Not only had the acquisitive strain run dry by his generation, but the years devoted to committees and debates, the decade concentrated on the troubles with England and with upstarts in the colony, had turned his attention from the figures, details and calculations which form the backbone of commerce. His long stretches away from home had made Berkeley, for practical purposes, almost an absentee-owned plantation. Certainly Harrison lacked the time—and even the mood when he came home—to supervise his plantation with the attention to detail which the complex, interrelating operation demanded.

With the flow of cash no longer constant, slaves could not always be replaced. On his roster of "Negroes," under "Remarks" there was a discouraging number of listings such as, "Superannuated," "Mad," "Infirm," "Worthless," "Crippled," and beside their names, under "Value," he wrote a neat row of zeroes. They were mouths to be fed, bodies to be clothed and housed, for it was an unwritten law among planters that no man of honor would ever set free a Negro who could no longer work.

Finally, the first-born son inherited, along with the manor and titular clan-leadership, involved administrative work in settling the estates of brothers and sisters, their in-laws and children. It all comprised a full-time job, requiring unflagging concentration on details, and with Ben Harrison the obligations inherent in his class privilege superseded in importance his personal affairs. Planting and not politics had become avocational.

None of the traits and habits ascribed to the mythical Old Massa caused large Ben Harrison to face this decline of his fortunes. His only indulgences were in food and wine. He cared little for shooting or the hunting field, though he was a magnificent rider, and the only money he spent on horses was for utilitarian purposes. He was addicted neither to gambling nor wenching, and his personal wardrobe became so skimpy that he joked with a servant who asked him what he wanted laid out for a trip. As with his forebears, he enjoyed most the companionship of his family, all the interlocking branches, and of friends who were likely in some way to be related. In brief, the affable gentleman fulfilled the requirements demanded by Julius Caesar:

*"Let me have men about me that are fat;*
*Sleek-headed men and such as sleep o' nights."*

These men are not the stuff of revolutionary plotters. The revolutionists come from the lank Patrick Henry type, which Caesar summed up with—

*"Yond Cassius has a lean and hungry look;*
*He thinks too much: such men are dangerous."*

Tom Jefferson, pragmatic idealist and affectionate younger kinsman of Harrison's friend Peyton Randolph, recognized that both types were necessary for a successful colonial movement. The revolutionists were necessary to shake apathy into excitement and to give voice to bold concepts that would set the progressive conservatives to thinking. When action came, the solid men of prudence would get the job done. Certainly without the most solid of them, George Washington, the radicals' secession movement would have aborted quickly indeed.

Washington turned out to be simply the biggest where the Colonies needed it the most. Ben Harrison, checking with an overseer the measure of his corn crop and, being a man of sanguine temperament, diverting his mind to the pleasant details of helping arrange Christmas boxes and provisioning powder for the firing of guns on Christmas morning, was not concerned about the future roles of himself and his friends as rough weather struck eastern Virginia in late December and kept the family around the fireplace.

4

From the quiet fall and early winter of 1774, family-man Harrison faced the new year with no premonition that in 1775 the gathering forces would rush toward the climax. Verbal exchanges would become physical combat, and the leaders of the Colonies—with their deep and immutable differences—would grope through what might be called The Year of Indecision.

War became a reality in all except name because the conservative colonial majority *did not wish to secede from England* and would not admit that "incidents" involving firearms constituted war. All the inflamed oratory of schoolbook heroes, and all the dedication to independence of those who became the heroes of egalitarian historians, could not without the blunders of the British ministry have moved the coalition of Southern planters ("haughty Sultans of the South") and Eastern financial powers. Jefferson and Richard Henry Lee from Virginia, Sam and John Adams from Massachusetts, *used* the incidents and the attitudes of England to work on the seemingly immovable body of wealthy conservatives, but the British government rather than patriotic inspiration provided the impetus.

The British ministry had committed itself to a belief in the rightness of might, and refused to take seriously the protests based upon theories of political liberties and human dignity. The fact was, as the British saw it, that a motley group of colonial dependents had become self-assertively troublesome, and must be coddled or whipped back into line—or both. The British lacked a clearly defined policy because the ministry arrogantly refused to consider merits in the colonials' petitions for self-government. In the eyes of the British ministry the Colonies lacked the power to support their pretentious claims, and that's all there was to it; the laboriously reasoned colonial protests were no more than the words of a stubborn child threatening his parents.

There *were* an awful lot of words, as the colonial writers kept redefining their grievances and the nature of their status, and in time the British Ministry even stopped reading the repetitious declarations. This was their mistake of omission. The various declarations only appeared repetitious to a bored party. Each paper went just a little further than the one before. The more the writers were ignored the stronger became their protests, and an interested observer (as some ignored Britishers were) could recognize the enormity of the change in a 1775 document from Richard Bland's first temperate definition a decade earlier.

In their smugness, the British finally missed the local purposes for which Jefferson (the most tireless and effective of the writers) was using his various documents. Widely distributed, the protests continued to keep the populace aroused (as Jefferson said, the citizens sometimes tended to forget their grievances) and, by constant elaboration and development of a single theme, the papers served as a guide for united action in Virginia and among the Colonies. Jefferson was to write thousands of words, and the conservatives like Benjamin Harrison were to attend hundreds of sessions of conventions, congresses, committee meetings and private meetings, before there was either unanimity or action.

In retrospect all such breaks seem inevitable and a long time in getting to the point. Even with perspective we are conditioned by early history reading which represents a few fearless patriots stampeding the righteously indignant Americans, with the rallying cry of "equality for all," to a sudden fourth of July rush to "independence" from a hated tyrant. Of course, there was a small segment of Tories, those loyalists to England who refused to join their fellow colonials in a secession movement; and a little reading beyond schoolbook history reveals an inexplicably minute proportion of able-bodied Americans who fought for independence. However, the heroism of Valley Forge usually glosses over those statistics—unless one asks why were there so few at Valley Forge and why, in a fat agricultural country, were those few starving?

The answer to that question reveals that the break was not inevitable through the nature of the revolutionary movement or the personnel structure of the Colonies. Had the intercolonial divisions been stressed instead of the myths, "democracy" would not have become such a cheaply used word, nor the heroes of the democratic movement bloodless symbols of a generality that is taken for granted as if, indeed, the emergence of a republic on this continent had been a simple inevitability—a matter of a few grandiloquent phrases, a few faceless patriots suffering one winter under a leader as de-personalized as a bad statue—and suddenly there was *America, the beautiful,* with the "American dream" that guaranteed equality to everybody and responsibility to nobody.

This treacly falsification has removed the colonial independence movement from the frame of its time. Despite a growing self-awareness among the colonials, most of the colonies were composed of *citizens who considered themselves British and who were not preoccupied with severance.* Though their troubles were with a British Ministry which refused them the rights of those other Britishers who lived in England, these citizens by no means included all England in their resentment of Parliament, nor was the average Englishmen preoccupied with keeping down distant colonials.

Englishmen were enjoying that last century of pleasure in the Western World, which was in a way characterized by Casanova (born one year before Benjamin Harrison), then running out the string of his curious career in 1775. In that year Sheridan, a young Irishman, introduced neo-Restoration drama in London with *The Rivals,* and two years before another Irishman, Oliver Goldsmith, had delighted audiences with *She Stoops to Conquer.* Virginians were eagerly buying those plays, and English novels and clothes and furniture, and writing to English relatives and to sons in college and to friends and business associates. Societal cleavage between American and British was not a fact in most colonies, and in Virginia least of all.

Instead, the cleavage existed among the colonies. Their clashing differences in economics and culture, in character and customs, formed groups so antithetical that some of the individual regional representatives regarded others with an abiding hatred.

Carter Braxton, Harrison's extremely conservative cousin and a later replacement in the Virginia delegation, said of New Englanders, "I hate their government—I hate their religion—I hate their *level-*

*ling.*" That harshly intemperate spokesman for the aristocracy did not italicize his oddly modern description of the people's rule.

From the other side, John Adams limited his sectional prejudice to personalities, and recorded spitefully inaccurate observations on Benjamin Harrison as a member of "the cold party"—not as advanced as Adams's Virginia friends Jefferson and Richard Henry Lee. With all of Adams's superior qualities, he was ill-natured and a hater, and his judgment of men was often warped by his personal feelings. He and the large planter were antithetical types, with nothing remotely in common, and their mutual dislike was instinctive and courteous. But Adams was compelled to derogate this bluff, self-possessed gentleman who carried a homegrown feud with Adams's ally, Lee, to Philadelphia. Perhaps Adams was ruffled a little, too, when, in one of the bickerings between jealous regions, Harrison jokingly suggested that Congress vote New England three million dollars a year and let them fight the war in their own way.

Brooding over this imperturbable Virginian, Adams confided in his diary that Harrison was "an indolent, luxurious, heavy gentleman, reported to be . . . at home . . . a cornerstone in which the two walls of party meet." Though certainly Adams did not mean this as a compliment, the description of Harrison's function in revolutionary times would describe a very useful citizen, and his fellow Virginians so regarded him. Adams did not let it go at that. In denial of facts, he confided that his enemy was "of no use in Congress of Committee," though Harrison was appointed to the chairmanship of the most important committees as long as he stayed in Philadelphia, and almost continually was made chairman of The Committee of the Whole, second in importance only to the president's chair.

Although later Adams conceded Harrison's contributions and "many pleasantries" that steadied rough sessions, the clashing passions involved in united action are illustrated by venomousness of even John Adams to a fellow patriot whose views differed from his own.

Since these typical personality differences occurred between the two powerful colonies which were the most strongly allied and the most advanced as groups in their demands on England, it can be imagined what differences existed among the representatives of colonies which were lukewarm to the whole idea. Because of these deeply rooted, intercolonial antagonisms and antithetical aims, no movement from within would have united the colonies. When united action came, it was against a common enemy, not the alliance of friends.

Let us say, the events came as an amalgam of the British and colonial reactions to each other and as even events need personalization, in Virginia the events leading to the end came in the short person of the governor, Lord Dunmore.

5

Until the spring of 1775, the amenities had been observed between the courteous natives and the socially trained nobleman, whose three young daughters attracted Tidewater bucks to the Palace in droves. Virginians were accustomed to liking their governors, with whom lasting personal friendships had been formed, and Dunmore—acting something like a pompous gentleman in evening clothes with a burning hot potato in his hands—was determined to preserve at all costs the dignity of Britain and its lords. Since every time the Assembly met, its complaints and resolutions grew more seditious from his viewpoint, Dunmore prorogued that representative body with such regularity that Virginia had in effect no official government—except that symbolized by His Lordship, isolated in his Palace in Williamsburg. What the proud-minded Scotsman had succeeded in doing was to eliminate himself—and the Ministry he represented—from the government of Virginia. For the Virginians went right on conducting their own affairs in their own way.

During this period without official government, the unsettled colony revealed the striking effectiveness of the oligarchy as a *de facto* government. Even with no courts meeting and no law-enforcement officers, and even with the potential menace of a population of black slaves, life in Virginia flowed without incident in its accustomed channels from the centers of the plantation. There was no increase in crime, no violence. At the county level, representatives of the oligarchy formed committees to control affairs. With the stimulus of a sense of emergency, county militias multiplied in number under the patriarchal command of the county "colonels," like Benjamin Harrison; and younger men with some fragmentary military experience—such as Harrison's brothers, who had fought with Washington and Braddock—took command at the lower levels and began drilling the jocular bumpkins in earnest. For all practical purposes, because of Dunmore's ineffectual measures, Virginians had achieved their goal of self-government under a nominal monarchy.

In late March, virtually the same body that composed the Assembly met for the second Virginia Convention, with the purpose of designing measures for the solution of their ambiguous situation, of electing delegates to the second Continental Congress at Philadelphia, and of instructing them on the basis of the resolves. Since the Burgesses' wing of the Capitol at Williamsburg was closed to them, the members of the Convention met in the little city of Richmond, straggling up hillsides from the river with scattered houses perched above warehouses and wharves and taverns.

The only public building was small, white-framed St. John's Church, of the established Church of England and the state religion. It was pleasantly situated on the plateau called Church Hill (in honor of St. John's) but inside the pews were narrow and too close together for the large Benjamin Harrison and his well-fed friends. Harrison and the Tidewater grandees were very sharply distinguished from the up-country representatives by their attire: the big planters wore British-imported clothes, delivered to their wharves with mercantile cargoes, while the "Westerners" wore homespun, sometimes buckskin.

The lines between political positions were more difficult to determine. At one extreme were the radicals, young Jefferson, stately Richard Henry Lee, the coarser Patrick Henry and the liberal-minded George Mason. At the other extreme stood the Old Guard, the *status quo* conservatives: vigilant of Virginia's rights, they were equally vigilant against allowing in power those revolutionaries who would lead to secession from the mother country.

Between the extremes was not Benjamin Harrison alone, as the "cornerstone" mentioned by John Adams, but a group—including Harrison, Washington and the convention president, Peyton Randolph—who might be described as progressive conservatives. They shared more native sympathy with the Old Guard, but they were less set in their political ways and more open to *gradual* change. They were most typical of the Virginia character over its whole history in that they resisted sudden change, and all change for the sake of the change. But, though their susceptibility to any change had to be measured by light-years rather than observed by the naked eye, they *would* change—if not crowded.

The lines between the three undefined parties were very dim. It must be remembered that most Convention members were kin to one or several of the others, that they were a homogeneous people of roughly a single background, and each according to his convictions was dedicated to the welfare of Virginia. No man was there solely to make a reputation. Many (like Harrison) were there at severe personal sacrifice, and all were there not as politicians but as Virginians with a responsibility to the land they loved. Because of their dominating sense of personal honor ("sacred honor," as they said, and meant it), they were not motivated by "party" loyalty in voting. Voting by conscience, individuals formed fluid and shifting majorities.

Sometimes the Harrison progressive-conservatives would vote with the Old Guard, sometimes with the radicals; less arteriosclerotic old-liners would sometimes vote with the middle group. Occasionally one of the stiffest traditionalists would grow enraged at some British insult which he took personally and would out-do any radical in a single action. Then he would return to the *status quo* as if his impulse had never happened. The farseeing radicals like Jefferson would conciliate the middle group, recognizing they held the balance of power.

With all representatives seated without grouping in the church, the proceedings began in orderly enough fashion with the reading of various innocuous resolves by President Peyton Randolph. Then came a "Resolve" to express gratitude to the Jamaica Assembly for its efforts to re-establish harmony between Britain and her Colonies, and to assure the Jamaicans of "the most ardent wish of this colony . . . to see a speedy return of those halcyon days, when we lived a free and happy people."

The representatives as a whole nodded in satisfaction over this expression of their sentiments, but not Patrick Henry. With all his slothfulness and indifference to study, his instinct for a people's temper had deepened as the hostile forces became joined, and he knew that the time had passed for such pious generalities. When he arose he had a prepared resolution of his own which, following the decorous memorial, came like a counter-resolution.

He proposed, in substance, the establishment of a permanent

and "well-regulated militia, composed of gentlemen and yeomen," as "the natural strength and only security of a free government." This standing force would make it unnecessary for the mother country to keep among the people an "army of mercenaries" and "obviate the pretext of taxing us for their support." With that preamble, in bolder words he came to the real point.

Mentioning that Dunmore's refusal to call them together in legislative capacity "renders it too insecure, in this time of danger and distress," to rely on England "to secure our inestimable rights and liberties," Henry then resolved that "this colony be immediately put into a state of defense."

Since this military defense could be directed only against England, all the conservatives arose in a body to protest this harsh repudiation of the resistance-policy that aimed for a reconciliation. Benjamin Harrison and Richard Bland, then grown old and half blind, joined with other middle-roaders of the oligarchy and argued that such a threatening tone would undo all the progress made by the hitherto gentlemanly statements of their demands and would equally vitiate any effect on the British merchant class of the boycott of British merchandise. After all, the purpose was not to antagonize the friendly Britons who argued their cause in England, or to show rebelliousness to the Crown, but to wring concessions from the current Ministry and their mercantile supporters. And, they pointed out, Lord North was even then preparing a conciliatory offer in answer to their last petition. It was not that they disagreed with the principle, but the timing was off.

Then, they argued, suppose Great Britain took up the gauntlet, and sent its established armies and navies against a scattering of unarmed people without military organization or the stores of war? The defenseless people would fall "an easy prey to Great Britain," and the result would be "to convert the illegitimate right which the British parliament now claimed into a firm and indubitable right by conquest."

Though the plantation masters did not mention reprisals in the destruction and confiscation of their estates in war, nor their own humbling in the world in the heat of defeat, they spoke from their hearts when they said that military defeat would forever remove "the strength and luster which we derived from our connection with Great Britain" and "the domestic comforts which we had drawn from the same source." This was the crux of the moderates' position from New York to Georgia: this was the human stand of the men of property with everything to lose and very dubious gains.

For the first time the crux of the moderates' position was answered by an argument that went to the heart of the whole matter. When Patrick Henry arose, he was not restrained by the need of presenting a logically arranged progression of arguments, or of trying to match legalities and learning with the orderly minded. As a true revolutionary, Patrick Henry was convinced of the truth of his vision, and out of this conviction he hurled his impassioned oratory at the august body as though they were a county jury to be swayed not by reason but only by his vision.

Though the ambitious man rose to higher estate later, this was his supreme moment. He made the greatest speech of his life; it was probably the greatest speech made in the revolutionary movement.

He started quietly, like an old pro, acknowledging the patriotism of the gentlemen who had spoken, and said, "Mr. President, it is natural for man to indulge in the illusions of hope." Then he began to warm up a little, and asked what in the past ten years of the British Ministry justified hope? "Is it that insidious smile with which our petition has been lately received? . . . Suffer not yourselves to be betrayed wth a kiss. Ask yourselves how this gracious reception of our petition comports with those warlike preparations whch cover our waters and darken our land. . . . Have we shown ourselves so unwilling to be reconciled that force must be called in to win back our love? . . . These are the implements of war and subjugation—the last arguments to which kings resort."

From here on he began to soar. "We have done everything that can be done to avert the storm which is now coming on. We have petitioned . . . remonstrated . . . supplicated . . . prostrated our-selves before the throne, and have implored its interposition to arrest the tyrannical hands of the ministry and parliament. . . . In vain, after all these things, may we indulge the fond hope of peace and reconciliation. There is no longer any room for hope."

Then, to the hushed gentlemen cramped in thc pews of the little church, his voice bugled out the words that not one of them had ever expected to hear on this earth.

"If we wish to be free . . . we must fight! I repeat it, sir, we must fight!! An appeal to arms and the God of Hosts is all that is left us."

One of the listeners, in recording his sensation years later, wrote a friend, "Imagine to yourself . . . the Roman senate, assembled in the capitol . . . imagine that you heard Cato addressing such a senate —imagine that you saw the handwriting on the wall of Belshazzar's palace—imagine that you heard a voice as from heaven uttering the words, '*We must fight*,' as the doom of fate . . ."

Sensing that he had his audience, Henry demolished the arguments of the Colonies' physical weakness. When would they be stronger un-der British rule? But, "there is a just God who presides over the des-tinies of nations . . ." and ". . . the battle is not to the strong alone; it is to the vigilant, the brave, the active." Besides, he shouted, they had no choice. "Gentlemen may cry peace, peace, peace—but there is no peace. The war is actually begun! The next gale that sweeps from the north will bring to our ears the clash of resounding arms." This was an accurate prophecy.

It was then, himself as carried away as his auditors, that Henry, his arms flung aloft, shouted the deathless words. "Is life so dear or peace so sweet, as to be purchased at the price of chains and slavery? Forbid it, Almighty God. I know not what course others may take; but as for me, give me liberty or give me death!"

He walked back to his pew in a profound silence. The men sat motionless, as though transfixed. Their trance was only broken when Richard Henry Lee arose to support Henry. Though Lee spoke eloquently, the fidgeting representatives could barely hear him out. They had had enough of words. They wanted the action of a vote.

Alas, even the most powerful speech of the Revolution did not cause colonials to jump to their feet, shouting, "Liberty, democracy, equality." On the issue only of whether to arm for any eventuality, the vote was almost even—65 for to 60 against.

However, once the balance-of-power moderates committed them-selves to any measure, they wholeheartedly put their backs to it. They might not be convinced that war had actually begun but, in their eminent common sense, the conservatives had been convinced that practical intelligence dictated preparation for all contingencies and not dependence on the British Ministry's compromise. Also, though not wanting a war of separation, the planters had been touched on a point of pride: they would not admit they feared the consequences of war if it came, and they were well aware of the consequences.

Later in Philadelphia, large Ben Harrison said to Elbridge Gerry, a small New Englander, "When the time of hanging comes, I shall have the advantage over you. It will be all over with me in a minute, but you will be kicking in the air for half an hour after I am gone."

Recognizing the work that the moderates would do once they were won over, for the committee for action on the resolution to arm, the convention appointed Benjamin Harrison, George Washington and other big planters, along with Jefferson, Henry and Richard Henry Lee.

Of Harrison's group, Jefferson said, "These were honest and able men, who had begun the opposition (to Britain) on the same grounds, but with a moderation more adapted to their age and experience. . . . Events favored the bolder spirits," but the older men, "differing nothing from us in principle, quickened their gait somewhat beyond that which their prudence, of itself, might have advised . . . and by this harmony of the bold with the cautious, we advanced, with our constituents, in undivided mass, and with fewer examples of separation than perhaps existed in any other part of the union."

Unanimity at home had been won on a crucial issue, really a turning point, and the delegates to Philadelphia were instructed to offer a resolution for "the taking up of arms" in all the colonies. Then the convention, aroused by its own daring, threw down another gauntlet on a local issue. They resolved to defy the British prohibition on manufacturing and not even ask for parliamentary permission to begin.

All this was quite too much for his Lordship, the governor in a Williamsburg that had become disturbingly silent. Earlier, probably on instructions, he had forbidden Virginia's civil authorities to appoint delegates to the forthcoming Continental Congress. When his proclamation was ignored, Dunmore faced the reality that Virginia's civil officers were responsible to the oligarchy who met in Richmond and not to the King's governor. The damn Virginians acted as if he weren't even alive. Once the outraged nobleman decided to show the colonials that he was very much alive, Dunmore began a series of at first inept and then barbarous actions, for which the best that could be said was that they reflected the Ministry's determination to teach the dogs a lesson.

6

Dunmore's first act intended to show his authority actually ended it. In April the governor secretly by night, like an *opéra-bouffe* plotter, smuggled into the Palace some armed sailors from a British man-of-war in the York River. Before dawn these worthies stole across the dark Public Square to the octagonal brick building which housed the colony's powder. This they transferred to the governor's wagon and gleefully scurried back behind the high walls of the Palace.

Early in the morning the citizens' guard for the magazine showed up for their duties and found most of their powder gone. The reaction of the populace demonstrated that Patrick Henry, with his sensitivity to the people's pulse, had correctly gauged their temper. Militia, armed citizens and excited young men came pouring into the wide streets of Williamsburg, where the trees were in full spring foliage and early flowers in bloom. Within hours, the armed crowd was ready to storm the Palace and seize the governor.

Portly Peyton Randolph, preparing for his trip to Philadelphia for the Continental Congress, hastened from his house to make personal appeals to the crowd, which included his young nephew, Ben Harrison's teen-age son. As a moderate who wanted of all things to avoid "incidents," the jowly gentleman managed to restrain the leaders and sent instead a formal protest to Dunmore. His Lordship, frightened by the menace, offered the lame excuse that he had appropriated the powder because of a threatened slave insurrection and promised to return it.

Not knowing of the governor's capitulation, a group of mounted militia collected in Fredericksburg, a planters' shipping center on the Rappahannock in mid-Virginia, fifty miles north of Richmond. George Washington's mother lived there, and the colonel of the First Virginia Regiment brought his prestige and massive presence to bear on the "cavalry" to restrain them. His Majesty's representative was being protected from British subjects by the Virginia oligarchy!

At his realization of this indignity, Dunmore in his panic swung from craven to blusterer. While Washington had held the cavalry at Fredericksburg, the governor sent Lady Dunmore and their children to a British vessel in the York, swelled his personal force by arming the house slaves, and threatened the mayor of Williamsburg with freeing the colony's slaves if his person were harmed, "and (to) reduce Williamsburg to ashes."

This weak bombast aroused in Virginians more contempt than anger, but Patrick Henry—lusting for the real glory in the field and anxious to precipitate incidents—seized on the tumult to march a body of Hanover County militia toward Williamsburg. This private army was composed largely of Henry's old hunting companions, and though he knew no more about military matters than did they, he fulfilled the role of leader in the true patriarchal sense. When he heard the news that this ferocious body was advancing, Dunmore swung back to conciliation. Declaring that the powder had disappeared, he sent a bill of exchange for its value with authorization for the force to acquire more.

Then, when Henry's country sharpshooters dispersed, Dunmore swung back once more and proclaimed Patrick Henry a "rebel." Ninety-nine years before, tough old Governor Berkeley had proclaimed Nathaniel Bacon, Henry's earlier prototype, a rebel and brought on civil war. The difference in the times was illustrated by the fact that nobody, not even Governor Dunmore, paid the slightest attention to the proclamation against Henry.

On the first of June, Dunmore was offered the opportunity to escape from his anomalous position by calling the Assembly to session for purposes of hearing the long-awaited proposals for conciliation from Lord North. During the spring turmoil, the Virginia delegates to the Continental Congress had been acting on two fronts—at home and in Philadelphia. When the Assembly was called by Dunmore, Peyton Randolph took leave of his chair as president of the Continental Congress and hurried back to Williamsburg to assume his post as speaker of the house. In Philadelphia, Benjamin Harrison and George Washington, who shared quarters with Randolph in a private house, represented his interests in Congress while he represented theirs in Williamsburg.

By then, also in April (as Henry had predicted), actual fighting had broken out in Massachusetts. British regulars had marched in daylight after a powder store at Concord and—with no one certain which side precipitated the action—the armed citizens and the redcoats opened fire on each other. The rebels scattered at first, but when the British returned to Boston, the troops came under punishing fire from running snipers on their flanks. This skirmish which began at Lexington was supposedly "the shot heard around the world," but the sound evidently came somewhat muffled to the members of the Continental Congress in the State House in Philadelphia, for they went on debating and trying to reach agreement on a resolution on "The Taking Up of Arms."

The outbreak must have impressed Lord Dunmore more than it did the colonials. After he called the Virginia Assembly to the capital in Williamsburg, his fear in a few days overcame his judgment and he joined his family, seeking sanctuary on the warship in the river. From the beginning, he had feared the Virginians, and his dignity lay in the externals of a lordship and not in the center of his character. Ten years before, when a crowd formed over the Stamp Act to mob the revenue collector, Francis Fauquier had walked among them to the porch of the Raleigh Tavern, and quieted the people by his personal dignity and by the force of the understanding affection he felt for Virginians. None of that was in Dunmore. When the Assembly adjourned in late June, he was scared to show up even to make the traditional closing speech.

On that day (June 20, 1775) England's original colony, after 167 years, in effect ceased to be a part of the British Empire. The outward forms were maintained for one more year, while the fugitive governor led armed slaves, renegades and British regulars against the citizens, and legal exchanges continued the fiction with all due regard for the conventions and the feelings of the Old Guard Anglophiles.

The first exchange concerned those proposals of Lord North for which the last Assembly had been called. Actually, the proposals were conciliatory, and offered exemption from taxation to Virginia, or any colony, under specified conditions which met with parliamentary approval. Setting here a "too little and too late" precedent, the British government—overruling protests from enlightened Englishmen—simply revealed that North's Ministry had missed the point by dismissing the resolutions on the nature of the compact.

Several years before, exemption from taxation for revenue had constituted the basis of the colonial command; by 1775, it was too late for that: the people had come to deny the right of Parliament to govern the Colonies in their internal affairs. On that rock, the Colonies and the home government at last, definitely and permanently, split. Too many colonials still wanted to patch things up for the split to be recognized formally for another year, and in that year the advanced revolutionists devoted their energies to moving the more prudent toward unanimity for the final step.

Thomas Jefferson, then appointed an alternate delegate to the Continental Congress, wrote Virginia's answer to Lord North's proposal and then hurried on to Philadelphia to collaborate on writing the Colonies' joint answer, on the resolution of "The Taking up of Arms," and on any document ostensibly designed for the British government that could serve to arouse the laggards at home.

7

In Philadelphia, debates were going on and committees were meeting for resolutions even though in Massachusetts a state of war already existed. In mid-June the Massachusetts patriots, emboldened by their Lexington-Concord affair and chafing beyond fictions with an occupation army in Boston, tried with the bold stroke of Breed's Hill (called Bunker Hill) to bottle up the British in the city. In driving away the militia, the redcoats suffered heavily and, adding no luster to their own reputation by clumsy front-order attacks on crack shots behind works, added no clarity to the situation by merely securing their position in Boston. Nor did the Bunker Hill action stir the delegates in Pennsylvania's State House to common cause with Massachusetts. In fact, some were inclined to permit Massachusetts to pull her own chestnuts out of the fire.

Before the Bunker Hill news reached the Congress, the delegates had already agreed to arm the Colonies for defense under a single command and had appointed George Washington commander-in-chief, with the rank of general.

The big, pock-marked plantation-master, who stoically suffered the experiments of colonial dentists on iron and wooden teeth, has come across time more as an abstraction than as a person. *First in war, first in peace, first in the hearts of his countrymen*—this alone is enough to dehumanize any man. Certainly he is not first in the hearts of people who inhabit the country he won, and George Washington personally would regard the nation that has evolved since his day with cold incomprehension.

First of all, George Washington was a product of the ruling class of Virginia's aristocratic republic. His antecedents were English, his affiliations were with English people and the Virginia-English. His experiences were largely limited to the plantation world of Eastern Virginia, and he had no real desire to extend his experiences beyond these limits. Like his close friend, Benjamin Harrison, Washington loved the planters' life and enjoyed with an earthy zest the physical details of living. Like all his friends, too, his obligations in the oligarchy required him to devote his services to his state. When his state allied with others for mutual defense, his ambition and sense of authority motivated him to seek leadership in the area where he felt best qualified to serve—in the military.

The plantation master suffered no delusions about his military gifts, nor did the Continental delegates who appointed him. Nor was the greatness he revealed in the ordeal presaged in any way at the Congress. Washington was picked, for a variety of sound political and practical reasons, primarily because he was a Virginia aristocrat, and not because he was some vaporless distillation of "The Patriot."

Any New Englander was eliminated from leadership because many of the delegates from other colonies (especially the rich conservatives) regarded them as troublemakers. This elimination made a Virginian the logical choice. Virginia was the largest and oldest colony; it had been a leader on principle in the struggle with England over colonial rights, and its representatives were as a group the most distinguished. Finally, despite all the later-day talk about democracy, the colonial representatives in 1775 agreed that an aristocrat, habituated to and a symbol of authority, should lead. This made *a* Virginian at least one inevitability of the movement.

The choice narrowed to George Washington partly because, in those realistic times, the delegates associated aristocracy with wealth (since all the colonial aristocrats were new enough to be aware that their positions had been won by financial power), and Washington had become the richest man in Virginia, perhaps in the Colonies. Not only was he richer than the other Virginia leaders, but while they were essentially men of the lamp, tall Washington, strongly built and superbly conditioned, looked as he was, a man of the field. Among a people without military organization or tradition, then, Washington, as a civilian, possessed all the attributes of natural leadership. Along with that, though his actual military experience was limited, it was at least as extensive as anyone's else, and he had evinced a taste for warfare.

In selecting Washington for these considerations, the Congress could not have known they had selected a man with the most enormous capacity for growth under pressure. In the literal definition of intelligence as adjustment to conditions, the big-boned planter was a highly intelligent man. Lacking the mental brilliance of the outstanding civil leaders, ungifted in self-expression (excepting awesome swearing when enraged), he conceived largely and soundly, and growing in the revolutionary war as the war demanded increasingly more of his gigantic character, Washington was the apogee of the progressive-conservative of his class and his state. He was the most dramatic vindication of the oligarchy's theory of producing from the plantation society superior individuals for leadership.

## CHAPTER IX

# THE "SIGNER"

1

*After* George Washington had been appointed commander-in-chief of Continental troops, the Virginia planter set out for Massachusetts to take command of the colonials besieging the British regulars in Boston, and Benjamin Harrison was left without a roommate. His brother-in-law, Peyton Randolph, returned later from the Virginia Assembly, but that close friend and political ally was soon to die in the strange city.

Randolph's place as president of Congress was taken by John Hancock, and when the time came for Hancock to take his seat, powerful Ben Harrison gave a display of his easy assurance among his peers. Thirty-eight-year-old John Hancock was distinguished not only as a Boston merchant and early activist against revenue enforcers, but as one of the proclaimed rebels specifically excluded from pardon by Britain. As the young man hesitated to take his seat in the president's chair, Harrison picked him up bodily and placed him in the chair. Then, smiling, he said to the Congress, "We will show Mother Britain how little we care for her by making a Massachusetts man our president, (and one) whom she has excluded from pardon by a public proclamation."

Harrison seemed to lose none of his good spirits by living alone, after Washington left and Randolph died. The high-living Virginian delighted his Northern friends with the lavishness of his entertainment and he was extremely busy in the ever-burgeoning committees. His talents were particularly suited for the work in one of the more constructive committees—that entrusted with the responsibility of transforming the various militias into something resembling a "national" army and preparing the force for mobile defense against any threatened area. Actually, they were organizing a military establishment where none grew before. Harrison enjoyed this work.

He neither liked to write nor talk in public, though, without shyness or self-consciousness, he was reasonably facile in either if put to it. A throwback to his great-grandfather—that second Harrison who established the family's position—he enjoyed the personality interplays and manipulation of committees. Here his bland self-possession soothed the friction between individuals and minimized those small details which in any committee some member seizes upon as important as life itself. Harrison was one of those sound, unoriginal men whose vision of the woods was never obscured by the trees.

His gifts were summarized (as well as recognized by his contemporaries) in the name of the important committee of which he was chairman—The Committee of the Whole. Having no personal ambitions and obviously happy in the interchange between male companions, Harrison was liked as a man. As a worker he was (as was Washington a leader) a perfected product of his class and state, a less heroic-sized but more typical vindication of the oligarchy's cultivation of superior individuals for government service.

With his intimate friends gone from his rented lodging, Harrison continued at the table in a city tavern with his feuding cousin, Richard Henry Lee, and others, with Tom Jefferson taking the seat of the absent George Washington. Across time, now that these mortal men have entered mythology, it is interesting to speculate on their conversation over food and wine. Certainly they did not talk constantly of their troubles with England. They were men away from home, and the nights ahead loomed no less long and lonely because their names are known in history. Even when they did talk of their reasons for being in the small-roomed city of Philadelphia—away from families and plantations—they undoubtedly indulged in discussions of personalities, discussions which their sense of dignity excluded from written notes on the occasion that became historic.

One of the most bedevilling personalities was John Dickinson, of

Pennsylvania. No great figure in the Revolution's mythology, Dickinson was very large in his day as a powerful, respected, and most dedicated *status quo* conservative. Since no one could question his patriotism, all deferred to his convictions, which personally epitomized on the continental level all that the Old Guard Virginians had felt back home.

It happened that Jefferson, as a young newcomer to Congress, had been placed (as the best writer from Virginia) on the committee suffering such difficulties producing that declaration on "The Necessity of Taking Up Arms." The unabashed young scholar immediately wrote one along the lines of his by then familiar theme: British injustice and (the rights of) colonial liberties. Dickinson, the conciliator, found it too strong, and rewrote a milder version. In its weakened form, the Declaration proved satisfactory to the majority of delegates, including independence-minded John Adams. To the Virginians, it was their own March convention in St. John's Church all over again on a continental scale—only in Philadelphia there was no Patrick Henry to galvanize the moderates.

John Dickinson, pleased with the reception of his rewrite of young Jefferson's version, then drafted a follow-up petition to the King, in which he bent the knee in all traditional humility. The members of Congress, as Jefferson said, "of their great desire not to go too fast for any respectable part of our body," resignedly passed the humble petition. This was too much for Benjamin Harrison.

When the petition had been voted on, Dickinson, though out of order, was compelled by his gratification to arise and say, "There is but one word, Mr. President, in the paper, which I disapprove, and that is the word *Congress*."

Since order had been broken, Harrison then arose and said disgustedly, "There is but one word in the paper, Mr. President, of which I approve, and that is the word *Congress*."

This came from a moderate, who only a few months earlier in Richmond had been opposed to "the necessity of taking up arms." But arms *had* been taken up and Harrison, like Washington, was the ultimate realist. Once in at all, as they said, one might as well be in "body, boots and britches." Everything was on the line, and you can only hang once.

But your family can be impoverished, and this dread possibility must have occupied Harrison's mind when, during a break in Congress in August, the husband and father returned to the plantation at Berkeley. There, in his large study, he awaited the discouraging piles of papers which represented his broken tobacco trade with England, bills for last year's imports, and notations on crops made with no market for shipping. There in the mute figures stood the high cost of secession to the Berkeley family.

For the returned family man, the need of familiar comforts came first and accounts could be settled later. In the smothering month of August in Tidewater, all actions, even worries, were slowed by nature. The sometime planter took solace in the companionship of his wife, who had been the great beauty, in talking with his older children about their futures, and in walking around the plantation with his youngest son, two-and-one-half-year-old William Henry, who was to be president of the nation his father was helping bring to birth.

2

In September, all too soon, the master of Berkeley was back in rented quarters in the city of uniform houses, and beginning again the round of committee meetings and restaurant dinners. Taking things as he found them, Colonel Harrison was not disturbed by the atmosphere of unreality provided by the representatives of jealous colonies trying to wage a war that did not exist and trying to act like a confederation without being one.

There was nothing remotely revolutionary about the delegates in the small city of Quakers. Without a defined goal or a practical purpose, various groups puttered through the days according to their personal interests or assignments. Those assigned to money-raising through the printing of paper bills ("Continentals") showed such an unawareness of any urgency that General Washington wrote, from Boston, "What an astonishing thing it is, that those who are employed to sign the Continental bills should not be able, or inclined, to do it as fast as they are wanted. They will prove the destruction of this army, if they are not more attentive and diligent." Then as his wrath rose, he added, "such a dearth of public spirit, and want of virtue, such stock-jobbing, and fertility in all the low arts to obtain advantage . . . I never saw before, and pray God I may never be witness to again. . . ." Then he pled for the last sum voted, "as $100,000 will be but a flea-bite to our demands at this time."

Those members with nothing much to do, believing that any action was preferable to none, decided that General Washington should open the ceremonies with an attack on the British troops in Boston. They reasoned that, since the local militia had done so well at Bunker Hill, Washington's army should be able to drive the British regulars from Boston. To determine why their commander-in-chief preferred to send in complaints about Congress's inaction on such mundanities as money instead of doing something himself, Congress dispatched Colonel Benjamin Harrison, Dr. Benjamin Franklin and Hon. Thomas Lynch, as a committee of three, to make a trip for a personal conference with the smoldering general.

Ben Harrison found his old friend in the most rebellious mood of his life—not against the British but against the Americans. The big man's outrage strained against his self-control as he denounced Congress, the troops and the whole mess. Washington was doing his duty, according to his background and training, and he expected every other man to be motivated by the same self-sacrificing sense of responsibility. He forgot that he was dealing with citizens who were not identified with any emotional attachment beyond their immediate regions, and that the traditional military organization he was trying to build was foreign to the natures and experiences of illiterate farmers without any nationalism—no *patrie*, no *Vaterland*, no country. Yet, even allowing for General Washington's limitations in vision, matters in his motley collection of volunteers were palpably in a sorry state.

Washington was just beginning that losing struggle with politicians which was to prevent enlistments for the duration of the war. Reporting on "the egregious want of public spirit which reigns here," he wrote: "Instead of pressing to be engaged in the cause of their country, which I vainly flattered myself with being the case, I find that we are likely to be deserted, and in a most critical time. Those that have enlisted must have a furlough. . . ." In fact, ". . . such a dirty, mercenary spirit pervades the whole that I should not be surprised at any disaster that may happen."

New England was to produce splendid officers (like fat young Henry Knox, the Boston bookseller who became Washington's chief of artillery, and Nathanael Greene, the Rhode Island blacksmith's son who commanded brilliantly in the Southern theater) but at that time the "generals" were vainglorious and inept. As for attacking British regulars with his undisciplined horde led by clowns and fools, the very idea suggested the remoteness of Congress from the realities. Washington might have received no military education, but he recognized the vastly different requirements for attack and defense. At Bunker Hill, the men stood in works that protected most of their bodies and were required only to stand and shoot. Attack required highly ordered maneuver in the open against trained soldiers with artillery. Besides, what would he attack *with?* There was not enough powder for a skirmish.

Washington summed up his own feelings about the revolution at that stage with this line: "Could I have foreseen what I have, and am likely to experience, no consideration upon earth could have induced me to accept this command."

When the two Bens, Harrison and Franklin, with Mr. Lynch, reported the conditions to their compatriots, nothing was done. Nor was there any reason why much could logically be hoped for. Having no more nationalism than the soldiers, and no less self-interest than appears in any time or place, the assorted body of strangers was not vitalized by any passionate cause. All that electricity of independence sparkled, in glorious phrases, after the fact. Without real authority and no single boldly gifted leader, the members of Congress were tentative and uncertain, divided between secessionists and loyalists—divided, indeed, in their own minds.

Unlike the later French revolutionists, these men had no machinery of government, or of anything, to take over. As for building a government out of the air, many were not sure they wanted one, and those who were sure were not certain what kind of government they wanted. For all their efforts toward formal independence, the Jeffersons in Congress contributed nothing to administration. Washington and other men of capacity were in the field; the solid workers like Harrison did what they could in their own spheres, but the areas of assignment overlapped and conflicted and left gaping blanks. Harrison needed his wits and his energies merely to keep all his own committees straight, though it was an outrage to his sense of social proprieties that aroused him out of his routine.

In late November, Mrs. Martha Washington passed through Philadelphia on her way to join the general, and a group of friends planned a ball for her at the City Tavern. The general's lady was no heroine to the Tory ladies of Philadelphia, who could have supported such an event. Furthermore, the proposal to hold one fell afoul of a Congressional resolution against amusements, which was used by busybodies to prevent it. As there were threats of mob action, a committee with the backing of Sam Adams decided to call off the ball and so inform "Lady Washington." This pusillanimous action, flouting the principle of decorous pleasure and proper respect to a lady, shook Harrison out of his usual equanimity.

For this was not just any lady. Mrs. Washington's sister was married to Harrison's wife's brother, and she had come to Philadelphia from a visit with Harrison's brother-in-law in New Kent County in Tidewater. Big Ben Harrison stormed down to the lodgings of Sam Adams, where a group were congratulating themselves over coffee for having stopped the entertainment. It was the only time in his Philadelphia years that a witness reported Harrison "out of humor," as he argued for the ball to be held. When his arguments failed to move the negaters, Harrison left still raging, and turned his attentions back to the less controversial and emotional area of committee.

In November, he was appointed chairman of a new committee—the forerunner of the committee on foreign affairs (like the foreign office of the State Department)—which made Harrison more or less the Foreign Secretary. Having politically matured in Williamsburg during the territorial struggles that flared into the French and Indian War, Harrison was aware of France's smarting urge to curtail Britain as a colonial power, and the colonials were without illusions about horse trading in high diplomacy. The timidity of the committee's instructions reduced their actions to a feeling-out, but even this indicated a recognition of the drift toward a test by arms and the need of European allies.

With the turn of the year, 1776, several factors caused the growth of a sense of hopelessness over the possibilities of a reconciliation and more delegates became convinced, however resignedly, that the differences could only be resolved by asserting independence and attempting to resist armed subjugation.

First, the British Ministry antagonized many middle-roaders of high position by a rude dismissal of that petition which John Dickinson had written with such regard for British sensibilities; then, many waverers were won over by the timely appearance of Paine's *Common Sense*, which was just that: the plain statement of the American case. Finally, in the spring, matters came suddenly to a head in Virginia. Lord Dunmore, despite the hard core of loyalists and the power of the conservatives, succeeded in uniting a majority against Britain in the country's first declaration of independence.

3

When the British governor became a self-made fugitive from Williamsburg during the summer of 1775, he seemed driven chiefly by a vengeful spirit toward the citizens who had caused his indignity. Based on British warships in the great watery area of Chesapeake Bay, he directed landing parties composed of sailors and regulars, armed slaves and renegades, in destructive raids on plantations and outlying communities, stealing slaves and provisions. In the early fall, emboldened by success and grown aware of the strong loyalist sentiment in the Norfolk region, Dunmore conceived the strategic stroke of seizing the port city.

Norfolk had become the commercial center for the country south of the James River, three miles wide where it empties into Hampton Roads at Norfolk, and more than any other Virginia community it was populated with English and Scotch merchants and clerks. Like Philadelphia and New York, whose merchant-class loyalists later welcomed the British, Norfolk's native-born shipping and mercantile class were more closely linked by all bonds to England than to local revolutionaries. When Dunmore came, the poor and ignorant, caught under the joint rule of their economic betters and British force, signed loyalty oaths of allegiance and the city was British.

Dunmore at that stage had in his control a base which would have caused the colonial struggle an acute military embarrassment, as well as seriously weakened the revolutionary movement in Virginia. The probability is that he could have held this open port until the formalization of hostilities brought British forces in strength. But the vain nobleman, still motivated by vengeance for his humiliations and seeing his advantage only as a means of gratifying his personal spite, committed the one act guaranteed to lose the support of the conservative planter class. He proclaimed the slaves free and tried to incite them to insurrection.

Taking this from threat to actuality, he armed the several hundred runaways who reached his lines and, with loyalists and regulars, pillaged the countryside. In the late fall of 1775, Dunmore accomplished what all the speeches of Henry and the writings of Jefferson had failed to. He broke the back of the Old Guard resistance to the secession movement. If he represented monarchy, they would take their chances with revolution.

Until then, with Jefferson and Richard Henry Lee away in Philadelphia, Virginia's extemporized government in the Committee of Safety had been under the control of the less flexible conservatives of the oligarchy, who with political adroitness euchered Patrick Henry out of the play. Henry at that time—and not Jefferson or Washington, or any of those who were later to emerge in leadership—was the most popular man in Virginia. He had the people with him. While his fellow Virginians were away struggling in the mental miasmas of the Continental Congress, Henry's ambitions caused him to seize that hour to solidify himself in power at home. He made a tactical mistake.

Knowing, before the certainty became general, that arbitration by arms had then become inevitable, Henry wanted to be the Man on Horseback. Leaving the unglamorous duties of the Committee of Safety to the Old Guard, Henry blossomed out as colonel of the First Virginia Regiment (founded by George Washington) and came with his troops to Williamsburg primed for the heroics of war and the glory of freeing Virginia from the tyrant Dunmore.

The oligarchs had not the least intention of sitting by supinely while the rabble-rouser became the man of the hour. There was a *Second* Virginia Regiment, commanded by Colonel William Woodford, a politically safe gentleman who possessed (in the eyes of the conservatives) the inestimable advantage of military experience. The Committee of Safety, explaining their choice of Woodford on the grounds of his training for the hazardous enterprise, dispatched the Second Virginia toward Norfolk and put Henry's First Virginia to guard-mounting in Williamsburg during December's dreary weather. There was nothing either he or his followers could do, since the military operated under the authority of the civilian government.

Woodford showed an understanding of the rudiments of warfare and an extreme caution, which was probably suitable for one leading militia against a nucleus of British regulars, supported by cannons and their armed mob of loyalists and Negroes. In a succession of counter-offensives, after receiving attack, he permitted the British regulars to defeat themselves and in retreat to stampede their irregulars who—as Woodford must have realized—were deadly on a running enemy but would themselves run when the tide turned. They ran all the way out of Norfolk at the end of the year, 1775, and the Virginia port was saved without creating a people's hero. In fact, by the not very curious omissions, considering the emphases of American historians, Wood-ford, the Battle of Great Bridge, and the recapture of Norfolk are not even mentioned in footnotes as comprising a decisive Continental victory and the first forcible ejection of British rule from American soil.

Dunmore had one final act of spite to contribute to Virginia's rapid course toward independence. Back on his ships in the harbor, on New Year's Day (1776), he bombarded the city where the loyalists had given him refuge and, under cover of the heavy guns, sent in landing parties to set houses afire. The then thoroughly violent militia, while driving out the landing parties, set more fires indiscriminately—except for the warehouses containing whiskey—and Norfolk was no more. Dunmore lurked around the waters until July, ravaging the shore lines of Virginia and Maryland, before he sailed away to his native Scotland with his vengeance still unsated.

Long before his ignominious departure, things had moved very fast to a climax in Virginia. On May sixth, Virginia's Revolutionary Convention met for the last time—with Harrison, Jefferson and the others still away in Philadelphia—and the oligarchy-controlled Committee of Safety was ready to admit that it was all over between Britain and Virginia. They could no longer observe the forms of colonial dependence when the fugitive British governor was engaged in senseless pillaging of innocent people, when the courts had not been held for two years (with cases pending against British Loyalists), and when, in brief, Virginia existed in a state of *de facto* independence and England related only as a *de facto* enemy. The times demanded a government to fit the circumstance.

In designing a new government for an independent commonwealth in emergency alliance with other colonies, the Virginians revealed a casual pride in the unself-conscious awareness of their power on the Continent. Since they were to be independent, the Virginians instructed their delegation in Philadelphia to declare formally for colonial independence, for a confederation of the Colonies, and for foreign alliances. They expected all this to happen because *their* delegates suggested it, and it did. Richard Henry Lee had written home that nothing would be done until Virginia did it first.

The Virginians in Williamsburg, indeed, considered their instructions to their delegates in Philadelphia as tantamount to making independence an accomplished fact, and on May fifteenth solemnized the occasion by a Declaration of Rights. Written mostly by liberal-minded George Mason, the Virginia Declaration, first introducing as a government principle the rights of man, served as the model for Jefferson's more famous preamble to the Declaration of Independence and as the precursor of the Bill of Rights. As was said on its 180th anniversary by Dag Hammarskjold, Secretary-General of the United Nations, it "may be considered to mark the beginning of a series of declarations of human rights leading up to the Universal Declaration proclaimed in 1948 by the General Assembly of the United Nations."

At this time, the Virginians' awareness of their historic hour was expressed in a verse which, freely translated from the language of the day, ended:

*With just disdain and most becoming pride,*
*Further dependence on the Crown is denied,*
*And as long as freedom's voice can in these wilds be heard,*
*Virginia's patriots shall be still revered.*

Though they were somewhat optimistic about future reverence for Virginia's patriots, the exhilarated people gave the grandest celebration in the colony's history in the warm, shady streets of Williamsburg —again, as in the preceding year's last meeting of the Assembly, in full spring bloom. Combining the more riotous features of wedding and race meet, funeral and fair, Christmas and county election, the citizens fired guns and drank toasts and climaxed the day with pulling down the British flag and raising the Continental banner over their lovely red brick Capitol.

After all the evolutionary phases and changing eras since Jamestown, the English transmuted into Virginians had become a free people in an independent republic. The war that affirmed their position was a matter of details: the act of independence, the fulfillment of the revolutionary movement, came on May 15, 1776.

4

In Philadelphia, the members of the Continental Congress were in the mood to accept official recognition of their status. In March, in the trouble spot of Boston, a show of strength by Washington had inexplicably rid the city of British troops and given a stimulant to the colonials' weak sense of self-reliance. Washington's makeshift army had received the material support of forty-three British cannon, which young Henry Knox sledded down from captured Fort Ticonderoga, and with these armaments of war General Washington occupied the hills overlooking Boston and opened fire on the city. Instead of sending his troops out from their fortifications, the British General Howe sailed them away, out of harm's way.

Nobody has yet explained the enigmatic behavior of genial Sir William Howe during his three years of command. An able commander and trained soldier, he repeatedly defeated the colonials in battle and never followed up an advantage. Much has been made of his preference for luxurious city quarters over the rigors of camp, of his hedonistic pleasures in champagne suppers, and of his attachment to his Boston mistress, Mrs. Loring, whose complaisant husband used the liaison to fatten his pockets through purchasing departments.

Many British officers enjoyed the favors of American mistresses, and showed a pronounced leaning toward champagne suppers, but with Howe it was something more, something that went deeper. It was as if, a man of honor, he performed his job within the narrowest limitations of duty and, beyond that, he did not really want to defeat the Americans. Perhaps, believing in conciliation, he hoped the colonials would wear themselves out and return to the Empire without the dislocations and hatred brought on by suffering a brutal conquest. In any event, General Howe evacuated Boston before the war became official, and the city of the revolutionary incidents did not figure in the actual fighting.

In the Continental Congress in the summer of 1776 nothing was known of the pacific nature with which a British general was to go through the motions of subjugation by arms, and on June seventh Richard Henry Lee introduced Virginia's resolution for independence. A committee for drafting the declaration was immediately formed and, to Lee's bitter disappointment and to the rankling bitterness of his family, he was not chosen to draft the declaration. This slight to Lee has been attributed by some to cheerful Benjamin Harrison and his friends. If Ben Harrison, still resenting his cousin's betrayal of his class, did open the way for young Jefferson, he inadvertently performed one of his most distinguished services. For Lee was no writer, and Jefferson was the best.

Neither Lee nor Mason, who first expressed the idea, could have made of that preamble to the Declaration of Independence what Jefferson did nor written with his clarity and passion the now-forgotten and then controversial body of the Declaration. John Hancock, wishing to sit with the Massachusetts delegation, relinquished the president's chair to Benjamin Harrison and to the Berkeley plantation master went the honor of reading to Congress the Declaration of his fellow Virginian.

The large man, as if aware of the importance of *this* document, read slowly and gave full value to each word in the opening paragraph that placed the whole in context. "When in the course of human events, it becomes necessary for one people to dissolve the political bands which have connected them with another, and to assume among the powers of the earth the separate and equal station to which the laws of nature and of nature's God entitle them, a decent respect to the opinions of mankind requires that they should declare the causes which impel them to the separation."

Then Jefferson's preamble—picking up Mason's idea, sharpened by the skillful collaborators on the committee for the declaration—followed with the deathless lines: "We hold these truths to be self-evident; that all men are created equal; that they are endowed by their creator with certain inalienable rights [he originally wrote *inherent and* inalienable, but one of the collaborators changed that to the qualifying *certain*]; that among these are life, liberty, and the pursuit of happiness; that to secure these rights, governments are instituted among men, deriving their just powers from the consent of the governed; that whenever any form of government becomes destructive of these ends, it is the right of the people to alter or to abolish it, and to institute new government . . ."

Unfortunately for the spirit of independence, like the "shot heard around the world" that was so muffled in Philadelphia, these beautifully expressed sentiments were read in Congress by Benjamin Harrison without arousing a single "hurrah" or causing one Quaker to stop another on the street and comment on this new concept of equality. As a matter of fact, the historically ringing challenge lay on the table for several days, and several days more were spent in arguments over points in the body of the Declaration and in removing clauses that were offensive to certain colonies.

Jefferson, for instance, wanted to abolish slave trade. But Georgia and South Carolina opposed that and, as Jefferson recorded, "Our northern brethren also, I believe, felt a little tender under these censures (against slave trade); for though their people had very few slaves themselves, yet they had been pretty considerable carriers of them to others." Also, for once, the young Jefferson had allowed his passion over injustice to override the order of his intelligence and the discipline of his craftsmanship, and he was guilty of some rather purple passages as well as intemperateness. Benjamin Harrison changed the finality of Jefferson's "eternal separation" from England into the more reasonable "enemies in war, in peace friends."

All that happened on the glorious fourth of July was that by that Thursday the hot delegates, sweating from the sun which baked in through the high windows of the State House, came to agreement on a document officially proclaiming their independent status which they would sign. Some agreed reluctantly, and Pennsylvania's Dickinson would have nought to do with it.

To most of the harassed gentlemen this acceptance of a fact was probably a relief from indecision. The more optimistic probably hoped that the Colonies, finally united in a course of action, could proceed more vigorously and intelligently toward defending their proclaimed rights against England's applied might. For a certainty, they could openly seek foreign allies, like the French, instead of engaging in the pussy-footing forced on Benjamin Harrison and his foreign affairs committee.

Thomas Jefferson was mainly concerned with the pride of authorship. He was as touchy as a professional about changes in his copy, and went to considerable trouble to display his original against the edited version—which was a manifest improvement. No one else cared who got author's credit, and Jefferson himself soon went home to look after his political fences, where Patrick Henry had taken advantage of his absence to become Virginia's first elected governor.

During the war years the members of Congress were to see no more of Jefferson, the inspired writer, and Henry, the demagogue, who had done so much to get them in the fix. George Washington and hundreds of other Virginians were to spend years in dismal camps in strange country, but the secessionists' object had already been achieved: a confederation had been formed, in alliance with which Virginia could maintain her claims to independence. But first of all, they were Virginians.

Benjamin Harrison, after signing his name to the Declaration, was somewhat divided between the familiar affairs of Virginia and the continental affairs into which he had been nudged by the young radicals. Without Henry's personal ambitions and none of Jefferson's theories that were to make Virginia an experimental ground in humanism, heavy Ben Harrison's indecision was resolved by events. For a while they took him, too, back to Virginia.

# CHAPTER X

❊ ❊

# THE HOUR FOR HEROES

1

*At* the time Virginia's civil leaders were going home to erect the structure of the independent commonwealth (the war was to be largely conducted by independent state action), George Washington was experiencing a series of difficulties away from his native soil which, had the enemy been more determined to suppress the rebellion, might have placed Jefferson's and Henry's experiment in political theory forever in the purely academic realm.

In the first place, to Washington's limited military experience was most definitely *not* added an instinct for warfare at the level of high command. There was no reason why there should be. His supreme gift derived from his environmental conditioning was in patriarchal leadership. It was this gift, hardening and developing his tough character, which saved the Revolution.

It has often been said before, and it can only be repeated that the colonials did not *win* their war for independence. The movement was saved from defeat by the character of Washington and by the nature of the British fight, and the decision was awarded the colonials through the intervention of the French. Washington, the British and the French played their parts in the series of events which caused the

British to elect a new Ministry and to write off the Colonies as part
of the British Empire.

As there was no reason for the middle-aged Virginia planter
suddenly to display a vaulting genius in warfare, there was equally
no reason for the British high command to have at hand a ready-
made plan for the military conquest of three million quasi subjects—
some loyal, some rebellious, some indifferent—thinly spread over one
thousand odd miles of coast line. English-speaking people were two
generations away from conceiving of total war on a civilian population as a means of uniting the bonds of union, and it took Americans
to think of that. Some individual British commanders fought cold-
bloodedly against peoples in their way, like that young fury Balestre
Tarleton in the South, but Sherman and Sheridan later made his ex-
ploits seem like relatively mild mischievousness.

In brief, the British produced no leader willing to win at all
costs to the conquered, and the high command's essays in grand
strategy bore little relation to the realities of subduing a fluid population to whom the fall of coastal cities ("key positions") had no meaning at all. The Colonies militarily had no "vitals"—no capital, no
railroad junctions, no productions center, not even a place of sentimental attachment.

Against this more or less amorphous enemy, the British had two
courses for subjugation: they could have strangled the Colonies
with a naval blockade, which they failed to attempt; and they could
have captured George Washington with his small army, which they
failed to achieve. This failure was partly due to the British's lackadaisical prosecution of the unorthodox war, to General Howe's gallant
reluctance to finish a reeling foe, and to Washington's indomitable
courage and determination in the face of disaster.

As the disaster was sometimes of his own making, from lack of
comprehension of the fine points of war or even of the rudiments of
commanding a whole army, great spiritual poise was required to deny
himself the solace of bathing in the inner tears of confession to his
own limitations. He was not deeply religious. A conformist and no
self-student of the soul's relations to God, the planter subscribed to
the forms of the Established Church and took his faith conservatively
like a good Episcopal gentleman.

While struggling to overcome rather than to bemoan his limitations, Washington was continuously beset by the failures of others. He operated on the uneasy ground of shifting loyalties in his fellow Americans, and lived in an atmosphere of greed and intrigue, of deceit and outright treachery.

Congress never got him money, farmers refused the paper money and sold to the British; his army was constantly shifting in strength and personnel as patriots slunk off and bounty hunters appeared; outlaws operating on the periphery appeared and disappeared according to their needs. Men closest to him betrayed him by denial. Brother officers formed a cabal to oust him from command. Since he did not deign even to notice the attempted *coup,* the plotters became like boys shooting spitballs at a statue, and the conspiracy broke before the iron of his character. In a way, all disasters broke over him in the same fashion, and the "commander-in-chief" kept an army in the field—at least, a rebel armed force to be conquered—long after the disorganized and fainthearted Revolution should have been crushed.

Before the Declaration of Independence had been adopted, Washington, finding his uncontested occupation of Boston without profit, had moved into New York. Though military experts, like statisticians, can prove either side with facts, there does seem to have been no particular reason for him to have set up shop in New York. The city held nothing of its present importance and was no hotbed of revolution. There was its central location, the great harbor, the Hudson passage northward—and Canada assumed an importance in the calculations of both sides which is difficult to appreciate today. Able and aggressive Benedict Arnold was trying his hand at victory there, and the British would later launch an offensive from there.

The surface reasons for occupying New York would be outweighed by its strategic disadvantages. The British had the fleet to make the harbor an asset to them and the geography of Manhattan Island forced a division of forces on either side of the East River— on Manhattan and on Brooklyn Heights. Since Washington lost at New York, any armchair student of warfare can point out his ignorance of the elementary maxim against division of forces in the presence of a numerically superior enemy. Robert E. Lee divided an inferior force against McClellan and lifted the siege of Richmond, repeated this even more daringly against Hooker at Chancellorsville and achieved a masterpiece; even though Lee was audaciously knowledgeable, he would have been criticized for breaking the same maxim had he lost. Though Washington seemed not to know any better, he would have been praised had he won.

In the debacle, he exhibited one trait which many a technically more brilliant commander has lacked: in the rough going he kept his head, his heart, and acted with decision and effectiveness. He was a leader. He saved his army and got the so-called soldiers in one piece to upper Manhattan. There, after retreat became rout and rout panic, he rallied them for a stand that checked the pursuers. Then again, outmaneuvered by Howe, his troops outfought by confident regulars, he staggered on through Harlem into Westchester County. But the British never bagged him. Howe, who did not try too hard, called him the "old fox," and Cornwallis, who tried harder, used the same name.

In the late fall, with the cold biting across the Jersey flats, Cornwallis tried to pin Washington between the Hudson and Hackensack rivers. He slipped on southward, holding together by force of will his poorly armed, illy clothed and underfed collection of transient soldiers. Then on that historic Christmas night, he led his freezing ragamuffins across the river to fall on the drunken Hessians in the small triumph of Trenton. Militarily Trenton accomplished little, except the enjoyment of some captured stores, but a victory—*any* victory—lifted morale as does any good news received in times of depression and hopelessness. It did something to Washington, too. It gave him confidence as a soldier.

When Cornwallis came after him in Trenton, Washington evaded the ponderous grasp by a night move over roads solid with ice, fell upon the surprised British at Princeton while Cornwallis's force was starting out behind him, and won a less spectacular though militarily more heartening victory. Princeton enabled Washington to retire on a high note to undisturbed winter headquarters in Morristown, and prevented the revolution from coming to an inglorious end in the first year of the declared war.

In saving his pitiful little force as the armed symbol of the independent colonies, the exile from his plantation had also grown in understanding the nature of the whole experiment into which he had been drawn by the brave words of others.

Looking backward from a current viewpoint, it is always easy to simplify a struggle into black and white, villains and heroes, according to who won. George Washington, uprooted from all he knew and loved, was groping through a gray world. It was peopled with honest loyalists, who are villains because their side lost, and visionary radicals who are heroes because they had Washington. There were American traitors more insidious than Arnold (who committed a single act) and unsung heroes unmotivated by democracy. The greatness of Washington, surrounded by turncoats and self-seekers, by honest enemies and knavish friends, is demonstrated by his evolution into a real force *because* of these very pressures. This product of the Virginia oligarchy grew more in vision than any man in the independence movement.

It is a shame that the American heritage has missed the living image of this shy and generous man, this lonely and warm man, who gave the most pathetic eagerness to friendships and who, outwardly so assured, worked so self-consciously at self-development. He never presumed on the stature which his instinct told him he possessed.

2

Because of the unconquerableness of their absent conservative, Washington's smarter contemporaries were able to maneuver politically in quiet Williamsburg for control of the structure of an independent Virginia. In the evolution of the state's political character, it is most significant that Virginia, without consulting the Continental Congress, had declared itself free and independent of England or anybody! Then too, even while the Congress was drafting the Declaration of Independence, the same Virginia Convention that instructed its delegates to declare for independence was designing a government for its free people and producing for that government the first written constitution in the world.

This happened at a time when the democratic-minded, or progressives, were in numerical majority, and the power of the traditional oligarchy was weakened by the revolutionary movement. But as the defenders of the aristocratic rule fought hard and skillfully every step of the way, there were no radical changes made in the structure of government as it had existed for the preceding century. A House of Delegates and Senate replaced the House of Burgesses and King's

Council and, to replace the Committee of Safety, an advisory Council was appointed to work with the governor.

Since the two houses elected the governor, the essential change from the colonial government was the removal of the controlling authority that had become so irksome. This essential change went to the very heart of the Virginia Constitution. The powers of the governor were carefully defined and restricted, and all authority was allocated with acceptance of that semiautonomous status of Virginia counties. This gave the state, in effect, the limited powers of a central government in relation to the political-social entities of the counties.

Within this structure of government, power struggles over the social aims of the independent commonwealth immediately began between two former allies—Patrick Henry, the governor, and Thomas Jefferson, a member of the legislature from Albemarle County. These leaders, complementary during the secession, became antithetical when independence was established.

Essentially Patrick Henry, the rabble-rousing orator against the King, had accomplished his purpose when Virginia freed itself of Britain. He was, in truth, nothing of a social reformer; his unreflective mind conceived of no political philosophy, and there had been enough changes for him when he moved his family into the resplendent Palace recently vacated by His Lordship.

Actually, he preferred Virginia as it was, and in fear that anything of his familiar country might be changed, Henry wanted nothing to do with the other colonies beyond the loose alliance necessary for security against subjugation. Later, he was to fight as bitterly against union in a Federal government as he had fought against the Crown. Though he was a people's champion and the acclaimed leader of the progressives, his embrace of democratic principles was so listless that the Old Guard feared less from him than from the Lees, George Mason and young James Madison. Indeed, after his military career was thwarted by the oligarchy, Henry drifted back into his old indolent ways and for this Virginian, with his roots deep in the physical life of his land, the end of the struggle came with revolution.

For Jefferson, the Virginian, as embryonic cosmopolitan, the revolution was the beginning. Though he had seized as a catch phrase (a literary "hook") Mason's idea of the equality and freedom of mankind, *political* equality did express Jefferson's visionary idealism. He progressed from the championing of political rights within the British empire to an almost messianic zeal for social reform in freed Virginia.

When Jefferson returned to Williamsburg in the summer of 1776 as a member of the new legislature, he declined both another year in the Continental Congress and a place on the mission to France, and set his sights on replacing Henry's leadership of the progressives. This was not in indifference to the colonial military struggle. Rather, it indicated his limitations in realism, as he believed the struggle would be only a short affair. During the five more years of the fighting, the war remained to him a remote happening as compared to his concentration on changing the character of his native state. At bottom, thirty-three-year-old Jefferson intended to break the rule of the oligarchy and to change the conditions that perpetuated power for the privileged few.

In this repudiation of the class that made possible his own position, Tom Jefferson was not repudiating the production of the superior individual for rule. Jefferson never carried his equality theory to the point of accepting all men as equally fitted for rule, and he would have abhorred the elevation of the "average man" to position of authority in the lives of his fellows. What he wanted, or claimed to want, was a different method of producing the superior individual from that used by a propertied aristocracy.

He held that a landed aristocracy long entrenched in power grew stultified and protective of its own interest, without regard to the welfare of the commonwealth, and ceased to produce superior individuals. He conceived of a "natural aristocracy," of talent and of the mind, and his detachment from people in mass caused him to believe that he could erect an order where this natural aristocracy would supersede the aristocracy of inherited privilege.

While Jefferson was certainly right in his contention that a continuance of entrenched privilege could produce citizens whose fatuity and bloated pride rendered them anything except superior individuals, he curiously dismissed the historic fact that all aristocracies are based upon wealth and tangible power, and that the aristocrats of the mind and talent do not form ruling classes. Such aristocrats tend to an individualism which rejects the necessary conformity. Though superior individuals as individuals can adapt to and function within an established ruling group, as did Jefferson himself, a whole ruling group even of Jeffersons would bring chaos.

It is unfortunately true that it has always been hard for the natural aristocrat to rise in a society controlled by entrenched privilege, but the destruction of one *class* usually opens the way for another *class*, and Jefferson would seem to have been warped by the reformer's monomaniacal egotism in believing he could remake the character of society.

Even short of the natural aristocrat ideal, his attempt to change the nature of an aristocratic republic presumed a perpetuation of the Virginia as he knew it, and here again in this presumption is the limitation of the mortal ego. Though a product himself of the ferment of the eighteenth century, Jefferson could not conceive that the ferments would continue after him and changes would introduce elements in which his theories would be inapplicable. For his democracy was to be composed solely of Virginia's land owners, each with roots in and a stake in a homogeneous region—as the new constitution put it, citizens who had "a permanent common interest with, and attachment to the community." In the society with which he experimented, each individual grew up in relation to his land as a child in a family.

There is no reason that his imagination should have conceived an industrialized, money society of rootless urbanites. There is every reason for him to have recognized that in a changing world the qualities of the Virginian were the results of a stable and special kind of society, and he was tampering with the character of a people as well as with a political order.

As that society then existed, Jefferson also had every empirical reason to believe in its production of superior individuals for rule. No other colony matched its continental delegation, where each man, the best in his sphere that the state could produce, was allotted the role for which nature, training and opportunity had fitted him—Washington as a military leader, Jefferson as a writer, Henry and R. H. Lee as orators, Peyton Randolph as presiding officer, and Benjamin Harrison as committee workhorse. The younger men (Madison, Monroe, Marshall), who were to succeed this generation in the American Republic, were already on the scene.

If Jefferson wanted to protect this propertied aristocracy against future stultification and to broaden the avenues of opportunity beyond the limits of rich planting families, such aims would be healthful for the community's welfare, desirable for its individuals, and feasible in practice. But his plan of substituting the new natural aristocracy remained in the abstract realm of a complex educational system foreign to the people's nature and impractical for any people.

Jefferson made a blueprint for a society without considering the human material to be worked with. In practice, he only executed that part of his program concerned with weakening the oligarchic power of the landed aristocracy, and as a result, without substituting a new aristocracy for the old, Jefferson's social aims in Virginia hardened class lines for generations to come and deepened a political division in the state by, in effect, setting against one another the landed bourbons of Tidewater and the small landowners of the more egalitarian western counties.

As an apostle of that swelling of the rights of men in the heady intellectual atmosphere of the eighteenth century, Jefferson, for all the brilliance of his mind, was conditioned by that typical reformer's evangelism which finds virtue only in his own single concept of salvation. Much of proven value to the society, in individual attitudes and delicate balances, is lost in those total changes which come as panaceas for all the ills of mankind. As in medicine, it has been discovered that an excess of wonder drugs can bring harmful reactions, and in time even the cure-all loses effect: the patient, after many easy victories over illness, is sicker than ever.

Given the nature of Virginia's society, the situation was ideal for the introduction of true democratic principles (as *then* understood) into an aristocratic republic. But Jefferson, belonging to the future, tried to abolish the structure that had extended from a deeply rooted past and, when he returned from Philadelphia, the aristocratic-conservatives were little more popular in Virginia than they have traditionally been in the rest of America. Indeed, many historians, riding the wave of democratic fashion, have regarded even the most dedicated patriots among them as the villains of time for holding a minority conviction.

For their minority conviction was that men are *not* created equal, that Jefferson's theory of a ruling class of "natural aristocrats" was as vaporous as it has proven to be; and they certainly did not wish to be ruled by inferiors. It never occurred to the oligarchy to give the machinery of government over to professional politicians who would be front men of powerful interests. They had been trained in an aristocratic republic to believe that the class in power should do its own ruling, and very forthrightly without lurid appeals and empty promises. After all, elected at a county level in a parochial society, the candidates were talking to men they had grown up with and who would be around personally to see that each promise was kept. There was no such thing as a "campaign-promise." A man gave his word on his honor, and if he broke his word he became a man of dishonor.

The oligarchy made no tinny appeals to the common man in their defensive battle against Jefferson. The conservatives fought as they had traditionally fought, on the principles in which they believed and which had proven workable. Not only were they in a minority, but they were fighting something more than a majority. They were fighting a new fashion in the concept of man's relation to government and, as with any new fashion among Americans, everything before became old hat.

The leader of the new was Jefferson, and soon after his return to Williamsburg in the summer of 1776, he became the most powerful man in Virginia. He quickly won the power away from Patrick Henry, whom he succeeded as governor in 1779 (at the end of Henry's three legal terms), and during his three years as delegate and two as governor, Jefferson worked on that one half of his program which was to loosen the grip of the oligarchy.

With the majority support and with the tides of the time, Jefferson passed measures which shrewdly undermined those supports which had sustained the small oligarchy in power. He liberalized the land-owning restrictions on the voting franchise to increase the popular vote; he abolished the English-inherited laws on entail and primogeniture, which broke up the large landed estates; he separated Church from the State in a "Statute of Religious Freedom." Idealistically this statute permitted all dissidents from the established church (like Baptists, whom the planters called "religious fanatics") to worship where they chose, without being taxed to support the church of the state. Realistically, in the removal of state financial support from the Episcopal Church and the reduction of this church to the position of any other faith, the community power of the Episcopal vestries was broken.

[ 247 ]

All these liberalizing measures did weaken the power of the ruling class, but none of them changed an aristocratic republic into a democracy with modern connotations. Jefferson was fighting innate, immovable, traditional conservatism in the people. The weakened landed aristocracy went on the defensive and in their bitterly unyielding rearguard action they became, in the following generations, self-centered and provincial-minded, a class fighting to retain its privileges against fellow citizens and no longer to lead them. With few exceptions (none to compare with the giants of "the golden age"), leadership was produced only in the military where the habit of authority was still a useful trait.

All that was in the future when, while other Virginians were off fighting the British, the lines were drawn in Williamsburg between the forces of the man of the future and the forces of the gentlemen of an age that was dying. At the same time as Jefferson's first experiments in democratic government were introduced on Virginia's not entirely fertile soil, he was growing into an experimenter for the republic.

On the national level, no man's words have received so much lip service and suffered so much distortion. In Virginia, the republican element followed him passionately for what he was—a humanistic believer in the destruction of all entrenched privilege in order to provide an equality of opportunity for those able (as he said) to "*pursue*" it. Obviously, he believed that, given equality of opportunity, the superior would make use of it, and not that the superior would be leveled to the lowest common denominator.

As it turned out, the only place he hurt entrenched privilege was in Virginia, and that was because the plantation masters in their imperiousness refused to give lip service to the crowd any more than to the King. Preserving their sense of honor, they preached what they practiced, and they fought Jefferson and the tide openly and proudly.

It really was an unequal fight, but the Old Guard did not know it then. Jefferson did: he knew he was one with time. Despite mistakes in detail and his contribution to the confusion of understanding the democratic principle, he personified the spirit of his age; and, though visionary he might be in regard to mankind in mass, close up in dealing with his fellows he was unsurpassed in political astuteness.

3

In the same summer of 1776, Benjamin Harrison also returned from Philadelphia to Williamsburg, and in a very curious circumstance. Virginia's seven delegates to Congress had been elected for one term, with re-elections, and replacements for Washington, Peyton Randolph and Patrick Henry. When Patrick Henry became governor, for some reason of his own he reduced the number to five, and in the new election Benjamin Harrison and his cousin, Carter Braxton, received the insult of not being returned to Congress. Though Harrison retained his usual self-possession, he was outraged at the slap and moved right in to investigate what he recognized as back-knifing.

Thomas Jefferson, himself receiving the lowest number of votes of the elected five, expressed his feeling in a letter to a friend: "The omission of Harrison and Braxton and my name being next in vote gives me some alarm. It is a painful situation to be 300 miles from one's country and open to secret assassination without the possibility of self-defense."

The sudden and, as it turned out, brief uprising of a bloc of enemies against Harrison had possibly two causes. The split in the Virginia delegation, between the Harrison-Braxton group and Richard Henry Lee and his New England allies, had spread beyond them to the point where distant supporters of the two camps were whispering slanderous stories. For those who wanted to believe the worst of Harrison there was the appointment he obtained for his son-in-law, a doctor, as director of a continental hospital, although there was a more popular claimant. As part of the same split, there was a group strongly opposed to George Washington, and Benjamin Harrison, his closest friend in Congress, did not trust either his Lee cousin or John Adams in regard to the general. This deepened personality conflicts.

Also Harrison, to some of the new progressives, was tarred by the brush of his more conservative older kinsmen. In a revolutionary scene the ramifications of his family connections could operate against him, and between Harrison and then still powerful Henry there was no love lost. If the growth of the quickly blooming intrigue against Harrison lay in these causes, there is no question that the enemies took advantage of his absence, and that his staunch friends, assuming him safe, had been asleep at the voting. When Harrison came home, it was different.

That he still enjoyed at home a position of trust and prestige is indicated by his unanimous election to the governor's select Council of eight. But big Harrison wanted to face down those guilty of what his friend Edmund Randolph called "malicious insinuations." He refused to accept the seat on the Council until his honor was cleared of stigma.

His refusal to accept any office under the circumstances, and his firmness and composure in seeking to bring the character-poisoners into the open, won over "even those who were prejudiced against him." When a new election was called in October to fill Jefferson's place at Congress, the legislature showed its support of Harrison by electing him to the post by a 69 to 5 vote, and rebuked the intriguers by passing a resolution of appreciation for his past services.

Harrison could not write of his own vindication to George Washington so one of his friends did, and mentioned that the five who voted against Harrison were *"the remains of a certain party not unknown to your Excellency."* Whatever the anti-Washington party of five was, the incident served to elevate Benjamin Harrison to the point of highest esteem in his long public career and ultimately to the governorship of Virginia. There was an impressive dignity and force about the large gentleman when his honor was touched, an inner size that contemporaries were apt to forget in seeing him usually jovial and, as they said, "making pleasantries."

Harrison felt the slap deeply at the time but, once vindicated, his steady-nerved and cheerful extroversion sent him undisturbed back to his duties in Philadelphia. Shortly before he left Philadelphia, he had been appointed chairman of the newly created and important Board of War, and he was particularly interested in the board because it gave him the opportunity to work to free Washington from the maddening and picayune interference of Congress.

His confreres in Congress rallied to show him what they thought of the back-room intrigue in Virginia, and on the day of his arrival in town restored him to the chairmanship of the war board. There one of the members reported that he had the opportunity to observe in action Harrison's "firmness, good sense and usefullness in deliberative and critical situations; and much use, indeed, was required of these qualities, when everything around us was lowering and terrific." Congress also immediately passed a resolution to continue Harrison on all his standing committees and, illimitably inventive in creating committees, founded new ones for him to serve on.

His fellow Virginians, observing these honors heaped on Harrison, outdid themselves to show repentance for the lapse which had permitted local politics to deliver a slight to this useful citizen, for in the next election, in May of 1777, a joint ballot of both houses elected him first among their delegates to Philadelphia.

By then Harrison was beginning to suffer the pangs of homesickness. His personal financial affairs had fallen to such low estate that he was forced to take a short-term loan from his friend Willing, the Philadelphia merchant, in order to meet the cash expenses of living away from home. Then, too, he was continually being sent on trips to confer with governors and generals, and his love of luxury scarcely fitted him for this simulation of a commercial traveler. While Ben Harrison made friends easily—Benjamin Franklin among them—he was of an age when the familiar faces and proven intimates meant more to him than the most enchanting new companions.

National affairs, service to which kept him away from home, were in an equally dismal state. The war had slumped into a pattern of apathetic aimlessness that could manifestly drag on for a long time. With actually no central government or civil leader, no money and little patriotism, the colonials militarily could not conceive of any war plan, or even strategy, for its few forces in the field.

Washington, as commander-in-chief, could not hope to do more than try to check the British when they sporadically stirred out of their sluggishness and to make certain that his little army was not gobbled up. In his confidential correspondence with Harrison, Washington grew choleric with complaints at those things which *could* have been done and were not. In the summer of 1777, he even wrangled with his old friend over what at the time seemed a very minor matter—though it turned out to be epochal as regards the Colonies' defense.

On a June night there appeared at the Huger's coastal plantation in South Carolina a party of young French officers, led by a handsome eighteen-year-old boulevardier, who introduced himself as the Marquis de Lafayette. The personable young Frenchman explained that an American representative in Paris had offered him a major

generalship in the continental armies, that he was on his way to Philadelphia and had sailed this round-about way to avoid the British
warships. The captain of the French ship, however, had become
timid of landing on the strange Southern coast and the marquis had
run ashore in a ship's boat, and—*voilà*—there they were in the middle
of the night.

The hospitable Major Huger bowed as if everything had been
explained, graciously opened his home to the unexpected guests, and
later helped them on their way.

Everything the youthful nobleman had told his host was true, as
far as he knew. One of the American representatives in Paris, despairing of arousing the French to an active alliance, had blandly
offered high-sounding commissions to anyone who seemed receptive.
The young marquis, knowing little and caring less about England's
colonial wars, was stirred by the romance of becoming a division commander in a foreign war and impulsively left his pregnant wife for
high adventure. The trouble lay in the fact that the American representative in Paris lacked authority to commission even a lieutenant,
let alone to give an eighteen-year-old French-speaking society darling
command of a division of infantry.

In Philadelphia, the Lafayette party encountered no hospitable
planters, and were left lurking in the street until they were informed
their services were not wanted. Only shame at returning home, dismissed by Colonial Americans, kept the young nobleman hanging
around the strange city, and these days of his gloomy indecision
proved to be one of the most decisive periods in the war. For in that
time a letter arrived from Benjamin Franklin, in Paris, pointing out
the high connections of this marquis in a country run by a few
aristocratic families, and suggesting the influence on the French of finding some use for the young man's services. Immediately he was appointed major general by Congress, though they intended his commission to be honorary and not apply to field command.

Lafayette had been in Philadelphia long enough to form a hero
worship for the solitary figure of George Washington. When at a
dinner in Philadelphia in August he first met "that great man," as he
recorded, "it was impossible to mistake for a moment his majestic figure
and deportment." His warm admiration for Washington was returned
with an almost filial love by the childless planter, and this friendship—

between the adolescent European nobleman and the middle-aged Virginia aristocrat—formed one of the few bright threads in the drab struggle and was probably the decisive element in later bringing in the French as allies.

But in that August of 1777, Washington, not knowing what to do with a stray major general, could only offer him the hospitality of his headquarters and make him something of an unofficial staff member, until the marquis tactfully made it known that he was waiting for the troops of his command. Then Washington turned loose on his equable old friend, Colonel Harrison, and demanded to know what was what.

Harrison answered with his usual pleasant firmness, and said, "I remember well a conversation passing betwixt you and I on the subject of the Marquis de la Fayette's commission, and that I told you it was merely honorary. In this light I looked on it, and so did every other member of Congress."

It was up to Washington to resolve the situation tactfully, and this he did with such innate consideration that Lafayette went back to France to enlist his country's aid for the country of his friend. That happy end to the Lafayette problem was long in the future, when Benjamin Harrison's known intimate correspondence with Washington was used against them both by a forger and by a renegade. Though Ben Harrison would never be described as a sensitive man, this was the second occurrence in which his correspondence with his friend had been used against him, and the first had hurt him because of his family's name and his children.

Two years before Washington had written Harrison one of his raging letters in which he berated the mercenary spirit of the New England people, and Harrison had answered soothingly that troubles with New Englanders "are not more than I expected, knowing the people you have to deal with, by the sample we find here."

Harrison's letter was intercepted by the British, and a roguish propagandist—a forerunner of the abolitionists—decided to give spice to this commonplace exchange between intimates by inserting a detail of the carnal life which outsiders imagined existed between planters and female slaves. The since-proven forger attributed to Colonel Harrison a response to the pretty daughter of a washerwoman, whom he would have broken into love except for the untimely arrival of another woman, Sukey, and the forger had plain-spoken Harrison write, "and but for the cursed antidote to love, Sukey, I (would) have fitted her for my General against his return."

Now, nobody knows what Harrison and Washington talked about when alone, but it is known that Ben did not call George "my General," and the tone of the whole insertion jumps out from the rest of the context. However, since the inept forgery was not proven until years later, Harrison was understandably disturbed for his family's name —especially because the letter, with the insertion, appeared in the Virginians' favorite *Gentleman's Magazine*, from which the motto, *E Pluribus Unum*, was taken.

The 1777 letters contained no slander on Harrison's personal life, but on his and Washington's patriotism. A British printer in New York published the forgeries, purporting to be despondent exchanges between the two Virginians, with expressions of disgust at the whole Continental business. Since they were both disenchanted with the practical aspects of the revolutionary movement, these forgeries hit close to home. Washington, for instance, was appalled at the luxurious living of war profiteers in Philadelphia, and Harrison, the shipbuilder, observed with pain the fortunes being made by New England privateers. These adventurous sailing men did, in passing, contribute to the war by the harm in pocket they gave to British shipping, but Harrison used his docks for the construction of an eighteen-gun man-of-war for the Colonies.

The other letters were written by a former chaplain of the Continental Congress who, going over to the British, added innuendo to known information. It was a fact that Benjamin Harrison was the last of the original Virginia delegation in Philadelphia; it was innuendo that the others had gone home in despair and that Harrison soon would join them because "he is disgusted with his unworthy associates."

It is not known whether all this influenced his decision. His fellow delegates had gone home because they were Virginians, and the war was being fought at state levels—as by Clinton in New York and Rutledge in South Carolina. Harrison might have gone home sooner except for the point of pride over that gratuitous slight which sent him back to Congress. Or he might simply have become convinced that nothing could be done in a welter of committees without authority.

Then, as constantly with Washington and Jefferson, there was always the pull to his plantation, to Berkeley.

Perhaps the British decided it for him, but this too is conjecture. In the late summer of 1777, the British forces suddenly launched grand strategy. Burgoyne would strike down from Montreal and Howe would relinquish the fleshpots of New York for the undiscovered pleasures of Philadelphia. "Gentleman Johnny" Burgoyne, a gallant character who should have fared better, had run out by the time in October when, at Saratoga, he encountered a force commanded by Gates (the leader in the conspiracy against Washington) who was fortunately supported by tough Benedict Arnold and even tougher Dan Morgan with his Virginia Rifles. Though Saratoga represented the colonials' first great victory, the capture of a British army—with the repercussions in Europe that success always brings anywhere—things grew very dismal in Philadelphia where Benjamin Harrison was paying rent with borrowed money.

Sir William Howe, in his campaign to take the continental "capital" at Philadelphia, fared better than Burgoyne. Instead of hacking their way through the unbroken wilderness of the north, his soldiers took a boat excursion from New York, down the Atlantic, and up the Chesapeake Bay. Their land journey was short, over a most genial countryside, whose farmers provided them with tasty viands in exchange for gold. Where the pleasant Brandywine flows through this beguiling country, Washington essayed to check the British. Though he showed improvement as a general, it was not enough. Howe marched his troops on into Philadelphia, where Sir William was received by the rich Tory families as a deliverer. With that arduous campaign happily behind, General Howe devoted himself to the more appealing pursuits of discovering the blandishments offered by the Quaker City. Needless to say, no bluestockings prevented grand parties for his ladies, as they had two years before for Mrs. Washington.

This turn of events evicted Benjamin Harrison from even the transient comforts of what had become his "home-away-from-home," and with the other fugitive Congressmen he huddled cheerlessly in York. By this time he was convinced that he could serve more usefully in his native land. Although the conviction undoubtedly supported his desire to be home, it was a sound conviction. There was really nothing that a congress without power or leadership could accomplish, and daily it became more apparent that responsibility for successful resistance devolved on the separate colonies.

Benjamin Harrison did not leave until Congress passed the Articles of Confederation, which would make permanent the temporary compact between the Colonies. (It was years before the states ratified the Articles, the last in 1781.) It was more than three years since his carriage had first taken him northward in a hot August across the fat Pennsylvania countryside. As the bands later played it, "The World Turned Upside Down," all the personal world of Colonel Benjamin Harrison, of Charles City County, had changed in those three plus years beyond what he could have imagined before he recrossed that countryside going southward in the bleakness of early winter.

The cushions in his carriage were then worn, the lamps were no longer polished, and the homeward-bound planter, wrapped in a greatcloak, did not look—and probably did not feel—any part of the legendary master of a plantation.

4

Benjamin Harrison had the energy and endurance that supported his equanimity, and back at Berkeley he needed no "vacation" (an unknown word to him) to shift from the Continental Congress to the more relaxing atmosphere of Williamsburg. His plantation was beginning to show its rundown condition even in appearance, and in all likelihood it was a relief for the old politician to turn from financial problems that had become insurmountable to the familiar scenes at the capital.

This should not imply that the master of Berkeley was in any sense slovenly about financial obligations. On the contrary, Harrison was extremely meticulous about cash dealings. The reason for his economic situation was that cash was hard to come by. The planter, despite the later-day Virginian's scorn of trade, was a trader, and Harrison's trading markets were cut off. Plantation-grown produce caused the family to live high on the hog, but they were living off their capital. Harrison understood this, but it was too late in the game for him to do anything about it.

In this there was nothing unique about Harrison at Berkeley.

Washington's Mount Vernon suffered similarly, and Jefferson at Monticello became so poor in his old age that public subscriptions provided
for his subsistence. To repeat, running a plantation was a full-time job,
and in the struggle for the democracy which Americans accept so
casually as heritage many aristocrats impoverished themselves.

In the traditional revolution, the aristocrat was destroyed by the
people; in the American Revolution the Virginia aristocrat destroyed
himself, and the people, with little of the liberty-love attributed to
them later, profited by it. Yet, in the current timidity about admitting
any flaws in the leveling of democracy, the "people" have to be made
the heroes of everything. This has resulted in confusions regarding the
case history of the composite American—especially in regard to America's original colony, and the Southern states that derived from or were
influenced by it.

Benjamin Harrison, innocent of history's distortions, drove in his
carriage along the winding planters' road to a familiar environment in
which he had wielded power since coming of age. Back in those quiet
years, when he had been a tall, slender, good-looking young dancing
man, the young master of Berkeley had not gone to the capital to conquer the world (it was already conquered for him) nor to improve
society, as the society he knew existed in a state of perfection. He had
gone in obligation and interest in public affairs and part of his obligation had been to sustain his idyllic society, as well as to protect his vast
family in the matrix of that society. In each of those of his original
responsibilities, he had failed.

In order to sustain his society, he had been led step by step—often
reluctantly, sometimes protestingly—into his present situation where, if
his society were sustained at all, its idyllic quality was lost; and within
the broken idyll his family had lost security.

Along the way, there was nothing he could have done to change
events. When issues he had fought became facts, he had adapted to the
necessity and given of his time, talents and fortune according to the
course of events. From the act of doing his duty in the tradition into
which he was born, the aging gentleman derived no great moral unc-
tion. In no way did a sense of virtue give balm to the poignancy of
all that was being lost. Obligation to his birthplace went as deep as instinct, and performance in that obligation was by then as habitual as a
reflex.

Without philosophic reflection, then, Ben Harrison resumed his duties at the level where they had begun, his home place. The colony had changed, but he had not, and given his habit of adaptation to things as they were, the new problems became simpler to master because his duties were performed in familiar grooves. In a way, it was like returning to the same job with the old firm under new management.

The House of Burgesses was now the House of Delegates. Soon after his return, Harrison became Speaker again, defeating Jefferson for the chair in 1778. He looked on the faces of many strangers (some of whom had knifed him in the back) and he missed the faces of his close friends—his brother-in-law, kindly Peyton Randolph, dead in Philadelphia, and iron-willed George Washington, off holding together a few thousand starving ragamuffins at Valley Forge, in the bitter cold that descended on that country where the farmers took their produce to Howe's people, warm in Philadelphia.

In the Palace, where in his young manhood he had enjoyed the hospitality of British governors, the lights were often out as Patrick Henry, their native-born governor, took off for reasons of health to the countryside he loved and left the details of government to others. These details were little different from those of the days of his prime during the French and Indian War. Men must be recruited, fed, clothed, armed and sent off to distant places to fight again with George Washington. One of Harrison's brothers was away in the army, serving as colonel of artillery. The state was incurring heavy debts again, but there was a new class to share them—all those farmers in the western sections, and more farmers and merchants and artisans in Tidewater.

During Harrison's first summer at Berkeley, 1778, his absent friend, Washington, won an inconclusive military victory at Monmouth, New Jersey, though the repercussions were disturbing. British General Clinton had replaced hedonistic Howe and decided to return to New York overland. Overestimating the punishing effects of winter on Washington's troops, he marched across New Jersey with miles of inviting wagons, and Washington struck. Though Clinton lost the field, he lost little else, except any urge to counterattack; but, since he proceeded on his way without further molestation, he claimed a victory. As Washington won the field, though little else, he claimed a victory. Morally the victory would seem to lie with the Continentals.

Most definitely the Continental troops showed improvement. They had fought the British a full-scale battle *without losing*.

The repercussions came over Washington's second-in-command, a British-born, trained soldier named Charles Lee—no relation to the Virginia Lees, though he then resided in Virginia. This Lee was a great eccentric who imposed himself on the colonials, as did most professionals from Europe, citing the superiority of his military genius. At Monmouth, Lee, without authority, ordered a retreat which many students of the battle believe cost Washington a decisive victory. As it was, only the presence on the field of Washington, always heroic in the presence of danger and disaster, saved his army from rout.

For a long time, it was believed that Charles Lee was a traitor. Washington apparently did not think so, but the violence of his feelings over the retreat erupted through his famed control and he cursed, as a Virginia general at Monmouth said, "to turn the leaves on the trees . . . like an angel out of heaven." Lee, resenting Washington's public ire, wrote impertinent letters that led to his court-martial and ultimate dismissal from the army. The long fight over Lee, who found many supporters against Washington, obscured for a time the curious fact that, as far as battles and campaigns went, the war was over in the Northern states.

Clinton returned to New York, and Washington, who perforce had to skulk outside the American cities, encamped his army at White Plains—and the British and Americans were back where they were two years before. Then, while the state of war continued innocuously in the North, the fighting shifted to Georgia and the Carolinas, and then to Virginia.

The fighting in the South was more intense and continuous than it had been in Northern states. British commanders (with no Sir William Howe among them) more nearly approached the total war later levied on the Confederacy, both in intent to crack civilian morale and in savagery of execution, though with none of Sherman's systematic destruction of a people's economy "for fifty years to come." It was more personal than that. It was really more of a brother's war than the Civil War, since loyalists joined the British in plundering their neighbors and kinspeople, and individuals clashed with forthright hatred. The British did not steal jeeringly under the moral slogan of "freeing the slaves," nor insult citizens under the pious excuse of "preserving the Union." It was like the warfare between Indians and the first settlers had been, where nobody expected quarter and honestly avowed enemies fought to the death, knowing the consequences of defeat.

When the British first came, in the fall of 1778, they had it all their way. There was little organized opposition, with the Continental troops of the Southern states away in the North, and the few militia without experienced leaders were distracted by fears of slave insurrections. Savannah and Augusta fell early, and then the British thrust northward and South Carolina suffered its first devastation by invading troops. Charleston, which had repulsed an earlier assault from the sea, was taken from the land, but the British showed no intention of enjoying the captured cities, as in New York and Philadelphia. From their bases, they immediately struck out over the countryside, again shifting northward, to North Carolina.

There the going began to get tough. By that time some of the militia had become battle-hardened, and the region had developed ruthless guerrillas, like Sumter and Pickens and Francis Marion (the "Swamp Fox"). Experienced Continental troops came in small lots, and experienced commanders—magnificent Nathanael Greene, the Rhode Island blacksmith (whose chief of artillery was Harrison's brother Charles); Dan Morgan, Virginia's "natural" fighter; and the *beau sabreur* of the cavalry, "Light Horse Harry" Lee, cousin of Richard Henry Lee, father of Robert E. Lee, and husband of one of Benjamin Harrison's Carter kinsfolk and nextdoor neighbor.

The viciously fought battles in the Carolinas do not loom large in American history, but the men who later fought with Harry Lee's son grew up on first-hand tales of Camden, King's Mountain, Guilford Court House and Cowpens. At Cowpens the brilliant Greene divided an inferior force in the presence of the enemy, and natural-soldier Morgan (a precursor of Forrest) invented a unique battle plan for his half to give high-riding Tarleton a thoroughly bad going over (830 casualties to 73).

However, the British, then commanded by Cornwallis, though suffering heavy casualties and harried by irregular warfare, were shifting inexorably northward to Virginia.

In Virginia, though its loyalists had been under control since Dunmore's brutal private war, troops were as scarce as they had been in Georgia and South Carolina at the beginning. Also Virginia had a governor, Thomas Jefferson, who could not seem to concern himself with military affairs, even after advance warnings of the coming invasion in the form of raids into the state, heavier and heavier, and coming closer to the heart.

5

In 1780, when Tarleton's raids into the state began to bedevil people and destroy property, the capital was moved from Williamsburg to Richmond. That former trading post at The Falls in the James River, on the far edge of frontier when Williamsburg was made the capital eighty years before, had become the junction point between Tidewater and the West (which then included West Virginia and Kentucky) and was obviously destined to grow as a commercial shipping center, as well as a center for the small industries already beginning to operate. The shift was made under Jefferson's urgings on the grounds of Williamsburg's exposed position, and it was practical, but Jefferson seemed obsessed with the need to change everything associated with the oligarchy—to leave nothing as he had found it. (Instead of concentrating resources on his alma mater, the fine liberal college of William and Mary and second oldest in the country, he set up a rival in his own demesne far removed from Tidewater.)

In 1780, Richmond was not a city even in name and of its eighteen hundred population, one half were slaves. Besides wharves, warehouses and taverns, there was a rope yard for ships' riggings, a foundry, a smallpox hospital, two professional "physicks," and small houses cluttered near the river or hung perilously on the steep slopes of the hills. The site was extremely "picturesque," though according to future resident John Marshall when he first saw the village, "it will scarce afford one comfort of life."

Committees met in Mr. Hogg's tavern to plan the construction of a temporary wooden building for the Assembly, and a public square was created on which later would be erected the Jefferson-designed permanent Capitol. Under French influences then, Jefferson designed a magnificent building as different as possible from the Georgian Capitol where the oligarchy had reigned. While the members of the Assembly scrounged about to find furnished rooms, the governor temporarily took over the city home of an uncle, to which he brought house servants from Monticello, and complained of living conditions so oppressive in comparison to home. Actually it was more than temporary lodgings in a rude village that bothered thirty-seven-year-old Tom Jefferson. He was experiencing the first failure of his life.

As a wartime governor, the man of the future was simply not the man of the hour. Fundamentally, the range of even the most protean-minded must have limits, and with Jefferson the range stopped short of military affairs. Though Jefferson was a hard-working and able administrator, he was a doctrinaire and as chief executive in crisis he was more concerned about constitutionalities than physically protecting the community. Taking very seriously the new democratic principles of which he was the leading apostle, Jefferson operated by the strictest legalities within the newly built democratic machinery. By being among the first to demonstrate that democracy is a luxury which emergency cannot afford, Jefferson brought the state to the narrow edge of disaster, from which it was saved only by the drastic measures of others and a gratuity from fortune.

All Virginia's organized troops and military organization were outside the state, and "militia" had come to mean any willing and reasonably able citizens who would show up on call, receive arms, ammunition and victuals, and march in a body to a threatened point. As they invariably reached some desolated spot after the ashes of fires were cold and the marauders long gone, the men disbanded (usually retaining any weapon that struck their fancy) and went back home. For various reasons of constitutionality and economics, Jefferson refused to keep the units out permanently or to draft any standing force. The result of these sporadic and futile musterings was to quench the glow in the fainthearted lovers of liberty and to fill the stouthearted with frustrated rage and humiliation at the helplessness of Virginians. Materially, the destructive raids whittled away at the sources of supply in a state where the rich planters were already suffering and the government was in desperate financial straits.

At the end of the year (1780), the trying situation grew more seriously ominous when two thousand British regulars, commanded by the traitor Benedict Arnold, landed by boat at the mouth of the James

River, and began a campaign of ravagement along both sides of the river through the heart of the original colony of the Jamestown period. With the lion among them, the Virginians hastily dispatched Benjamin Harrison once more to Philadelphia, on one of his familiar trips of liaison. He was to plead with Congress to come to the rescue of Virginia, who had stripped her territory of troops for other colonies —and, he did not add, done nothing to insure defense with the men at hand.

Congress heeded the appeal of their old friend but, since they lacked troops to dispatch, some time was required before the first handfuls began the overland journey to Virginia and before professionals rode southward to take over the scattered and irregular "militia." (George Washington made the painful decision of holding his army outside New York, to immobilize Clinton, and not come to the rescue of his countrymen.) For the first months of 1781, Virginians, more outraged at their governor than at the British, were virtually helpless before the march of the heavy raiding force under rough, skillful Arnold —then as mean against his betrayed countrymen as the most vicious of the British.

Before leaving Virginia, Colonel Harrison had taken the precaution of moving his family from the exposed river plantation of Berkeley to the less accessible plantations of other members of the illimitable family. It was fortunate for the girls that he did. On January fourth, Arnold's hard-bitten force disembarked at the foot of the wide lawn of Westover, where the shade of elegant William Byrd strolled in the evening, and pushed across to neighboring Berkeley by the path that the Byrds and Harrisons had so often followed when visiting in the olden days.

Even under brutal Arnold, the British produced none of those house-burners who flourished in a later invasion, but Arnold did want to hurt a Signer of the Declaration and the close friend of the man he had betrayed. As a fellow American, he recognized the sensitive point of a Virginia aristocrat, and there was a subtlety in his cruelty which would touch Harrison without destroying his plantation's future usefulness.

He removed all the portraits from the walls and placed them on a bonfire in front of the mansion. That not only hurt the Signer's family—for the planters spent heavily on journeyman artists to preserve their likenesses into earthly immortality—but also future historians seeking portraits of the Harrisons.

The festivities of the portrait-fire incited the idling soldiers to practice target shooting on Harrison's cows, and frightened Negroes gathered in the nearby quarters. The British had no fixed policy on slaves and, since Dunmore's unauthorized attempt to provoke insurrection, individual officers ran some off or ignored them according to personal whim. Since the Berkeley slaves belonged to Washington's friend, Arnold directed his men to herd along forty of the likeliest, and unknowingly dealt Benjamin Harrison a deadlier blow than the hurt to his pride. This capital loss (one third of his active slaves) was more than the fading fortunes of Berkeley could absorb.

The Berkeley interlude was a passing fillip to Arnold who, in accord with British policy, was devoted to crippling resources and the people's will to continue the revolution and not permanently to destroy their economy. After taking out his spite on a Signer, Arnold restrained his more personal gratification as he marched his troops along the winding planters' road the twenty-odd miles to Richmond. On the fifth of January, 1781, the few hundred militia which Jefferson had collected at the last minute fled at the first sight of the regulars, and the pitiful little new capital offered no defense to the soldiers tramping along the muddy street that was to become Main Street.

In the presence of no enemy at all, Arnold divided his force: part pushed on several miles west of town to Westham, where they partially wrecked and partially burned the arms-producing foundry and the powder magazine; others burned the tobacco in the warehouses. Since most of the houses were frame, a number caught fire from the sparks and the citizens rushed about trying to save their city, while the soldiers searched in vain for anything else worth destroying. They understandably missed the new wooden building which served as temporary Capitol, and after inflicting a twenty-four-hour ordeal on the natives, Arnold withdrew his troops back down the river to their boats. Then they sailed to Portsmouth, near Norfolk on the south side of the James, and ensconced themselves there as a permanent menace.

When Benjamin Harrison returned from the North, he was forced to join his family in their temporary quarters with kinspeople, and snatched such time as he could to direct the rehabilitation of his home at Berkeley. Even this transient security did not last long. Despite the coming of inadequate reinforcements, the bottom was rapidly falling out of the defense situation.

Baron Steuben, the trained soldier and fine drillmaster, had been imported to transform the sometime militia into soldiers, but he became first bewildered at Jefferson's constitutional restrictions against military preparedness, then outraged and finally disgusted. Citizens began to speak out against the governor and demand action. Lafayette, back from France and entrusted with a force of less than one thousand, hurried the reluctant Continentals into the state from the North in the spring, but by that time dangers threatened from more than big-nosed Arnold's raiders.

An unexpected turn had come from the North Carolina area. Nathanael Greene had played a brilliant game of hare and hounds with Cornwallis, pulling the clumsy Britisher ever farther from his base. Cornwallis, awakened from his delusion that the progress of his army across country was subduing the people, retreated to the North Carolina port of Wilmington for a breathing spell and supplies. At this stage, Greene made a wrong guess. He assumed that Cornwallis would sail to his base at Charlestown. This was an entirely reasonable assumption (Cornwallis's superior, Clinton, in New York, made the same assumption), but Cornwallis was no longer reasonable. So, while Greene marched his toughened troops southward to be ready for Cornwallis in South Carolina, Cornwallis crossed him and marched his men into unprotected Virginia.

By this inexplicable military behavior, Cornwallis was in position to effect the military conquest of eastern Virginia (beyond the mountains the people were having their own troubles) and profoundly influence the course of revolution. By then, the Americans were worn out with the struggle, the British were despairing of the futile business, and whichever side won a decisive campaign would have won the war.

All unaware of these gathering disasters, Thomas Jefferson called the Assembly to regular session in early May. When Speaker Benjamin Harrison arrived, he found that less than a quorum of members had showed up. The delegates might not know any more of the military situation than did Jefferson but, with Arnold on a second raid destroying tobacco warehouses across from Richmond at Manchester (now South Richmond), they knew that Richmond was no longer safe.

Harrison and the other members who ventured to town agreed to meet two weeks later near Jefferson's home at Charlottesville, in the rolling hills at the foot of the Blue Ridge.

Even before the members reached Charlottesville, Cornwallis's small army had lumbered northward to within twenty miles of Richmond, and on May twentieth, at the shipping town of Petersburg on the Appomattox River, joined Arnold. Lafayette's own force, though in the process of growing, was entirely too small to contain Cornwallis. However, the personable young marquis acted with sound military instinct and drew Cornwallis after him, across a succession of rivers, to Fredericksburg in mid-state. Not to have a Greene trick played on him again, Cornwallis came to a halt at the Rapidan River west of Fredericksburg, in the thinly settled planting country and, while eying Lafayette, put his cavalry to good use. In early June he dispatched Tarleton westward across country to bag the fugitive Virginia Assembly and especially to capture Governor Jefferson, the author of the Declaration of Independence.

By indulging in such an unpatriotic movement as seeking a glass of ale in the tavern at Cuckoo, a powerfully built young militia officer named Jack Jouett was able to observe Tarleton's mounted force riding westward hard by night. Guessing their destination, Jouett, who possessed the fastest horse in Louisa County, took out across the dark country through the briery brush of summer. He was scarred for life by thorn lashes in making the night ride of forty miles through all physical hazards, but he pushed his lathered horse up the steep hill at Monticello as Benjamin Harrison and several other guests were sitting down to breakfast with Jefferson.

The people, disillusioned with Jefferson as a war governor, accused him of physical cowardice along with other defections, but with Tarleton's raiders approaching his house, the tall philosopher acted with complete coolness. It is true he did not make the senseless gesture of selling his life as dearly as possible, any more than Harrison and the others did. With nothing precipitate in his actions, Jefferson sent off his family and his guests, gathered his papers and belongings, and quietly rode down one side of the hill as the British cavalry rode up the other.

Benjamin Harrison made it back to Charlottesville, where seven of the assemblymen had been captured, and the rest of the harried, embarrassed body took off across the mountains down to the Shenandoah Valley town of Staunton (where Woodrow Wilson was born). On the way Harrison, Patrick Henry and others were insulted by citizens enraged at the humiliation to Virginia's government, and when the Assembly met in Staunton the most unpopular man in Virginia was Thomas Jefferson.

In the rush of events, Jefferson inadvertently intensified the violence of the revolt against him and contributed to the later calumny heaped on his war career. While Benjamin Harrison was his guest at Monticello, Jefferson had already decided not to stand for re-election. Feeling that the military emergency was desperate, that the people had lost confidence in him and that he could not change his legalistic ways to give what the crisis required, he preferred that some man of action succeed him. However, as his term was about to expire, Jefferson had made no official announcement of his decision to retire, and the assemblymen seething in the Valley sanctuary were left without a chief executive. For his act of omission, which created this mortifying confusion, Jefferson was accused (then and later) of "abdicating" under fire and fleeing the consequences of his failures.

Some of the assemblymen were sufficiently angry to pass a resolution of inquiry into his conduct, while others, disgusted with Jefferson's democratic constitutionalities in the midst of disaster, cried for a dictator. Sensible men of practicality, like Benjamin Harrison, effected a compromise and elected a governor who would take resolute, practical measures for defense. He was Thomas Nelson, Jr., one of Harrison's Carter cousins and a conservative planter who could be depended upon to act without Jefferson's tender regard for the legalities of the new democratic processes. The progressives, with their hero in disgrace, discreetly kept quiet while Nelson was given emergency powers to put out the fire.

Neither brilliant in mind nor trained in military affairs, Nelson acted with common intelligence and forceful energy and did those things which needed to be done. Purposeful action to meet the emergency revivified the people and the troops out of the apathy of shame and frustration that had settled over the state.

Lafayette's little force swelled to a size where he could at least make threatening gestures, and Cornwallis was not hard to impose on in those days. Bewildered by forces that kept springing up in a countryside which by right had been militarily conquered many times over, Cornwallis cautiously moved southward back to Tidewater, where its many rivers would make him handy to the British fleet. Passing Richmond again, he followed country roads into the ever-narrowing peninsula between the James and the York rivers, on past silent Williamsburg, to the port city of Yorktown.

If his navy commanded the rivers, as he expected, the peninsula would offer him a sound base for military invasion (as it would McClellan, with the U.S. Navy, eighty years later). If the enemy commanded the rivers, Cornwallis was in a bottleneck.

Until that time, the French warships and the five thousand French troops under Rochambeau at Newport, R. I., had not struck a single effectual blow against the British and very few blows of any kind—though the presence of a French force at Newport restricted Clinton to New York City. With Cornwallis at Yorktown, George Washington and the French saw the opportunity of gobbling up the main British army actively engaged in conquest.

Washington, with a slowly developed guile, fooled Clinton as to his destination, and in co-operation with the French fleet, marched and sailed his troops from Rhode Island to Tidewater Virginia. It was the only large-scale Continental action in which everything worked. Cornwallis, looking out onto the broad York, saw French and not British ships riding at anchor. When Washington joined Lafayette, it was like slipping a cork in a bottle. After the panoply of war was served by some gallant sorties back and forth from the redoubts, and heavy guns startled civilians for miles around, luckless, inept Cornwallis accepted the inevitable and on October 15, 1781, some sad wretch hoisted a white flag.

Farther south, Greene had already cleared the Carolinas of all the devastating forces and had the British besieged in Charleston. Clinton had belatedly sailed his troops from New York to come to Cornwallis's aid and entered Chesapeake Bay five days after Cornwallis surrendered. He could only sail away again. It was all over then except the dickering, which went on until the peace treaty was finally signed in 1783.

In Virginia there was a big bill to pay, with the social order disrupted and faith lost in the ability of Jefferson's progressives to cope with practical matters. Jefferson personally might have had no military instincts, but he followed that sound maxim of "a good general knows when to retreat." The repudiated boy wonder lay doggo at Monticello until he was called away as Minister to France. When he returned several years after his disastrous interlude as war governor, all was forgiven, and when he went on to the national scene with his cosmopolitan humanism, his glory rebloomed in his native state and his political power became almost absolute.

By then Virginia's power and glory were on the wane. The social order of the colony that spread from the Jamestown nucleus never recovered from the revolutionary movement.

As the aftermath of Cornwallis's surrender, the "liberal" element among the progressives was so discredited that Patrick Henry and Jefferson's former ally, Richard Henry Lee, fought for control of the conservative elements in the progressive party; then, perceiving that they were losing to the regular conservatives, joined forces. Even they could not stop the trend away from radicals. When Nelson resigned from office, after his war job was done, Benjamin Harrison came into his reward. He was elected as Virginia's first peacetime governor, to serve as chief executive while the ravaged and dislocated former colony set up in business as an independent republic.

*CHAPTER XI*

❀ ❀

# THE SETTING SUN

1

*Benjamin Harrison* V belonged among the "venerables" when, at fifty-five years of age, he settled with part of his family in a plain, commodious house rented by the state for their governor in Richmond. By then he was a planter only in residential background, and his home at Berkeley had drifted into a state of muted splendour which characterized many older plantations of Virginia from the upheaval of the Revolution to the destruction of the Civil War.

It was during this period that plantation life, observed by Northern visitors when already in decline, assumed its mythical character. At Berkeley an outsider would find the hot land and the crops, the great manor house and outbuildings, the gardens and the river-bordered lawn, grazing animals and playing children, and the Negroes, wearing bright-colored cottons and speaking in soft, liquid voices, but the scene began to hold the hushed, slightly decayed quality of the legend.

No boats were built on the fortune-making docks, and few ocean-going trading vessels rode the swells of the tidal river. The gristmill and sawmill, the blacksmith shop and what they called "merchant-mills," still operated, but on the lackadaisical schedule

[ 270 ]

of overseers. Produce was grown for the plantation's people, providing that lavish self-sufficiency which gave plantation life its air of indolent abundance. But for lack of cash, there was no supervisor to stock a Jamaica-bound ship as Harrison, when a fourteen-year-old boy, had seen his father load the *Charming Anne,* named for young Ben's mother: 487 barrels of Berkeley-cured pork, 250 of home grown peas and 70 of home grown corn, 58 barrels of Berkeley-ground flour and 30 of Berkeley beef, 15 of lard and 2 of tongue, along with 4,000 staves from the sawmill, plus whatever tobacco was smuggled under the cargo in those dear, dead days of British shipping restrictions.

Tobacco was grown again for export, but the British had adopted a harsh and arrogant policy toward Americans, making trade extremely difficult. There was an acrimonious confusion about planters' debts to factors and British reparations for destroyed American property. The thousands of Virginia slaves that had been run off so casually during the revolution were an item the bookkeeping-minded British wanted to forget in settling *planters'* claims, but Benjamin Harrison could not forget the two-thousand-pound minimal value of prime hands lost to Benedict Arnold's impulse.

At Berkeley, the governor still owned about one hundred slaves, of whom at least one fourth were nonworkers. Not more than a dozen were skilled artisans, and more than a dozen were diverted to the desirable status of house-people. The scale of planting operation then in effect was never long successful in supporting the great establishments without those commercial adjuncts which were becoming a thing of the past. That genetic drive to plantation mastery which spanned four generations in Virginia faltered in the fifth, and Benjamin Harrison's three sons did not want to *work* at planting, nor did any of his four sons-in-law.

They still wanted to work, for they were not yet the idle generation, but the plantation was no longer a challenge to them. It was a home to support, a way of life rather than a career. The youngest boy aspired to be a doctor, the middle boy became a lawyer, and the oldest—Benjamin Harrison VI, heir to the home plantation—had been trained in friend Willing's mercantile establishment in Philadelphia. Yet, Benjamin Harrison VI felt no inclination to invest that training in a plantation whose economic glory had been forever blighted by the troubles with England.

When Benjamin Harrison V became governor, his son came to Richmond as his secretary and looked around for opportunities to enter business in the new capital. Governor Harrison could not have been unmindful of the implication of his children's turning away from planting, any more than he could escape the awareness of decay under the façade of Berkeley.

When Benjamin Harrison and his generation were diverted from personal plantation management by the demands on the ruling class, their children were not trained, as the elders had been, to assume responsibility for the large-scale operation. In the first place, as the plantation seemed largely taken for granted by the fathers, so the sons accepted their manorial center as a matter of course. The shrewd, tight-fisted maneuvering of the founder of the family fortunes was incomparably more remote to them than to history. No oldest kinsmen of their vast family told any tales of early hardships, of the rough days; all the children knew was their position in a distinguished and powerful family, intertwined with the ruling class. As planned by their grandfather, the builder of the manor house, and their great-grandfather, Robert ("King") Carter, the Harrison boys and their well-married sisters were warp and woof of a social structure designed for infinite perpetuation—only the foundations of the structure had been shaken by revolution, physical and ideological.

At the ages when the boys would normally have been inducted into the details of plantation operation, their father was away from home struggling with matters far removed from plantation life. At home, trading ceased on their money crop and from their boat landing; local customers vanished and then the family scattered before invading soldiers.

When the family regathered after the war, no son felt urged to pick up the pieces of the once-flourishing shipping-trading enterprise with an England that now renounced them as aliens, and showed by every action the determination to make Virginia planters suffer for their ungrateful secession. The world of trade had changed since the simple days of their grandfather, who had been as intimate with British factors and government officials as with members of his own family, and who entertained at dinner sea captains like old Captain Taylor of the *Charming Anne*. All that was gone forever.

Different conditions would arise for succeeding generations, but the sixth generation was caught between two eras. Conditioned by and belonging to the old, they lacked the heart for change, and their blood had run too thin to accommodate the bold resourcefulness with which their ambitious ancestors had seized opportunity in crisis.

Nor were they motivated by the political ambitions with which their forebears had won their way into the councils of the mighty and into positions of colonial power. The colony was no more as their father and his father had known it. Now the Assembly was crowded with democratic people nobody had ever heard of, who already had pulled down the pillars which supported the oligarchy. Except for old men like their father—individual legatees of the past—there was no oligarchy, and few of the Harrison boys' contemporaries were going into politics. James Madison, four years older than Ben Harrison, Jr., was a protégé of Jefferson in the advanced group, but he was a student-type to whom politics was a science as it was to his mentor. *There was no hereditary position of obligation for the more typical planter's son to assume.*

The democrats had rejected government by a hereditary ruling class, and there was certainly no obligation to battle over theories of government with all comers, even if the aristocracy had been interested. For example, the Harrison boys had only to look at what happened to their father and uncles as a result of spending their lives in the political arena. The sons consequently had to begin new careers in order to look after themselves, and let whoever wanted to operate the new state machinery of government.

2

If their father was disappointed that none of his sons followed him in government—and he must have felt it—there is no record. Neither introspective nor aware of himself as an historic personage, Benjamin Harrison kept no records for posterity. It is inconceivable to think of the huge man, approaching three hundred pounds spread over a tremendous frame, talking to Diary. From his youth, he liked to talk to people, and the report of a visiting tourist in Richmond on the sociable governor's hospitality showed that Harrison worked as chief executive with no more strain than as committeeman. In fact, he probably welcomed the break in the hardest and most thankless work of his life.

In his three terms as governor, allowed by the law (1781-'84), Benjamin Harrison was confronted with the mundane details of setting up on a businesslike basis an independent republic suffering the dislocations of war and revolution, after the adrenalin of both had been spent. In the anticlimactic period of letdown, the people faced a disordered present of poverty and rebuilding, with no sustaining emotionality and an unsettlingly uncertain future.

Harrison's administration, which guided the state through these unheroic times, is one of the least written about of any Virginia governor. The painful period of transition represented no progress in "the march of democracy," and represented none of the humanistic ideals that later fashions could dramatize. Harrison was an old pro doing a professional job to which he had been trained, and to this detail work he brought such concentration and experience as his father and grandfather had given to the plantation operation of Berkeley. Whether or not the governor was aware of this, he was so totally identified with public office that he accepted his job as his life's role and, unlike Jefferson, was not forever pining for "private life" and reminding people what a sacrifice he was making in living away from his plantation.

In conscience, none of those who had participated in the revolutionary movement from the beginning could quit until the job was completed. As the first strong position taken against England twenty years before had led successively to more advanced positions and deeper involvements, so the solution of each problem caused by severance raised another. Even while Harrison was grappling with problems of currency and imposts to collect funds for back pay to Continental soldiers, he was pondering over letters from his friend Washington urging him to move toward making a federal union of the loose confederation of states. As a practical man and veteran of the futilities of a powerless Congress, Benjamin Harrison perceived the necessity of a central government for the Colonies. It was the nature of the potential union that gave him troublesome speculation.

With all the controls of Britain removed, the thirteen Colonies operated in something of a political vacuum. There were no national courts, currency, trade regulations, army or navy, and the confederation could easily have fallen prey to any determined foreign power, of whom there were two on the continent—England to the north and Spain to the south. The separate states were sovereign, autonomous entities, who worked with the whole according to their interests and whims. When these interests conflicted, as they often did, there was no national arbitrator, and it was the machinery of arbitration that concerned Harrison as he recognized that a union was the final inevitable step in progression.

Virginians, with no manufacturing, had bought from English markets before 1774; after the nonimportation boycott against British merchants, the people had largely done without or bought some articles from manufacturers in the Northern states. In the North, the manufacturers had opened up a home market, though profit and loss were confused by credit and paper money and the scarcity of gold and silver coins. When the war was legally over, the British merchants unloaded their overstocked inventories on the free colonies and the home manufacturers set up the same howl the colonial merchants had when the British tried to undersell smuggled tea.

This time, however, the manufacturers could not, as the tea merchants had, dump the imports overboard, since there was no national grievance to give "cause" to protection of local commercial interests. Immediately the manufacturing colonies began erecting tariff barriers, against England, against each other, against anybody who might undersell them. To Benjamin Harrison, governor of an agricultural state, it of course became obvious that tariff to protect manufacturers would merely substitute Northern economic discrimination for British, and Virginia was experiencing enough difficulty as it was in regaining solvency.

Virginia was not one of the states that had used paper money, but coins were as scarce there as elsewhere, and for trade the people returned to tobacco in barter or as substitute for currency. While tobacco served as a temporary expedient, some money standard was urgently needed in Virginia itself, aside from transcontinental and international trade.

Though Virginia had ceded her northwest territory (Ohio, Indiana and part of Illinois) in order that the Articles of Confederation might be ratified by other colonies fearful of Virginia's great power, and the territory of Kentucky would soon be severed to enter the union as an independent state, the Allegheny country reaching from the Cumberland Gap to the Ohio River near Pittsburgh was a long way from Tidewater, and the economic life of the peoples differed so widely that tobacco could not possibly serve as exchange for denizens of the hills. When it came to a money standard, then, Harrison did not want the citizens of a physically diminishing republic to be paying out more than they received.

Just such an unequal exchange with England, working a constant hardship on planters even where little cash was passed, had been a fundamental reason for their resistance to cash taxes. In a nationalized union, cash taxes would of necessity be higher than anything England had ever demanded, and Virginia's economic position would be most unsound if small farmers as well as planters were forced to put on a cash basis a system of selling cheap and buying dear. As it was, the big planters were going to need help in a near future.

Most of the Tidewater plantations had suffered, as had Berkeley, from slaves run off, loss of tobacco trade, and indifferently run overseer farming. In addition, after 150 years of tobacco-growing without refertilizing the soil, the low-lying land along creeks and rivers was becoming exhausted, and the limestone soil of the Piedmont and fertile Shenandoah Valley was unsuited for tobacco. That was the country for horses and cattle. In the sections west of Tidewater the drift had been steadily toward grain, fruit, poultry and truck-farming along with stock; hence, while the social eminence of the tobacco barons was still acknowledged, they no longer dominated the economic life. The trend was away from the monolithic one-crop economy toward a balance in agriculture. The planter, beset by the troubles of change at home, could not hope to sustain his life if dominated from without by the unequal exchanges which protective tariffs would create.

These problems of union were theoretical while Benjamin Harrison was governor. During those years the other colonies were too concerned with their individual post-Revolution depressions to be worrying about strengthening their confederation. When his third term expired in November of 1784, Harrison took the problems with him and they gave him deep personal sorrow because as a result of the solution, he and his old friend, George Washington, at last reached the parting of the political ways. All the other delegates of the Continental Congress had long since split over designs for the freed colonies, while the two large gentlemen of practicality had stood shoulder to shoulder. Now the fox-hunting friend was changing. He was changing over the concept of a union.

3

Though their correspondence was continuous, the two friends had seen each other little while Harrison was in Richmond and Washington in New York, where he remained until the end of 1783. In the November of the following year when Governor Harrison's term expired, Washington wrote one of his warm letters announcing a trip to Richmond, in which he said, "I shall feel an additional pleasure in offering this tribute of friendship and respect to you by having the company of the Marquis de Lafayette."

The return of the native hero and the visiting gallant gave the new little capital its first opportunity for a public festivity. The happily situated commercial center had grown rapidly since Benedict Arnold burned the warehouses. A theater and a race course had been built and a jockey club formed; there were also a Masonic building, an English school, the first great town houses with gardens on the style of plantation houses, and the sumptuous Bell Tavern where the visitors were entertained. Compared to Paris, it must have seemed a trifle provincial to the marquis, but he loved the people and they him, and the charming occasion was cherished in the memories of all who enjoyed it.

None enjoyed such conviviality more than Benjamin Harrison,

and it would have seemed like a recapture of old times except for the change in General Washington. Owing three years' back taxes on Mount Vernon, and faced with selling land to acquire the cash, the acquisitive planter was nevertheless caught up in the nationalism of the revolution which he had carried on his back. Washington had become despite himself *the* national figure. This status implied a destiny which in honor he could not avoid, and Washington's epic growth continued as he shouldered on a continental scale the obligations which he had assumed so long before on a Virginia scale as a modest member of the oligarchy. Remaining a Virginian, Washington was committed to the union of all the colonies for which he had fought. At that moment in time, Washington, of all the leaders in the Revolutionary movement, was one of the few who had progressed beyond native country to the whole—and the only one with his weight.

Neither intellectual nor average man, the Virginia planter was the ultimate pragmatist and his compulsion toward a union was most pragmatic and not democratic. Probably the absence of sweeping phrases about democracy lies at the bottom of Washington's lack of popularity. No social-justice cult could ever make a hero out of him. He had, as commander-in-chief, seen enough of "the people" to confirm his inborn convictions about the "average man" in the mass. Thus, the "father of his country" was not interested in theories of democracy: George Washington was interested in *making* a country of thirteen intransigent and defenseless freed colonies. In his determination to achieve this practical end, the greatest Virginian looked—now as during the fighting—to the whole and not the parts, not even that part to which he belonged.

Washington's eight years away from Virginia as commander of a continental defense had conditioned his thinking. Benjamin Harrison was still thinking as a Virginian, as were the revolutionaries, Patrick Henry and Richard Henry Lee, and the majority of the Assembly.

For the final action of their protest against the British—the forming of a central government for the confederation of states—Benjamin Harrison returned to his old place in the House of Delegates. He had one contretemps over his seat with neighbor John

Tyler, whose son and Harrison's son were one day to run as president and vice-president on the same ticket, but otherwise government life continued in the familiar grooves. In his one remaining coach he traveled from Berkeley to Richmond instead of from Berkeley to Williamsburg, and the shorter journey seemed longer, as ills of the flesh began to plague the massive man.

He suffered from gout, as had his grandfather, and a flush in his thickening face probably indicated a cardiac condition. When friends suggested causes and remedies for his ailments, he laughed them off by saying it all came from following the fashion and shifting to light French wines instead of "good old madeira." Away from the Assembly, the former governor stayed more at home, talking to his capable, intelligent wife about their children.

As Harrison had been away from Berkeley so continuously during the childhood of their youngest child, William Henry had come much under the influence of his gentle mother and seemed the most promising of the three boys. Though only twelve in 1785, he was being prepared in one of the academies then flourishing to enter college early, and in talking over his future William Henry and his father began to get more closely acquainted.

The oldest son, Benjamin Harrison, Jr., was a disappointment. He had a flair for the good things of life but not the mercantile business he started in Richmond, and he seemed unstable. Though he looked like a Harrison, his features were all softened, with a pretty mouth and weak chin. At the age of thirty, late for a Harrison, he married the daughter of Judge Mercer in 1785, and in the summer two years later Anna Harrison came to Berkeley to be delivered of a child. Eight days after the birth of Benjamin Harrison's grandson and future clan-head, the mother died in the heat of late August.

Then, though Benjamin Harrison, Jr., had appeared to be deeply devoted to Anna, within weeks after her death he made an impulsive marriage with Susanna Randolph, at neighboring Curles Neck plantation.

The Harrisons and Randolphs had intermarried until those two families, with the Carters and the Byrds, were like one large family, with the four surnames so constantly recurring in various combinations that a visitor to Tidewater would suspect he had stumbled into some sort of grandiosely incestuous group. Blood cousins did marry, as when Randolph Harrison married Mary Randolph, and one of Jefferson's daughters married a Randolph cousin. (The name, incidentally, is pronounced in Virginia *Rand*'uf—with no "olph" sound at all.) This would make it appear that they all liked each other, but such was not the case. It was more that they liked no one else, though among themselves dislikes could go very deep. Thomas Jefferson had no bitterer enemy than his cousin, John Randolph of Roanoke, a first cousin of the junior Benjamin Harrison's wife, and Harrison's new wife's family made him unwelcome even before he could take his bride to Richmond.

The quick break, by mid-November, between young Benjamin Harrison and Susanna Randolph's family belongs properly in the family's closet since, unlike the scandal which involved John Randolph's sister-in-law (also a Randolph cousin), the personal troubles did not become matters of public record. Facts are that the bride, with her husband's new baby by his dead wife, stayed with her family, while Harrison returned alone to Richmond and there wrote a drunken document in the form of a will.

The rambling confessional, with the handwriting growing larger and looser, showed death to be on his mind to the extent that, though a healthy man of thirty-two, he was obviously suffering suicidal urges. "I am impatient to be with my Anna," he wrote, in the Episcopalian's acceptance of an immortal life, "and I am sure she would be as impatient to be with me . . . I do not decline mentioning my wife Susanna and my baby at Curles because my affection for them is lessened, but from some things which have passed between myself and some of her family, I expect I should not be a welcome guest among them if hereafter we have any remembrance of our former state. . . ."

Then he veered off to "my dear friend Abby Willing of Philadelphia, to whom twenty guineas must be sent immediately on my death with a lock of my hair." (He wore his dark hair loose, brushed forward over the temples in the fashion, and was obviously vain of those romantic locks.) "God preserve my child," appeared as a sudden thought. "If I die, what will become of him?" Then he returned to acceptance of death, making various bequests, including to "my kind father my chariot and four of my best horses." This would be four more *good* horses than the father owned.

He closed the strange document with the mention that it was written "on the anniversary of my wedding with my deservedly beloved Anna." Then, there was a wild and mysterious P.S. concerning his second wife's sister: "Don't fail to give my watch to Betsey Randolph of Curles."

Perhaps he married the wrong sister. His impassioned night writing stood as a will and in a later codicil—still with no bequest to his wife—he wrote, "The Negro girl Sally that I have given Betsey Randolph is to be secured to her and her heirs forever. . . ."

These emotional didoes, untypical of all previous Harrisons, occurred to burden the father's heart in the winter of 1787-88 when Benjamin Harrison was already deeply troubled by what had become the open political break between him and Washington over the constitution for a union of the states.

4

The delegates from the thirteen separate colonies had worked four months over plans for strengthening the confederation with central powers and in September, 1787, had arrived at a design which went beyond the original intent of the states which had sent them. None of the old revolutionaries of the 1775 era worked on the formation of a central government. (Jefferson was in France as a minister and John Adams in England; Sam Adams, Patrick Henry and Richard Henry Lee stayed at home.) They were mostly men of business who put their heads together to form a working union. There was no need for inflammatory speeches nor for ringing phrases to define the rights of man. Man already had rights enough according to George Washington and the solid citizens who were concerned with an organization that would *work*.

As in any political assemblage where divergent interests and conflicting viewpoints must be resolved for a common end, the convention that produced a written constitution was a tedious procedure in compromise—that behind-the-door trading of "you give there, I give here"—the result of which is announced, when the door is opened, as an act of wisdom and humanity, wrought from the rock of ages as a rock for ages to come.

Because the small states wanted to protect themselves against the large, the senate allotted two members to each state; because the large states wanted the benefits of their size, congressional members were to be elected on the basis of population. Because the majority of the Americans feared that a life-appointed chief executive might develop kinglike tendencies, a four-year term of office was defined by law, though not the number of terms that could be served: that was a precedent set by George Washington and followed until Franklin D. Roosevelt, the first President to consider himself indispensable. With the legislative and executive machinery defined, a highest court was established as the ultimate authority for the judicial system of the states and of the union of states, though this Supreme Court was denied any "implied powers" not specified in its sphere of authority.

This government, even then more authoritative in centralized power than most Americans had conceived of as necessary, attempted to balance power between the states and the federal authority, with each sovereign within specified areas. The sober gentlemen of affairs who arrived at a written constitution to sustain this delicate balance were aware of its imperfections and aware that future changes in conditions would make constitutional changes needful. For this purpose they allowed for amendments that could be made by legislative majorities. Eminently practical for the future, the plan of amendments was also used as an argument to persuade state officials that they were not signing their rights away permanently by ratifying the constitution.

Benjamin Harrison was not among those persuaded, nor was Patrick Henry. The course toward nationalism had finally allied these two antithetical types, formerly political opposites. They believed a constitution should mean what it said, and not be subject to every passing wind of doctrine. As for changes under transient pressures, that could work against them as well as for them. They wanted a constitution which they could support *as it was*, and what Harrison and Henry gagged at was the provision over protective tariff for manufacturers. This, the most significant of the compromises, gave Congress the regulation of commerce on a majority vote, and Benjamin Harrison of an aristocratic republic distrusted numerical majorities.

The Virginia delegates to the Constitutional Convention had already compromised on many other measures. They agreed on a twenty-year extension of the slave trade, to please the other Southern states and the New England slave traders, when Virginians wanted to abolish slave trade then and there. A really practical compromise had been arrived at over the count of slaves for votes. The Northern states did not wish to count slaves as population for a representational basis, but they wanted to count them for purposes of taxation. The Southern position was the reverse. The compromise was to tax and count each slave as three fifths of a member of the population, though their individual status remained that of property.

Through such horse trades, each section (and each state within the section) fought to form a union in protection of its own interests, and yielded grudgingly only where it must. Benjamin Harrison and a majority of the Virginians at home thought their delegates had yielded too much, and trusting tariff to a majority in Congress became the point where they stopped. They felt that Washington's concern for a working union was blinding him to the interests of his own country.

George Washington and the drafters of the constitution recognized that the state governments were not going to be pleased by the nature of the compact of union, and it would need some doing to get nine states to ratify their form of central government. The job of convincing Virginians was undertaken essentially by two men—fifty-six-year-old George Washington, a Virginia figure for thirty-five years, and thirty-six-year-old James Madison, Jefferson's successor as a political manipulator on the home scene.

This small, courteous, scholarly Madison possessed infinite tact and illimitable patience in maneuvering quietly for his own goals. No protégé of Jefferson would make the mistake of stampeding the staid middle-grounders with appeals to gaudy generalities. In a democracy only the score (of votes) counted, and the point was to get votes by using methods acceptable to a conservative people, who were still a little jumpy after Jefferson's experiments in a new aristocracy. Madison busied himself unobtrusively before the Virginia convention for ratification met in Richmond in June, 1788, with realistic use of Washington's prestige.

George Washington personally wrote appeals to the powers of what by then had become the Old Guard—former governor Harrison, former governor Henry, and George Mason, who refused to sign even the constitution because it legalized the continuance of the slave trade. To Harrison he wrote, "My friendship is not in the least lessened by the difference which has taken place in our political sentiments," and from this patently sincere declaration, he pointed out to his aging friend the urgent necessity of ratifying the constitution as it was, with all its faults.

Benjamin Harrison was always praised for being a sensible man, for his firmness and conscientiousness, his cheerful equanimity in the most trying circumstances and the quick turns of humor that relieved tensions. Yet, in replying to his former ally (out of his uninspired clarity in regarding facts), he wrote like an ancient prophet.

Saying first he could form "no judgment of the necessity" of ratifying such a constitution, he wrote, "if our condition is not very desperate, I have my fears that the remedy will prove worse than the disease." In the honesty existing between longtime intimates, he confessed that "age makes men overcautious. I am willing to attribute my fears to that cause. But, from whatever source they spring, I can not divest myself of an opinion that the seeds of civil discord are plentifully sown in very many of the powers given, both to the president and Congress. . . ."

From there, he went to his prophetic line: "*If the constitution is carried into effect, the states south of the Potomac will be little more than appendages to those to the northward of it.*"

Six-year-old John C. Calhoun was to try forty-odd years later— and forty-odd years too late—to turn back the clock to that warm June when Virginians voted on putting their trust in a national majority.

With all of Washington's prestige and Madison's politicking, the convention most likely would not have voted to ratify unless, while they were debating, the ninth of the thirteen states had come over. New York, Rhode Island and North Carolina still held out, but the Virginia convention in late July, after nearly two months of hot wrangling, reluctantly accepted the inevitable and voted to ratify by a thin majority of five out of 170 votes cast.

For once, the defeated did not accept gracefully the will of the majority. Suddenly new revolutionary talk was heard around like echoes of the earlier times. As there was little elation among the majority, some of whom later felt that they had been trapped into ratifying, small determined parties of the opposition began to meet secretly to form plans of rebellion. When news reached Harrison of a large night meeting of neo-revolutionists, the gouty old gentleman performed his last outstanding act for his country.

Saddened as deeply as any of them over the terms of union, and fearful of Virginia's future, he appeared at the night meeting and took the floor. He was greatly aged then for sixty-two, for forty years of public life and plantation worries had taken it out of even his huge body. No longer wearing a wig, he appeared with his white hair neatly tied in back in the fashion of his young manhood. His face red and puffy, his heavy body held with effort in its accustomed erectness, he addressed the crowd without any of his famed good humor.

He appealed to their honor and, though disbelieving in it himself, urged them to seek redress through the legitimate channels of amendments to the constitution. He won them over and, when the news reached George Washington, his old companion wrote that "your individual endeavors to prevent inflammatory measures from being adopted redound greatly to your credit."

It was the only reward needed by Benjamin Harrison for doing his duty as one of the survivors of the Virginia oligarchy, as he had been trained to do it.

He had three more years to live, continuing in the House of Delegates where he had started when, under a king, it was called the House of Burgesses. Disliking the turn of history, as he had disliked much before, he adapted to things as they were and brought his best to the work to be done.

In April, 1791, two years after George Washington had been inaugurated as President of the new nation, the old political veteran was still pleased to be returned to the next session of the Assembly. He celebrated with one of the big dinners that had characterized life at Berkeley for all his memories, and friends crowded into the large rooms. Harrison never seemed in more jovial spirits, but as soon as the guests left he turned seriously ill.

Since his grandfather's day, some trust had developed in men who practiced "physicks," and a houseboy was sent hurrying for a doctor. But the boy had to ride a distance for the doctor, and Harrison had not abandoned the planters' practice of home medicine. He directed Molly, one of the old housemaids, to prepare a potion for him.

Molly came in fearfully and said, "Here, sir, is the medicine you asked for."

The practical man looked at the old woman and answered matter-of-factly, "And here, Molly, will soon be a dead man."

Again he was a sound prophet. The next day, with all the composure with which he had ever directed a committee meeting, Benjamin Harrison relinquished consciousness of this life.

5

With Benjamin Harrison, "the Signer," died the "golden age" of plantation Virginia. In signing the Declaration, he signed away the birthright of the past.

International-minded Virginians (Jefferson, Madison, Monroe) were, one term after Washington's presidency, to occupy the White House for twenty-four successive years as the Virginia Dynasty, while the great John Marshall constructed the Supreme Court according to Marshall, and these Virginians comprised a "golden age" of the state's power and prestige on the national level. But at home the sun was setting on their land even while the Dynasty ruled the country through the War of 1812 that finally convinced England that America was here to stay; through the Louisiana Purchase that opened the west to Americans, and the Missouri Compromise which was the first step in fulfilling Harrison's prophecy of the South's future position in relation to the North.

Then he was long in the grave at Berkeley, near where the first band had established the Hundred when the first Harrison was a boy in England, dreaming of a future in the unconquered wilderness. All the successive ages of Virginia had been born and had died on that land by the tidal river, but no great age would be born of the death of the planters' oligarchy. The Virginia Dynasty, perfected products of the undemocratic process, devoted their lives to the new democracy that was to deny and then physically destroy the world of the landed aristocrat.

Americans came to revere new aristocracies built on money, because money they understood. They would also come to revere the foreign aristocracies built on land, because titles were something they lacked. But a landed aristocracy in monied America was intolerable. It stood convicted of the sin of being different without the *cachet* of being foreign.

Virginia became different because the "early adventurers" came with an Old World dream that, while realized with mutations in Tidewater, was antithetical to those migrant waves that rolled from Europe after the Revolution. The later people came fleeing the Old World in renunciation of all its castes: they wanted an "American dream" America and not a Virginia America. It would seem there had been room enough for both, but perhaps that is sentimental.

At the end of the post-colonial period, the planters' own twilight was gathering over the land where the gods had played, whose ghosts would haunt forever the minds of those who came after them. Since Benjamin Harrison's death, Virginia has lived within the union for almost as long as its life before, and during that time has suffered more physical destruction and more disastrous dislocation to its economy and society than any state in the country. Yet, so deep went the roots of the plantation culture in those first two centuries that Virginia has never changed in essence from the character formed in the great age of the plantation. That character derived from an old dream that perhaps does seem quaintly archaic and even exotic in a world devoted to material progress: it was a dream that molded the environment for the individual and not the individual for the environment.

The environment was not to be a fluid quantity in a ceaseless transience for improvement; it was to be perfected, like any masterpiece, for the permanent enrichment of the individuals who supported it. The masterpiece was achieved at Berkeley, but the larger environment in which the Virginia microcosm lived became, as the dead master of Berkeley had foreseen, hostile to the perpetuation of tranquillity.

❋ ❋ ❋ ❋

# THE AFTERGLOW

❀ ❀

## CHAPTER XII

# THE TWILIGHT OF
# THE GODS

1

*The* twilight was slow in settling over the day of the great plantations in Virginia. The Harrisons remained in occupancy at Berkeley
for half a century after the death of Benjamin Harrison V, while
Virginia underwent a gradual shifting of inner balances and stresses
during its transition from an oligarchic dominion in the British Empire into a conservative state in a politically democratic union which
grew hostile to its interests.

The absolute power of the planter oligarchy had been broken in
government, economic security was no longer certain on the plantations, and the concept of *noblesse oblige* faded from the landed families as a new struggle for power, along lines more than a century old,
began in Virginia, surrounded by a changing America.

To the north and in the central government, under the Utopian
concept of the Jeffersonian democracy of self-reliant farmers, a new
aristocracy of monied interests was forming, an aristocracy quite regal
in regard to what Mrs. Washington privately called "filthy democrats." Very sketchily the lines were being drawn for the class struggle
between a newly vested money power of industry, commerce, banking, and finally railroads, and what would gradually become the numerical power of "the people."

In the far south, the eighteenth-century growth of the Virginia plantation was to be repeated with dramatic suddenness in the new lands of what became the Cotton States. There, the new cotton princes would also duplicate Virginia's eighteenth-century political structure of planter-caste rule, with one fundamental difference. The late-arriving Bourbons, with *noblesse oblige* undeveloped, lacked that inherited sense of responsibility to the whole which had characterized the Virginia oligarchs, and the planters controlled power (like the new monied aristocracy of the North) for their personal interests.

With the cycle of rule completed in Virginia, its landed aristocrats were again fighting for control out of personal and parochial interests, and politically the Virginia powers of the early nineteenth century shared common lot with the new vested interests both North and South.

Gradually, however, the money powers of the North gained control of the dominant areas of population by extending their interlocking interests of banking, industry and railroads into the new sections developing west of the Alleghenies. Virginia, by its nature outside the new combination of industrial-money interests, with characteristic gradualism entered an evolutionary stage toward a balanced economy —of trade and small manufacturers to supplement an agriculture changing from the one-crop plantation to general farming along *with* the money crop. As an illustration, Richmond developed tobacco, flour and iron manufacturing from neighborhood products, shipped them from its river and canal (and later its railroads), and in turn—replacing the old plantation center such as Berkeley—supplied the farmers' needs.

When the Northern powers (under the high principle of abolishing slavery) sought to gain undisputed control of the central government in promotion of their interests, Virginia perforce allied herself with the Southern states whose economy was based upon the plantation. Virginians, wishing to preserve the nature of their society, wanted agriculture at the base of the triangular balance, and resisted the combination of an industrialized society already in the process of fulfilling Harrison's prophecy. On the slavery issue, the alliance with her sister slave states was made less because of a threat to capital investments in land and slaves should emancipation come—there were then relatively few large slaveholders—than because of the problem of ignorant blacks turned loose in a white agricultural society. As she did against the British, Virginia formed protective alliances against oppressive outside movements which were hostile to her welfare.

The adjustment to these shifts to the north and the south of Virginia was made at irreparable cost to her manpower, retarding the development of economic balance, and immobilizing Virginia's mental processes in practical affairs.

The landed families fought to retain control for a humanly selfish purpose—essentially that of maintaining their own positions. They possessed the immense intangible influence of perpetuating a pattern of life which had formed the people's character and which symbolized the ideal of the society. Hence, many families with no stake in the rule of the landed aristocracy supported their order and, of course, all who emerged to privilege instantly took oaths of allegiance to the traditional.

When cities such as Richmond arose as commercial centers, including some manufacturing, even the successful urbanites subscribed to the codes of the plantation society, which represented America's nearest approach to a hereditary nobility. In fact, social life in Richmond was indistinguishable from that at Berkeley, and the Richmonder's idea of a really gala event was a visit at a plantation. The time came when a Richmond manufacturer or international trader could have bought Berkeley with the cash on his person, but he could not buy with all the cash in the United States the quality that lured him to Berkeley or Shirley or Westover, to Sabine Hall or Mount Airy, to Brandon or Rosewell or over one hundred other plantations cut in the same pattern and offering the same "life in thrall."

As a republic of plantation centers (agricultural city-states) became anachronistic in a nation growing into industrialization, such was the appeal of the plantation that Virginia remained (as it does today) under the influence of a culture based upon a static serenity as opposed to dynamic progress. Of itself this is not a wicked thing, except to those who identify all human virtue with progress *per se,* and identify all human evil with the lack thereof. With all the obvious negative effects of the plantation system on the individual—its brutalizing of some, stultifying of others, and its tendency to promote overbearing pride—at its best, the culture contained a nobility of spirit, an expansiveness at once generous and gentle, a regard for the intangible values, a trustful respect of fellow citizens and, of all things, an appreciation of the journey of life for itself.

However, the frame of the times was not suitable for the evolution of the Virginia society into yet another phase of balanced economy in which the influence of the plantation culture would be preserved in the character. Virginians would have adapted to that as they adapted to the wilderness, to the Revolution and, with reasonable reservations, to the world wherein they now find themselves. But changes came too fast for a society with the hostage of an anachronistic plantation economy, and the planters themselves went on the defensive, carrying the thinking of the state with them.

Because this preservation of an eighteenth-century *status quo* in a nineteenth-century world emphasized the importance of land, people without good land began to go where they could get it. This migration out of Virginia marked a curious switch on revolution. In most revolutions the people overthrow the aristocrats and take over; in the Virginia revolution, the aristocrats overthrew themselves and the people got out.

Those migrations went back to the flight from England of "the common sorte," who came to Virginia for land unobtainable at home. Their descendants took up the trek after a two-hundred-year pause in Virginia. Small tobacco farmers had worn out their hundred-acre plots and wanted new land, new crops—and a new society. There was little sound reason for the young on the wrong side of privilege to cast their lots with an old caste society in an expanding new country. This migration drew the blood out of that stalwart middle class, whose members carried their manners with them into other states—Kentucky and southern Ohio, Mississippi and southern Indiana, and Texas, where the migrants included Houston and Austin and fifty-five signers of the Texas Constitution.

This drain of human resources was not limited to the yeomanry. As was the case with the early English settlers, younger sons of the privileged also left their native land. Now that the twilight had fallen on the great plantations and there was no oligarchy to absorb and use the upcoming men of promise as it had the second Benjamin Harrison, the young George Washington and all the others, the younger sons with energy and resourcefulness began to leave the state.

They went out in two ways. One group went to the New South,

as their English ancestors had come to Virginia, to enter a class of landed gentry that was closed to them at home. A descendant of John Woodlief, the first captain of the Berkeley Hundred plantation in 1619, went into the Alabama government by way of California. Another group went to non-Southern sections, in order to duplicate in the terms of those new sections what their ancestors had enjoyed in Virginia.

Of the group who went to the New South, probably the best known is Zachary Taylor, President of the United States and father-in-law of the President of the Confederacy. Of those who migrated to a totally new area, the most representative—with typical Harrison adaptiveness—was the youngest son of Benjamin Harrison, the Signer. President of the United States and grandfather of another president, William Henry Harrison caused big Ben to be the only man in the history of the country whose grandson was the son of one President and the father of another.

2

Nothing would indicate more keenly the fading glory of the plantation than the choice of the son of the master of Berkeley to migrate west of the Alleghenies—the dividing line between civilization and the wilderness.

William Henry Harrison was an eighteen-year-old medical student in Philadelphia when his father died and left him a tract of land in the original Berkeley Hundred. Beginning from the bottom as a planter held no appeal to a boy who had grown up in the casual luxury still provided in the Berkeley manor house, nor could he perceive any practical value in the sound classical grounding he had received in the academy and the new Hampden-Sydney College. That was standard background for all planters' sons and in his case had pointed toward medicine. In his day there was scarcely such a thing as working one's way through college and, though various friends of his father offered him help, the young Harrison was too proud to accept it.

There was also in the slim, well-made six-footer a strong strain of self-reliance. A child at home during the impoverishing dislocations of the revolution, he had heard from his mother the tales of his ancestors' greatness, and had formed early the ambition to excel on his own. The physical tumult of the revolutionary fighting on his own land also exerted an influence on the impressionable boy, who at the age of eight had seen Benedict Arnold's redcoats.

When William Henry was facing his future in 1791, the British, in defiance of the peace treaty, still occupied outposts in the western territories; organized Indians were carrying war to the settlers, and the new little American republic retained something like a standing army west of the Alleghenies. Added to a natural hatred of the British, was the glamour of soldiering as epitomized by the career of his father's friend, then President of the new union. After casting about, the younger son without fortune, like many an English fore-bear, selected the military establishment as "the way toward promo-tion and pay."

President Washington was cold to the idea of a military career for the youth to whom he acted as an unofficial guardian, and Mrs. Washington, who felt particularly close to the boy who was her sister's nephew, also wanted finer things for her old friend's son than soldier-ing in a wilderness. Like his adaptive ancestors, the youngest Harri-son had an instinct for his times and anticipated Greeley's "Go West, young man." When the Washingtons found his mind to be made up, the President obtained for William Henry a commission as ensign, then the lowest commissioned rank, and eighteen-year-old Harrison cut loose from all the advantages of connections and name to make it on his own in a new land.

For a new country, however, he possessed the same type of per-sonal advantages that had driven Benjamin Harrison II to the top in early Virginia. He belonged with his times in the new place. Less good-looking than his father and oldest brother, he had the strongly marked features of the early Harrisons, with a long face, high fore-head and thin, firm mouth. His chin was strong and his expression, like his father's, was kindly. Also like his father, his gaze was clear and direct, indicating that self-possessed, uncomplex and practical intelligence which had characterized the Signer. Though his six-foot frame was not constructed on the massive scale of his father, he car-ried himself well, moved with an easy vigor, and was blessed with great endurance. In sum, the Harrison émigré was self-assured and ambitious, practical and energetic, and very brave. Just as his oldest brother inherited all the softening traits of social inbreeding, William Henry inherited the vestigial toughness.

He rose very fast in what Virginians still call "the West." When he joined the regiment at Fort Washington, on the present site of Cincinnati, he found the small army demoralized by defeat and poor discipline, with the men of a most unglamorous military establishment seeking escape from ennui in the bottle. It was a depressing atmosphere for a Tidewater grandee but, like the earliest Harrisons in Virginia, the planter's son saw in the poor conditions opportunity for ambition to be realized and he applied himself to learning his new profession.

His application won him advancement to lieutenant and when General Mad Anthony Wayne took command in April, 1793 (eighteen months after Harrison's arrival), he made the industrious lieutenant his aide-de-camp. William Henry served, as they say, "with distinction," during Wayne's two-year campaign which brought a semblance of peace to the territory and accomplished the withdrawal of the British posts. On General Wayne's death in 1796, twenty-three-year-old Harrison, with the rank of captain, assumed command of Fort Washington.

It was later, in another war with Britain, that Harrison won larger fame as a soldier. As a young captain, this practical-minded throwback to the early Harrisons perceived that the military had served the purpose of establishing him in the new country, and he went on from there. An interesting genetic study in inherited traits, Harrison built his career on land and politics. He married the daughter of a judge from New Jersey, a large landowner in Ohio, and was appointed Secretary of the Northwest territory by his father's old enemy, John Adams, who had succeeded Washington in the presidency.

Carrying his Virginia influences with him, William Henry assisted in founding an Episcopal Church (the present large Christ Church in Cincinnati), on whose first vestry he naturally served, and built a twenty-two-room house of logs covered with white clapboards that he might duplicate on the new frontier the standard of hospitality by which he had been raised at Berkeley. Obviously, he dispensed the abundant life as judiciously as gracefully for, when a representative for congress was elected from the territory, twenty-six-year-old Harrison was sent to the new national capital named for his father's friend, George Washington.

In that year, 1799, his forty-four-year-old brother, Benjamin Harrison VI, died a self-aware failure at Berkeley. He had abandoned his Richmond mercantile venture after his father's death. His mother died soon after her husband, and Benjamin Harrison, Jr., established himself as master of the home plantation.

There, free at last to indulge his true gift for gracious living, he revived high style in the manor house as if land and slaves could be sold off forever. To this weak beauty, caught between ages, Berkeley owes the lovely Adam woodwork with which, in a gesture of gallantry, he replaced the sturdier and simpler paneling deemed adequate by his vastly rich grandparents. For this sort of thing, the Signer's oldest son had a flair. Berkeley was never more splendid than during his brief reign. Although of no consolation to this man of inner disorder, he too reflected his time.

Just as William Henry typified the energetic and resourceful young man of ambition who left Virginia, so brother Benjamin typified the unambitious and unresourceful planter heirs who lived under the spell of plantation life. Yet neither was typical of the Virginia character that adapted to the changing world of the approaching nineteenth century.

### 3

From the poorest yeoman families to the most land-rich descendants of the oligarchy, the typical Virginian tried, as he had all through colonial history, to adapt his life to his time and place, and to prosper according to the nature of his society.

Despite all the historic changes in the political system and the distant threat of Northern economy to his own, the yeoman loved the mellow land still holding its timeless quality. Even tobacco-exhausted land gave its easy yield of corn; hogs and chickens thrived, fish still ran the shadowed streams; game still abounded in the silences of the brushy woods; friends still gathered at the county taverns; fairs were still held, and it was a poor man who lacked a piece of silver to bet on a horse in a race meet.

Many plantation owners met changing conditions by changing methods, and somewhile later Edmund Ruffin's introduction of marl as a fertilizer brought fine yields in general farming. Energetic men, whose plantations had not suffered the neglect of absenteeism or the ravages of invasion as had Berkeley, continued to maintain great establishments—though for many even of the most industrious it was difficult to sustain plantations on the colonial scale.

On the small and middle-sized plantations, operating with less than twenty field-slaves, a modest prosperity and a gracious style of living was maintained by those adjuncts to planting which had formerly formed the commercial centers of the great plantations as they did at Berkeley in its hey day. Sawmills, gristmills, distilleries and even country stores were run on plantations; people of the humbler sort helped support their plantation by working as artisans in the neighborhood, and the educated turned to law and medicine, from the home base of the plantation.

From all classes went thousands of sons with a love of their home place and without a gift for planting to work in nearby cities, and the declining fortunes of many a tobacco-planting family were revived by a city son who went into the tobacco business or tobacco manufacturing. With no gaudy fortunes to be made, Virginia cities were soundly prosperous. Then, later in the nineteenth century, when the permanent military establishment acquired respectability, outdoor-loving Virginians turned to the honorable profession of arms as a career which would support plantations.

To the materialistic observer from the outside, Virginians seemed slothful and bemused to continue a plantation system which so obviously needed all these expedients to support it in the new century. What the observers missed then (as do those today who decry as backward a resistance to industrialized progress) was that the Virginians willingly tried all expedients to support the plantation culture long after the system of the large plantation centers was archaic economically, because they *liked* it. The plantation *was* Virginia.

The element that confused the continuance of the plantation as the agricultural segment of the evolving balanced economy was, of course, chattel slavery. Of all the aspects of the plantation culture that persisted from the Jamestown period, the labor system of using slaves as workers was the one archaism that removed the society from the realm of economics into an overlapping realm of human values.

Nobody would have cared how archaic the plantation system was without the moral aspect of slavery. Professional frontiersmen, shifting ever westward from Virginia, continued into the modern technological world as heroic symbols of the individual archaist in a world grown drab. So would have the plantation except for slavery; and slavery came to explain everything. But Virginia was not lacking in progressiveness because some people owned slaves; Virginia was irrevocably committed to non-progressiveness *and* some people owned slaves. If this seems an oversimplification, slavery has been extinct for nearly one hundred years and Virginia inherently has not changed in the least—only in superficial details.

As a matter of fact, despite the people's unshakable gradualism, Virginia was changing before the turn of the nineteenth century in her attitude toward slavery both as a labor system and as a moral problem. Slave labor could be profitable only on the large-scale operation of a single money crop, and on practical grounds alone the institution of slavery in Virginia began to decline with the decline of the great plantations. On humanistic grounds, Virginians were extremely advanced: the country's first emancipationists, they were the first to experiment with the touchy problem of the Negro in a white society.

There is no question that this humanistic movement was given a fateful check by outside moralists who, without responsibility for the society they attacked, agitated for total and immediate freeing of all slaves. Historically, the forcible removal of one injustice frequently substitutes another (as in the Russian Communists' replacement of the Czars); the abolitionists' high principle would have replaced the institution of slavery with the impoverishment of Virginia's representative families, with an upheaval in its economic structure, and finally with the still human problem of what to do with the black in a white society—and a society already suffering its own dislocation.

Since the Virginians lacked a ready-made solution for the freed slave, they turned from their humanistic gradualism in regard to the Negro to defense of their *total* society against disruption imposed from without.

However, while the emancipationist movement was checked by defensiveness, individuals continued to try personal solutions. More and more planters gave freedom to their own slaves in their wills, thus cutting off heirs from inherited capital. Many small planters gave Negroes their legal freedom and, to cover themselves for the financial loss, worked out agreements that amounted to share-cropping. Many planters solved both the moral and the economic problem by selling slaves South, and these have been historically excoriated for refusing to rob their children of any inheritance.

The very existence of the Negro—slave or free—was probably the single most important element retarding the already congenitally slow Virginian in his attempt to adjust to a new world; the Negro was deeply involved in the emotional and financial fabric of Virginia and outside agitators were using him to threaten the whole. For the first time the Virginian was not ahead in the game; for the first time he was on the defensive, only he wasn't quite sure what for.

At Berkeley, the son of Benjamin Harrison VI, twelve years old at the death of his father, inherited a life of grandeur with no way of maintaining it. The intermarriages of planter families, which had formed the oligarchy, had by his day formed an inbred society trying to sustain privilege. In a static world, they doubtless could have prolonged into some indefinite future a fading plantation world by selling slaves and land and by combining estates through intermarriage. But twilight was deepening over the world on which their society was built. Like the members of any privileged class with tomorrow gathering at their gates, they knew only to enjoy the moment.

To their everlasting credit, it must be said they lost none of their pride or generosity or style. Unaware that they would be damned and glorified as symbols of an unjust and beautiful life, the ladies and gentlemen danced and entertained, bred horses for the nonutilitarian purposes of chasing the fox and racing one another, instilled in their children the worthless grace of good manners, and committed their lives and their class to a belief in the golden moment of life. The measure of their success in gallantry is that not one descendant of any of them would have wished that they had turned their talents for graciousness into amassing wealth.

4

Still patriarchal within their narrowing spheres of influence, the Virginia products of the dream of a landed gentry presented the strange spectacle of a decaying aristocracy within a new country just beginning to expand toward continental and material power. In the yeasty expansion, William Henry Harrison, a product of this fading aristocracy, continued his rise in his new world by the same methods his ancestors had used in their rise in Virginia. As his frontier world became absorbed in the new national sweep, it became extremely unfashionable to be identified with privilege and breeding. A man of his times, Harrison became a man of the people, and never said "boo" about Berkeley Plantation.

William Henry had built his version of the plantation manor house, a brick Georgian mansion at Vincennes, Indiana, before he was thirty, but he recognized that the surgent new country, which he had come to represent, wanted nothing to do with the castes of the effete East. Unlike the Virginia adventurers to the first frontier who dreamed of a hot-country extension of a landed gentry, the pioneers from Virginia and the East Coast states became assertively vain of the frontier, as though it were something discovered by them.

When the second Benjamin Harrison had launched himself against his seventeenth-century frontier, he had perceived that to survive he must go the way of the big planters, then emerging from the class of the yeomanry, and in time his descendants would seek proof of his right to the purple by birth. Before that desire for antedated family distinction became a phenomenon of democratic America, Harrison's descendant in the Middle West perceived that to be among the big he must identify himself with the very class from which his great-great-grandfather had risen two hundred years before. As the Ohio senator's goal of bigness was the nation's top honor, the presidency, he acted with the sane practicality that had characterized his ancestors.

Not merely identifying himself with the people, he made a presidential campaign issue of his presumed folksiness and, passing himself off as a denizen of log cabins, introduced into presidental elections the campaign carnival. While to some this might seem a more ephemeral contribution than his brother's installation of Adam woodwork in the plantation house, still none can deny the effect on American life made by this son of Tidewater plantation masters who first publicly (and spuriously) identified virtue with humble beginnings.

Physically, William Henry Harrison was ideally cast for his role as the nation's first "log-cabin president." He had inherited his father's cheerfulness, generosity and forthrightness and, with his Harrison adaptiveness, it was simple to express his innate courtesy in the plain manners of the frontier. Too self-assured to be snobbish and truly liking people, it was his communicated pleasure to put others at their ease. All of this, in his frontier habitat, caused him to be accepted as a simple son of democracy, "plain as an old shoe." As in the day of the big planters his ancestors became the biggest, in the day of the plain man William Henry became the plainest.

Honest Harrison had not realized the asset of his folksiness when he first ran in 1836 and lost to Andrew Jackson's hand-picked successor, Martin van Buren. During the next four years, the Whig party managers observed that van Buren liked to do well by himself. He dressed elegantly in the high fashion of the East Coast, using pomades and perfumes some said, and he liked to preside urbanely at well-served dinners. It happened that Martin van Buren, born above his father's saloon north of New York City, had risen from the bottom by his own wily efforts and was rather innocently enjoying the worldly fruits of his success. Also, though strictly a politician, he had evolved democratic theories and practices in government, and ran as a Democrat.

The Whigs, desperate for a day in the sun, nominated William Henry Harrison to run as himself—or really a fictional version of himself. In the War of 1812, where Harrison had fought with competence as commander-in-chief of the army of the Northwestern Territory, he had endeared himself to the roughhewn population by a victory over the hateful Indian chief, Tecumseh, at a battle called by the catchy name of "Tippecanoe." So the son of a three-time governor of Virginia and an old Roman of the aristocratic oligarchy, entered the lists as the people's hero, "Old Tippecanoe." Thousands of campaign picture-handkerchiefs were distributed, revealing the likeness of the stalwart Indian conqueror in a field of blue, and on a white border were touching pictures of Harrison's imaginary log-cabin birthplace and the Signer's son in shirt sleeves at a plough behind a team of horses that looked like elongated Percherons.

Having passed off one of Virginia's sons as "The Man with the Hoe," the Whigs then went for the Virginia and Southern vote by naming as running mate John Tyler, a Democrat and Harrison's former neighbor in the demesne of the lords of the James, where Tyler's plantation was among those still flourishing in opulence. As a Democrat on a Whig ticket, and a Virginia aristocrat on a people's ticket, Tyler was kept as muffled as Harrison, and these items were resolved by the happy alliteration of his name, which made the campaign slogan "Tippecanoe and Tyler too."

Instead of giving speeches, the Whigs gave hard cider to the crowds that gathered around the log cabins built on wagons. To emphasize the backwoods element in Harrison, a raccoon on a chain cavorted about the cabin, and the Whigs chanted a nonsense song called "The Same Old Coon":

> "As I walked out dis arternoon,
> To get a drink by de light ob de moon,
> Dar I see that same old coon,
>   A sittin on a tree . . ."

When Van Buren Democrats tried to exhort the crowds with reason, the Whigs chanted, "Van, Van, is a used-up man," and then choruses sang a marching song:

> "Let Van from his coolers of silver wine drink,
> And lounge on his cushioned settee,
> Our man on his buckeye bench can recline,
> Content with hard cider is he."

It was the greatest free show in the young United States, the biggest traveling crowd-gatherer until the circus, and no recipient of this hearty good fellowship would vote for any dandified New Yorker, "on his cushioned settee," against the honest son of the soil, Tippecanoe and his log cabin, too. Van Buren lost in the campaign that made shrewd use of the people's dislike of anything that smacked of aristocracy, and the son of one of Virginia's distinguished families won by keeping silent.

On his way to Washington, William Henry made a sentimental

journey to his birthplace. He perhaps knew that Berkeley would not
be much longer in the family. His fifty-four-year-old nephew, Benjamin
Harrison VII (that grandson of the Signer whose mother had come to
Berkeley for his birth), had deeded the remnants of the plantation to
the Bank of the United States for a twenty-thousand-dollar debt, the
top loan that could be made on the deteriorated property. All shrewdness, ambition and acquisitiveness having been bred out of the line,
the governor's grandson was living on in such fashion as he could
sustain in the manor house he no longer owned.

In a way, William Henry Harrison also belonged to that vanishing
age of Berkeley's colonial Virginia. All his formative years had been
spent in that manor house and the youngest son had come under the
influence of plantation colonials while developing his values and concepts of the world. In making his way in a frontier country, Harrison
lived in a society that was repeating early colonial phases of Virginia.
Though the emphasis was on the common man ("everyone's as good
as anybody else") instead of the production of the superior individual,
by happy chance for him William Henry belonged more among the
average than in a society seeking the superior.

On a new frontier the problems to be met were of a relatively
primitive nature and, with all the democratic concepts, were remote
from the problems of a central government in a society changing with
almost frightening speed. Then, as the life of the mind was the last
aspect of civilization developed in any frontier, Harrison had probably
read nothing since the classics he was raised on and he had substituted
an ingrained hospitality for any deep thinking on the philosophy of
politics—just as his campaign featured a log cabin, hard cider and the
"Same Old Coon" song in place of a platform. In all truth, his election was a triumph for the kind of campaigning that would change
forever the use of the voting franchise in America, and he was really
not qualified to serve as chief executive of a growing nation about
which he knew little.

When he returned to the great-roomed house of his longest
memories, the sixty-eight-year-old front man of a political party and his
elegant, ne'er-do-well nephew each typified phases of a lost America.
By then, in February of 1841, Washington and Jefferson and all the
great men of the Revolution were long in their graves, and the country
had quickly forgotten why those men had led a revolution.

[ 305 ]

The industrialized North, already expanding into and drawing allies from Harrison's old Northwest Territory, was forming power alignments to contain the Southern states and make of the region that appendage which Harrison's father had feared. John C. Calhoun, a child born in the Revolution, was fighting his bitter, futile rearguard action to form a Southern alignment for the protection of the plantation system. In Virginia, young men (Randolph cousins by marriage) were renouncing the whole experiment in central government and seeking to return Virginia to its status as an aristocratic republic on the Greek model.

Of all these realignments of power, as the forces in the republic shifted for the showdown fight over control, old Tippecanoe knew nothing. A good man, of good cheer and good heart, he had outlived his day as his home place had outlived its age.

It was fitting that William Henry Harrison went into his mother's bedroom, where he was born, to write his inaugural address. From there he could look across the idle land to Westover, where the Harrisons and Byrds had strolled in interchanging visits, and where Benedict Arnold's hard-bitten Britishers had marched in another time. In that eastern room he took the books which he had studied in that other time and, for lack of any constructive program to outline, he filled his speech (as was typical of those days) with quotations from the classics.

When Daniel Webster, a man of the industrial age, later edited the speech, he confided to a friend that, "I have killed seventeen Roman proconsuls as dead as smelts."

Harrison did not relish these cuts from his speech, but he was an innocent in the hands of the shrewd men who belonged to the new America. The Lord was good to William Henry, the younger son, to the end. Harrison was spared the humiliation of trying an impossible adaptation to the capital of "a world he never made."

In the inaugural parade, the hardy old-timer spurned a carriage and rode a horse, doffing his hat and exposing his head to the damp, cold breezes that blow in March across the flatland along the Potomac. He took a cold, which went into pneumonia, and within a month of taking office, the kindly stooge of a political campaign joined his fathers.

He had met his hour in his mother's bedroom full of the honors of the highest office and with none of the disenchantments—dreaming over the scenes of his childhood, where he had watched slaves follow the ploughs that legend caused him to follow. A typical Harrison in non-reflectiveness, the old William Henry probably saw no disturbing contradictions for his country between the fact and the myth.

5

Berkeley remained in William Henry's family only a few years after his visit. His nephew, that uncharacterized seventh Benjamin Harrison, died the following year (1842), leaving the decayed plantation and its insurmountable debts to his eighteen-year-old son, Benjamin Harrison VIII. Where in past generations, the Benjamin Harrisons, on coming of age, had assumed control of the great plantation operation, on *his* coming of age, it passed out of his hands. The Bank of the United States found a customer for Berkeley in its nextdoor neighbor, Hill Carter of Shirley, distant cousin and descendant of a family who for two centuries had shared the social life of the Harrisons.

The eighth Benjamin Harrison followed his dozens of kinsmen into obscurer destinies than that of plantation master, taking with him (as had the emigrants out of the state) his manners and values and memories of a golden age. He and his kinsmen became absorbed in a society that would soon be forced into a new and painful adaptiveness whether they wanted it or no, but persisting even through that was the character formed in the great age of the plantation.

The plantation they left was worked by a succession of owners who tried with slave labor to work tobacco-exhausted land largely for general farming. The establishment was too grand to be supported by operation on a modest scale, and as it was the grandeur of the establishment that attracted the new people, each sold out rather than lower a standard they could not maintain. There was a certain sense of honor involved in sustaining the tone of a historic plantation, and each family tried honorably to "keep up appearances." Outwardly the house-unit of Berkeley, with all its outbuildings in good shape, looked as impressive as in its palmiest days, and even by 1861 loomed physically as a majestic symbol of plantation Virginia.

One of its transient owners was in residence when the long struggle between the agricultural South and the industrialized North reached its climax in a trial by arms. Such a test was an old story to Virginians: they had been fighting somebody for the land since the first adventurers were wounded by Indians even before they got off the boat in 1607.

The slavery issue, which covered the Northern side with moral principle, did not confuse Virginians, barely ten per cent of whom then owned slaves. They had been confused by the problem of the Negro for a long time, but they knew that no country sent in invading armies simply to "free the slaves." They did not need to be privy to Lincoln's private correspondence, which admitted that his emancipation edict served the purpose of giving a moral principle to the then lagging war to preserve the union.

As for this union, as was said by one of the impoverished planter's sons who had turned to a military career, "A union which has to be supported by bayonets has no charms for me." That was Robert E. Lee, who was helping support the plantation of his wife, a granddaughter of Martha Washington.

Like Lee, the Virginians regarded a forcible return to the still young union as a violation of Jefferson's "consent of the governed," and they prepared to defend their soil against strangers from the North as they had, in Lee's father's day, prepared against Britishers over the same principle. For Virginians defended themselves against armed invasion on the principle expressed in the opening line of Jefferson's preamble to the Declaration of Independence: "When in the course of human events it becomes necessary for one people to dissolve the political bands which have connected them with another, and to assume among the powers of the earth the separate and equal station to which the laws of nature and of nature's God entitle them . . ."

The course of human events had, for Virginians, made dissolution preferable to enforcing union on the Southern states which had seceded. Virginia, not having seceded and drifting away from dependence on the plantation center, dissolved the political bonds on the same principle with which Benjamin Harrison had risked his planters' world when Virginia allied itself with Massachusetts against Britain. The planters' world had never recovered from the first alignment; it, and the whole society spreading from its center, was finished when Virginia allied herself with the states that formed the Confederacy.

In the Revolution, the destruction was in property and a ruling class. In the Civil War, the destruction—along with property and the whole economic structure—was in those men who represented the last, post-colonial flowering of the plantation culture. Of the Virginia planters' sons known to history who were killed outright or never recovered from the war were Lee, Jeb Stuart, Joe Johnston, A. P. Hill, "Prince John" Magruder, George Pickett, Dick Ewell, Jubal Early, and the Gettysburg trio of Kemper, Garnett and Armistead. These at random are known products in leadership of a society dedicated to producing the superior individual (along with Stonewall Jackson, of the yeomanry). There were also other natural leaders, unknown to history, who were lost to the land that produced them—and exist only in the memories which replaced the tangible contributions they might have made in an orderly evolutionary phase of their society.

6

When the invading forces came from the North, Berkeley lay in the pathway to Richmond, as it had in the Revolution, and as had the original Berkeley Hundred when Richmond was the seat of the mighty Powhatan. To military experts who devote after-the-fact rationale to old wars, a critique of the Union forces long in fashion was that the armies invading Virginia stupidly followed the traditionalists in seeking to capture the Confederacy's capital of Richmond. Actually, Virginia was a physical buffer to the Coastal South, and the war lasted as long as Virginia held out; Virginia held out as long as Richmond did, four years.

Richmond was truly the capital of that vital state, as is London of England and Paris of France. The core of that economic balance which grew with the decline of the large plantation, the city was a railroad terminus in a fertile region of supply, with train connections (however skimpy) throughout the South to facilitate troop movements. It had the buildings, warehouses and shops to make ready conversion into a wartime capital, and its arsenals provided more war material than any production center in the Confederacy. In the first year it provided more than all the others together, and always provided more artillery than all the others. Sentimental symbol it might have been, Richmond was also a war center without which the Confederacy's effort at self-determination would have been considerably briefer.

Its physical situation for defense was only fair, neither weak nor strong. South, at its back, the James River provided a water barrier; to the west, the hilly, sparsely settled agricultural country lacked the roads and railroads to support an invading army. The obvious road to Richmond was straight down over present Route One from Washington, about one hundred miles across flat country, with four rivers to cross between Fredericksburg and Richmond, the last half of the way. Though it was the obvious course, it was also the simplest to defend, once the Confederate army in Virginia found, in Lee, a bold and skillful general to play off the invaders with counterthreats to Washington and the North.

The attacks over that route kept coming in the last three years of the war, when military imagination was supplanted by the brute force of superior manpower and material. This unequal pressure slowly ground away Lee's army by attrition, and it was these three years of destruction by invading armies concentrated in a single area that devastated sections of Virginia beyond hope of ever recovering.

The only imaginative attempt to capture Richmond was made by McClellan at the end of the first year of the war. He devised a giant pincer movement with one prong closing in from Fredericksburg in conjunction with the thrust of the major army straight up the planter's paradise of the Virginia peninsula. In following the old Pocahontas Trail, McClellan used for supply and support the U. S. Navy which had—in fighting a state of planters—control of the York River and the James River to within five miles of Richmond. There a hastily improvised river fort checked the gunboats for the whole war. That control of the James River placed hostile ships in front of Berkeley, and white and colored stared at the ominous-looking armed vessels patrolling the waters where "the big boats" of England used to ride.

McClellan's army, sweeping westward from Yorktown in a reverse of Cornwallis's course, sent civilians before it like game before a forest fire. With all able-bodied men of anything like military age in the army, only the old were left to help the women and children into carriages, buggies, wagons, carts, anything that moved, to join the somber cavalcades that jammed the five roads funneling from the east into Richmond.

The Virginians feared the Yankees' actions against civilians as they had never feared the British; the Northern people were foreign to them while their English cousins had not been. Virginians had split off from England in the same fashion as the Episcopal Church had split off from the Church of England while remaining in the Anglican Communion. In withdrawing from the sixty-odd-year-old American Union, Virginians left neither common roots, common blood nor deep attachments with the Northern and Western states. The invaders were alien enemies, and their hoodlumism among civilians was shocking to a people who had regarded Benedict Arnold as cruelly vindictive.

The British, who had been avowed enemies, were a different breed altogether from these hordes who were supposedly invading for the purpose of restoring a common union. Perhaps nothing offended a traditional people more than the grave robbers, who desecrated tombs in search of gold and jewels on the dead.

This was in the early days when the war was still "soft" and McClellan, with many close friends among Southerners, was trying to defeat the armed forces of a rebellious movement and not take war to civilians. Like some British commanders, he wanted to restore the bonds without leaving scars. The sadists, hooligans and arsonists were loosed later when the Union policy turned frankly to a total war of subjugation and entered the phase of systematized despoilization; but the elements of hate and brutality were present even when they were not incorporated officially in McClellan's policy. Families whose ancestors had withstood the Indians and the British to build their homes were made "refugees" from them. The Indians, too, had been avowed enemies, admittedly savages. These invaders, of the same race and— as they claimed—the same country, acted with a personalized viciousness and meanness that left a more lasting impression in four years than had nearly two hundred years of Indian fighting.

By the time that personally honorable McClellan reached the outskirts of Richmond, scarcely any people except slaves were left on the plantations in the swath of the Union army. Berkeley and other great houses were locked and left deserted, while the slaves on the whole remained in their quarters, apprehensive and curious, still performing such chores as feeding the animals and chickens, picking the ripe fruit and gathering the vegetables. The unworked fields baked under the June sun. Berkeley might have been the scene of that song, "The Year of Jubilee":

*We seen the smoke way up the river*
*Where the Lincum gunboats lay . . .*
*The Massa run, ha ha,*
*The darkies stay, ho, ho . . .*
*It must be now that Kingdom's comin'*
*In the year of Jubilo. . . .*

The Lincum gunboats came closer in late June, and by the first of July heavy transports began to dock at the old wharf that had, in the great days, been called "Harrison's Landing." McClellan's superb army had been turned back from the gates of Richmond by the first of Lee's great counterstrokes and, in the campaign known as "The Seven Days Battle Around Richmond," McClellan was maneuvering his heavily materialed army backward over those narrow, shaded roads that fanned out from Richmond. As he retreated, fighting, toward the river and the fleet, Harrison's Landing was aroused out of its slumbrous memories by such activity as never dreamed of by those Harrisons in their long sleep in the nearby family graveyard. The plantation, where the early adventurers had planted their dream of empire, was swarmed over by one hundred thousand muddy men in blue uniforms, who were turning the manorial center of a dynasty into a base from which to invade all that the plantation symbolized.

Rain had been falling steadily when the Union army retreated to Berkeley, and the plains spreading out from the house were, according to a Union army officer, "reduced to paste" by men's boots, horses' hoofs and wagon wheels. The wheat fields and corn fields, the vegetable gardens and the flower garden, all disappeared within hours, and a later arriving Union soldier reported that "every sign of vegetation is trampled out, and its broad acres are as bare and hard beaten as a traveled road." If the destruction was not enough "to wake the dead," it was enough to awaken the ghosts for one sensitive soldier with McClellan.

He said of Berkeley, "It is a noble plantation . . . broad and beautiful . . . memorable for being the birthplace of General Harrison. . . . The house is an ancient brick edifice, quite large, and flanked by two smaller ones. At a distance are the slave quarters, more comfortable than I have usually found them. . . ."

It was the damage in "the noble mansion" that disturbed him most deeply. With thousands of wounded (and hundreds of others already abandoned), the harried medical corps turned the manor house into a temporary hospital, though the merest fraction of the wounded could be accommodated there. The soldier watched in protest as "the elegant furniture" was treated as firewood and "the rich carpets . . . completely covered with mud and soaked with human gore."

He lamented that "the genius of destruction is let loose in war. Soldiers acquire a passion for destruction. It made my heart ache to see them break mahogany chairs (more than a century old) for the fire, and split up a rosewood piano for the kindling. But any protest is immediately received by the soldiers with cursing of the Rebels and all who sympathize with them."

A signer of the Declaration of Independence and the Father of his Country had used those chairs, when they talked of freedom over a glass of madeira, and grandees and their ladies had sat in them at the three-hour dinners and between dances in a three-day rout.

> *And we, that now make merry in the Room*
> *They left, and Summer dresses in new bloom,*
> *Ourselves must we beneath the Couch of Earth*
> *Descend, ourselves to make a couch—for whom?*

Those soldiers who were not disturbed by the ancient ghosts built signal posts out of the chimneys, one of which held the 1726 date stone, where the initials of the Signer's father and the daughter of "King" Carter were enclosed within a heart. On the great lawn, where the primeval trees had been left for shade and beauty when the house-unit was first carved out of the wilderness, the sound of axes came across the water in a grim re-echo of those first axes that struck to build a "pallizado" for the original Berkeley Hundred. Save for the one big poplar, which shaded the cook's stove outside the manor house, not one tree was left standing on the three-mile river front.

This desolation was not a part of the "soldiers' passion for destruction." The trees went for camp fires. Camp fires were necessary for an army preserving the Union, and it was no concern of the soldiers what happened in the future for the people who were being forcibly restrained in that Union.

While the callous transients were delivering the *coup de grâce* to the dying order at Berkeley, the phase of chivalry ended in what some called "the last war of gallantry." President Lincoln, in one of his two wartime trips from Washington, came personally to Berkeley to interview General McClellan on the prosecution of the war.

While Lincoln was there, McClellan delivered to him the famous letter that finished the general with the administration. Intemperate and egotistical, the letter presumed to advise the President on policy. Had McClellan been winning, the pragmatic Lincoln would probably have overlooked the insolence. But McClellan's hurting army was huddled in the mud under cover of gunboats and actually in a state of defense.

Despite the behavior of his soldiers, McClellan, like Sir William Howe, still wanted a defeat of the armed forces that would cause a collapse of the independence movement and return the revolutionists to a union without bitterness. Lincoln wanted a general who would win at any cost, and that was not McClellan. In their split over policy, it must be stressed that McClellan was not winning on his methods, and without a winner Lincoln's administration would lose home support for the war of subjugation. (As it was, he needed the Emancipation Proclamation that autumn to put heart in the ugly business of killing fellow countrymen.)

It was fitting that handsome and gracious George McClellan should be the Union commander whose day was ended at Berkeley. For he, too, was outside the mechanistic forces that strove for domination over the corpse of the plantation South. The "young Napoleon," as he was called when in favor, fundamentally wanted to preserve a union at the expense of no region and with all the best characteristics of all regions preserved in it. This of course is romantic, but McClellan personalized a romanticism that existed also in the North. But there seemed no room for romanticism left in the whole country if the union was to be preserved by destroying a region which wished to be separate.

As if to dramatize what McClellan personalized and what Berkeley typified, a curiously apt incident occurred on the great lawn which served as an army base. Raffish General Butterfield, one of the three opprobrious "Dans" in the Army of the Potomac, happened to have an amateur's ear for simple music, and encouraged Norton, his bugler, to experiment with notes.

One twilight there by the James River, where the Harrisons and their friends used to stroll, Norton came to Dan Butterfield excited about a few new notes for his bugle.

Fascinated, Butterfield had Norton blow the notes as a substitute call for "lights out." When the officers of other divisions heard the informal call, they hurried to Butterfield's tent to get the notes for their buglers. In time, the melancholy notes that Butterfield's bugler first played in the twilight at Berkeley Hundred, became the U. S. Army's official call of "Taps."

# A POST SCRIPT

When McClellan's army abandoned Berkeley (and went chasing Lee's ragamuffins in the North), the owners did not return to the desolated land, in the midst of which stood the seared and ravaged house, relic of a lost time. Few planters returned anywhere in Virginia. There was nothing to return to except, as at Berkeley, a ravaged house —and in many places that too had gone up in the pyre of an age.

No plantation, under conditions then known, could be worked without a system of slave labor. Since the slaves represented capital, and their emancipation amounted to confiscation without reparation, the planters lacked cash to replace stolen stock and destroyed equipment, or to pay wages to the freed slaves. Most of the planter families drifted into the cities in search of primary subsistence.

On the plantations that had been outside the area of systematized despoilization, enough equipment, stock and fertile fields remained for many of the owners to transform themselves into farmers and evolve of necessity a crop-sharing labor system with the displaced and starving Negroes. By this grim expedient for survival, the paternalism of the plantation was extended into the present.

After the death of Lincoln, when the bully-boys in Washington took over with the avowed purpose of reducing the South to "a mudhole," the bayonet-supported occupation government was filled with jackals who came to Virginia to batten on the dead society. Once in control of the tax bureaus, these worthies without difficulty found plantations in tax arrears for the four years of the war and claimed them in default. Even if any family had wanted to resurrect a wrecked plantation, conditions made it virtually impossible.

The result was that these large holdings were subdivided, and tracts were sold cheaply to individuals who, in an agricultural country, still wanted to farm. In almost all cases, these buyers came of nonplanting families who, during Reconstruction, found the opportunity to acquire some of the river land closed to them "before the war." Those people were practical farmers. They felt no faintest sense of responsibility to the traditions of a plantation. Lincum's soldiers had finished plantations for all time, and these rural Virginians were concerned only with obtaining a modest subsistence in terms of the harsh, postbellum conditions.

Eighty percent of the population of unindustrialized Charles City County was (and is today) composed of Negroes, freed slaves and their descendants, who formed pools of cheap labor for the farmer with little cash and simple tastes. In the struggle for survival shared by a few white farming families and thousands of landless, bewildered Negroes, a new pragmatic paternalism developed to replace the relationship between plantation master and slave—and this, too, has extended into the present.

Again Berkeley was typical. The farmer who inhabited the great rooms where the American Revolution was plotted viewed the formerly dynastic manor house only as fortunately spacious quarters. He covered the patina of the gorgeous old brick with red *barn paint*, and obscured the classic lines with double galleries that encircled the whole house. In lieu of trees, he used the outbuildings for firewood. Yet this man of his terrible times probably prospered as abundantly as any farmer in Tidewater Virginia, and provided work for the Negroes abandoned by their saviors.

In the early years of this century, any daring motorist, braving the mud of the old planters' roads, could have chugged into the fields of Berkeley without receiving a single impression to suggest the glorious episodes of American history that had been enacted on those then lean acres. It seemed like any other farm in Tidewater, where courteous people still offered hospitality according to circumstances. Instead of madeira, you would receive buttermilk or hot chocolate, according to season, always cake, and in really spirited times a spiked lemonade would be served in a Waterford bowl, which somehow had escaped all ravages of Indians, British and Yankees.

For the spirit of the plantation still lingered with the timeless scent of the jasmine and honeysuckle, in the shade of the grape arbor, in the shadows of the running stream, and most of all in the memories of men and women, and in the tales told to children when they drove in a disreputable carriage from the wooden depot across hot, murmurous fields and through the sweet-smelling, brushy woods. Because the men and women could not forget, the plantation could not die. Its greatest age had been officially buried with a Union-played "Taps," but another age was to be born through the persistence of the plantation dream across all times and all regions.

With irony equalling that of William Henry Harrison's election as a plain man, the new rich of the North fell under the enchantment of the plantation life their fathers had destroyed and, in what Virginians call "the second invasion," began buying up with cash those physical vestiges of an age of the dream. On the whole, the Virginia plantations have fallen into the hands of families who truly revered the past they were buying and, with fine feeling for the original spirit that built them, have resurrected the manor houses into simulacra of their days of glory. Also, most of the new residents, like many British emigrants in the Colonial days, became converts and are indistinguishable from the native.

In the case of Berkeley, as always a typical example, the brief farm phase was ended by Mr. John Jamieson, a New York Scotsman who, in 1905, bought for a summer place the disfigured manor house and the fourteen hundred acres still attached to the house-unit. As if in unconscious imitation of the original purchasers of Berkeley Hundred, Mr. Jamieson's acquisition of the property carried with it little perception of the dream inherent in the land. The dream was born in his son who, without supporting statistics, is probably the only living American who *grew up with* the ambition of resurrecting a Virginia plantation.

For Mr. Malcolm Jamieson, the present owner, the dream was as personal as for that Benjamin Harrison III, who first settled Berkeley as a dynastic center—and the early going was probably even rougher. With no central heating system in the eighteenth-century mansion and no nearby wood for the great fireplaces the slaves once stoked, at nights young Jamieson kept from freezing to death by chasing away the rats whose muffled padding was too too real to pass for ghosts. The days he passed in chipping away at the red barn paint that lathered the bond-laid bricks and in making his first modest experiments in cultivating the wornout land.

Like the planters, he learned by doing; and, like the early Harrisons, he adapted to his day in a complex, interrelating operation that the Harrison settlers of Berkeley would have admired. With liberal use of fertilizer, he has restored six hundred open acres, some in crop production (corn, barley, and soy beans) and some in grassland which supports three hundred Hereford cattle, fifty of which are the nucleus of a pure-bred herd. Where the field hands used to bend in the sun, tractors and a hydraulic sod drill roar across the sun-baked land, and his own experiments have developed a silage system for the winter as demanding in attention to details as the Harrisons' shipping.

For beauty and shade, Mr. Jamieson planted more than twelve hundred trees to replace those lost in long-dead campfires, and for beauty and profit, he planted thousands of boxwood hedges which not only suggest the past but sell in the present. As a final twist, a herd of two hundred sheep find good forage in the weeds around the boxwood and, while fattening, perform the weeding chores that once occupied the days of the less powerful slaves. The acres of pinewoods that had overgrown the old tobacco fields are cropped and pruned according to modern forestry practices, and instead of ships, which used to sail from the old wharf at Harrison's Landing, trucks now roll over the private driveway where the Harrisons once rode in carriages to Williamsburg.

All these strenuous devices to continue Berkeley as a working plantation represent the resourcefulness and hard work, the money and concentration to details, which would make a fortune for an individual if applied in other fields. But the enchantment born of the old dream at Jamestown reaches across the ages, and to the Virginia plantation owners today, as to the planters of the great ages, the plantation represents more than a way of earning a living: it is beauty, expansiveness and dignity, and a perpetuation of that graciousness which America has discovered can exist in a democracy.

## Acknowledgments

I wish to express appreciation to Mr. Stewart Richardson, formerly of Rinehart and Company, Inc., for suggesting the idea of the book, and for his enthusiastic and intelligent support during the work; to Mr. Dudley Frasier, who edited the manuscript, for a meticulous, painstaking and highly sensitive performance; to Mr. Malcolm Jamieson, the present owner of Berkeley Plantation, for placing at my disposal material in his possession, for sustained interest in the work, and for the hospitality of his home; to the Reverend Mr. Edward Gregory, for placing at my disposal his late father's library of Virginiana, with its invaluable records of the early colony; to the staff of the Virginia State Library and individuals at Colonial Williamsburg; to the staff of the Virginia Historical Society, and particularly to its director, Mr. John Jennings, for his most generous, patient and knowledgeable co-operation; and finally to those friends—particularly one—and companions on field trips who gave unstintingly of their time and knowledge.